INTERVIEWS WITH
MONSTER
GIRLS
Volume 3

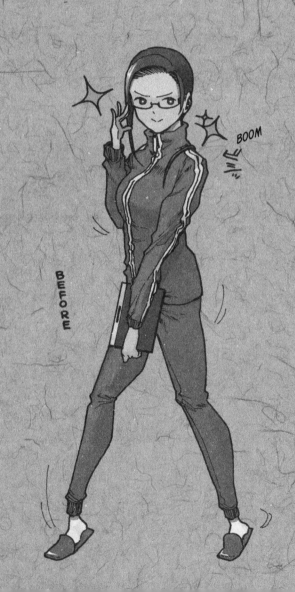

BOOM

BEFORE

INTERVIEWS WITH MONSTER GIRLS

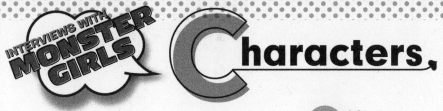

Characters

Vampire

Hikari Takanashi

Class 1-B

- Likes liver, tomato juice.
- Receives blood from the government once a month.
- Opinions on romance: plenty; actual experience: none.

Tetsuo Takahashi

- Biology teacher.
- Fascinated by demi studies since college.
- Tries his best to understand demis.

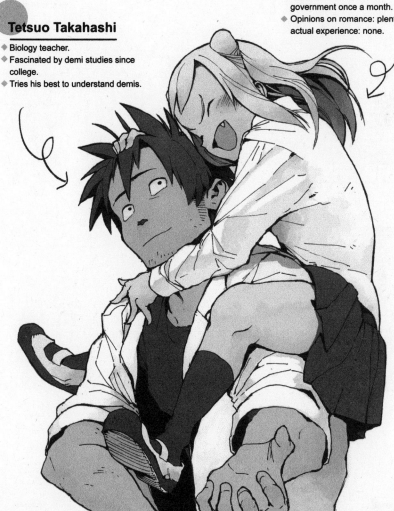

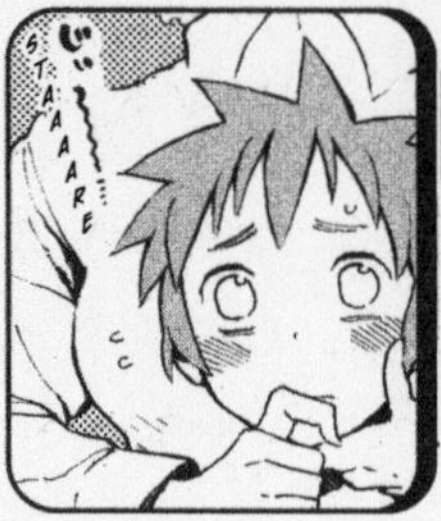
じぃ～…
STAAAARE

Dullahan

Kyoko Machi
Class 1-B

- A demi from Irish folklore whose head and body are separate.
- Likes her head to be held.
- In love with Takahashi-sensei.

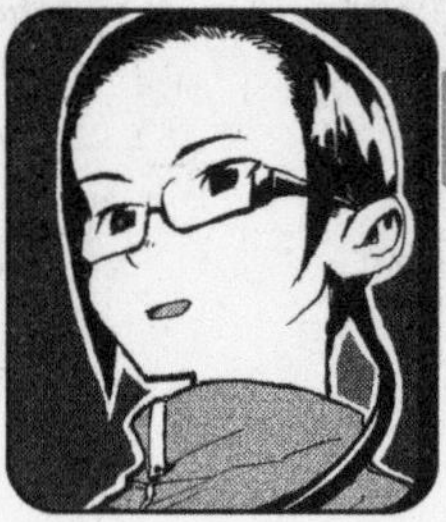

Succubus

Sakie Sato

- Math teacher.
- Lives in an isolated, dilapidated house so as not to unintentionally arouse anyone.
- Romantic history: zilch.
- Has a crush on Takahashi-sensei.

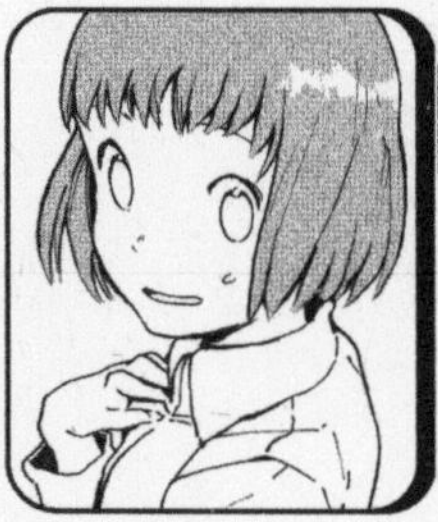

Snow Woman

Yuki Kusakabe
Class 1-A

- Exudes cold air and weeps ice under stress.
- At first, avoided contact with others due to doubts about her own nature.

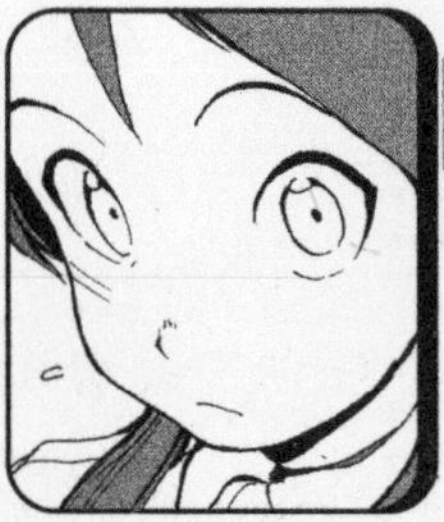

Himari Takanashi
Class 1-C

- Human
- Hikari's younger twin sister.
- Good grades, mature attitude—polar opposite of her sister.

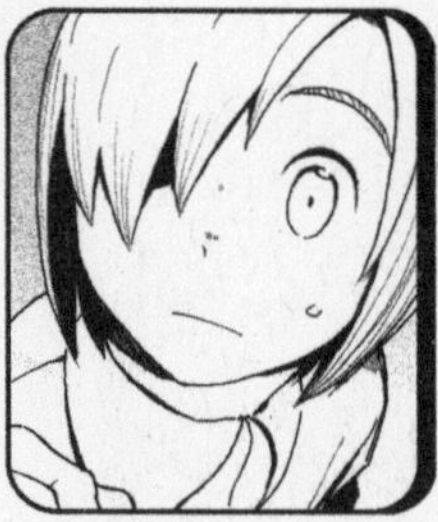

Kurtz

- Junior detective under Ugaki.

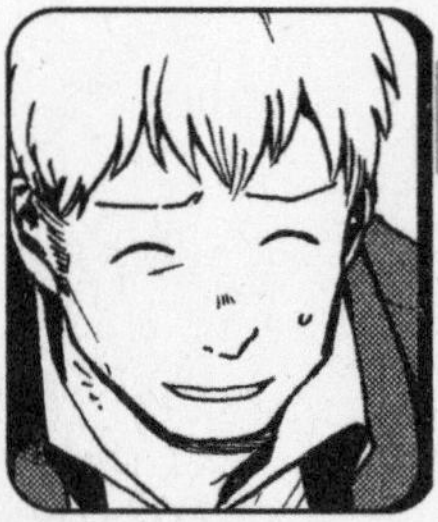

Ugaki

- Detective
- Acquaintance of Sato-sensei, apparently.

"Demi-humans" are just a little different from us—
these days, they go by "Demis."
Their problems are as adorable as they are.

*DEMIS: SHORT FOR "DEMI-HUMANS."

INTERVIEWS WITH MONSTER GIRLS

CONTENTS

3

INTERVIEWS WITH MONSTER GIRLS

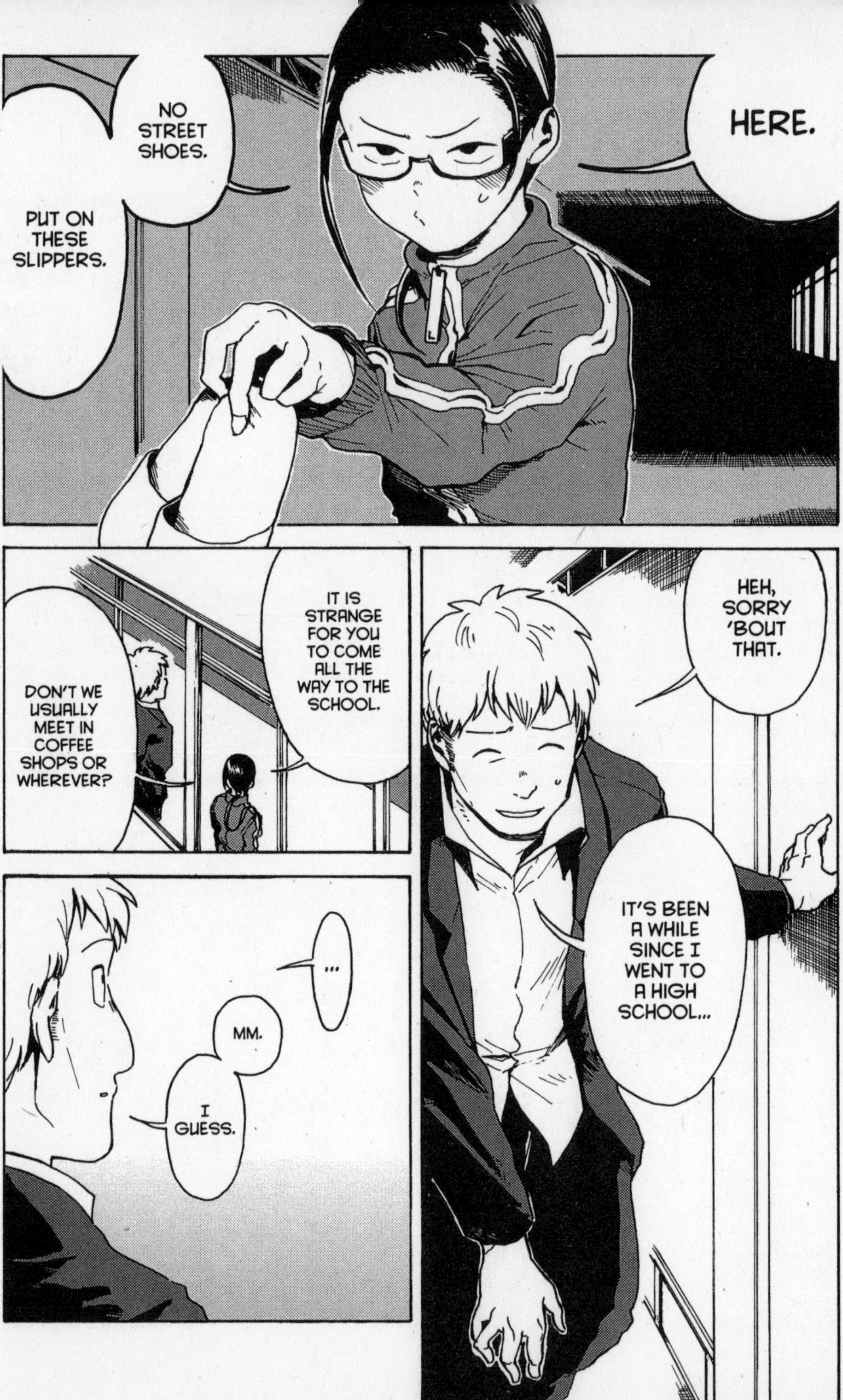
HERE.
NO STREET SHOES.
PUT ON THESE SLIPPERS.
HEH, SORRY 'BOUT THAT.
IT'S BEEN A WHILE SINCE I WENT TO A HIGH SCHOOL...
IT IS STRANGE FOR YOU TO COME ALL THE WAY TO THE SCHOOL.
DON'T WE USUALLY MEET IN COFFEE SHOPS OR WHEREVER?
...
MM.
I GUESS.

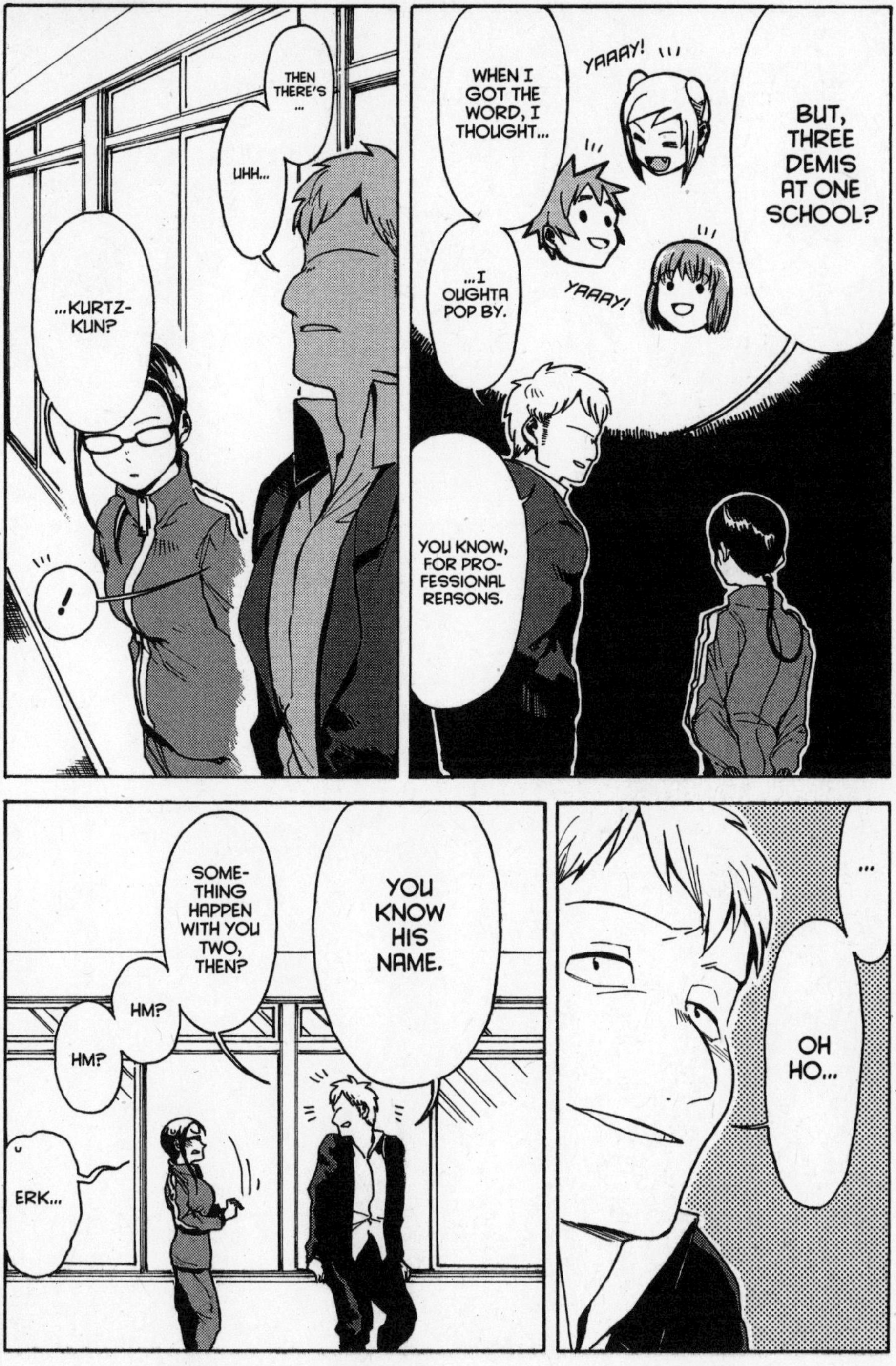
BUT, THREE DEMIS AT ONE SCHOOL?
YAAAY!
WHEN I GOT THE WORD, I THOUGHT...
YAAAY!
...I OUGHTA POP BY.
YOU KNOW, FOR PRO-FESSIONAL REASONS.
THEN THERE'S ...
UHH...
...KURTZ-KUN?
!
...
OH HO...
YOU KNOW HIS NAME.
SOME-THING HAPPEN WITH YOU TWO, THEN?
HM?
HM?
ERK...

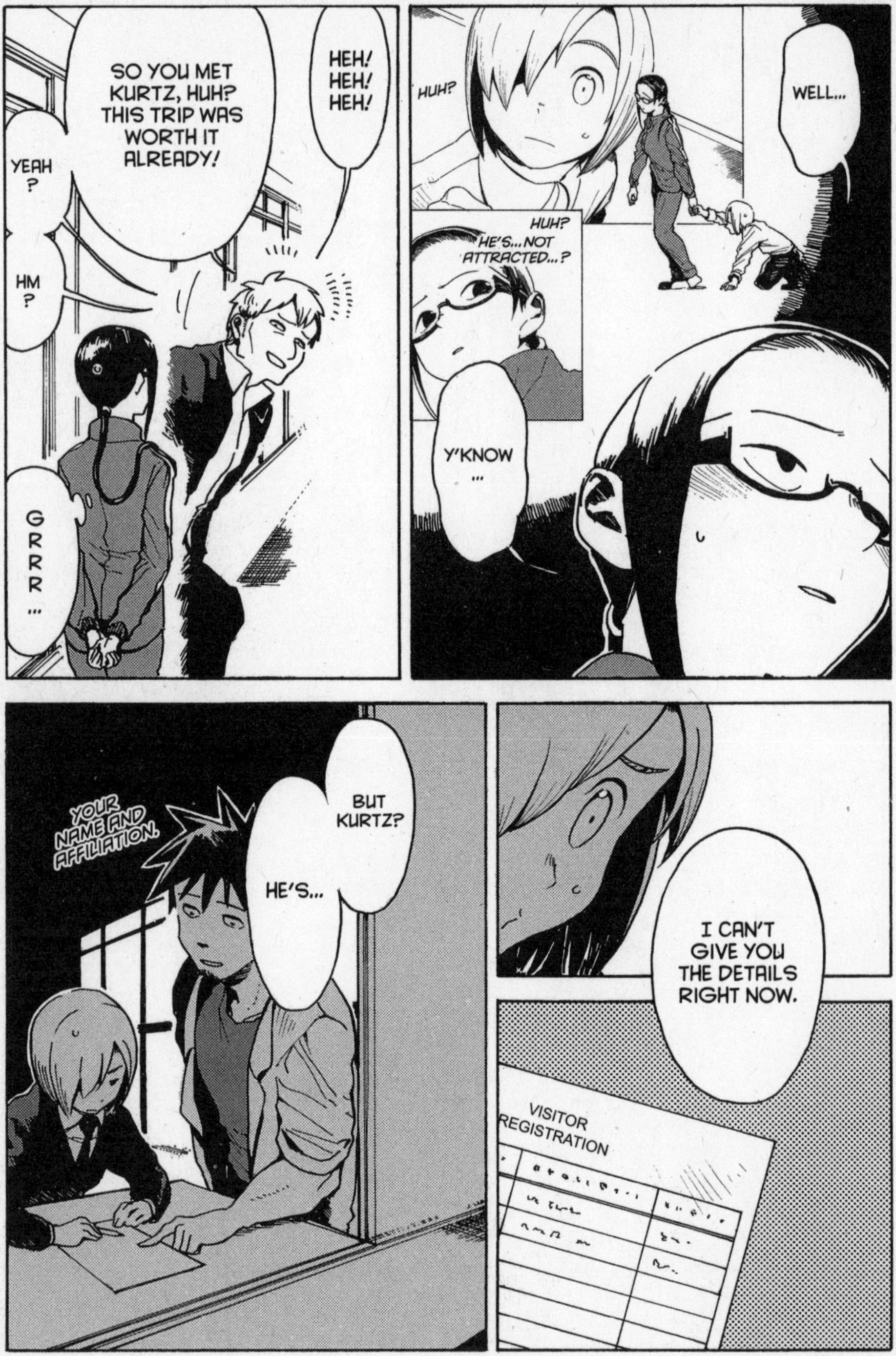
WELL...
HUH?
HUH? HE'S...NOT ATTRACTED...?
Y'KNOW ...
HEH! HEH! HEH!
SO YOU MET KURTZ, HUH? THIS TRIP WAS WORTH IT ALREADY!
YEAH?
HM?
GRRR...
I CAN'T GIVE YOU THE DETAILS RIGHT NOW.
VISITOR REGISTRATION
BUT KURTZ?
HE'S...
YOUR NAME AND AFFILIATION.

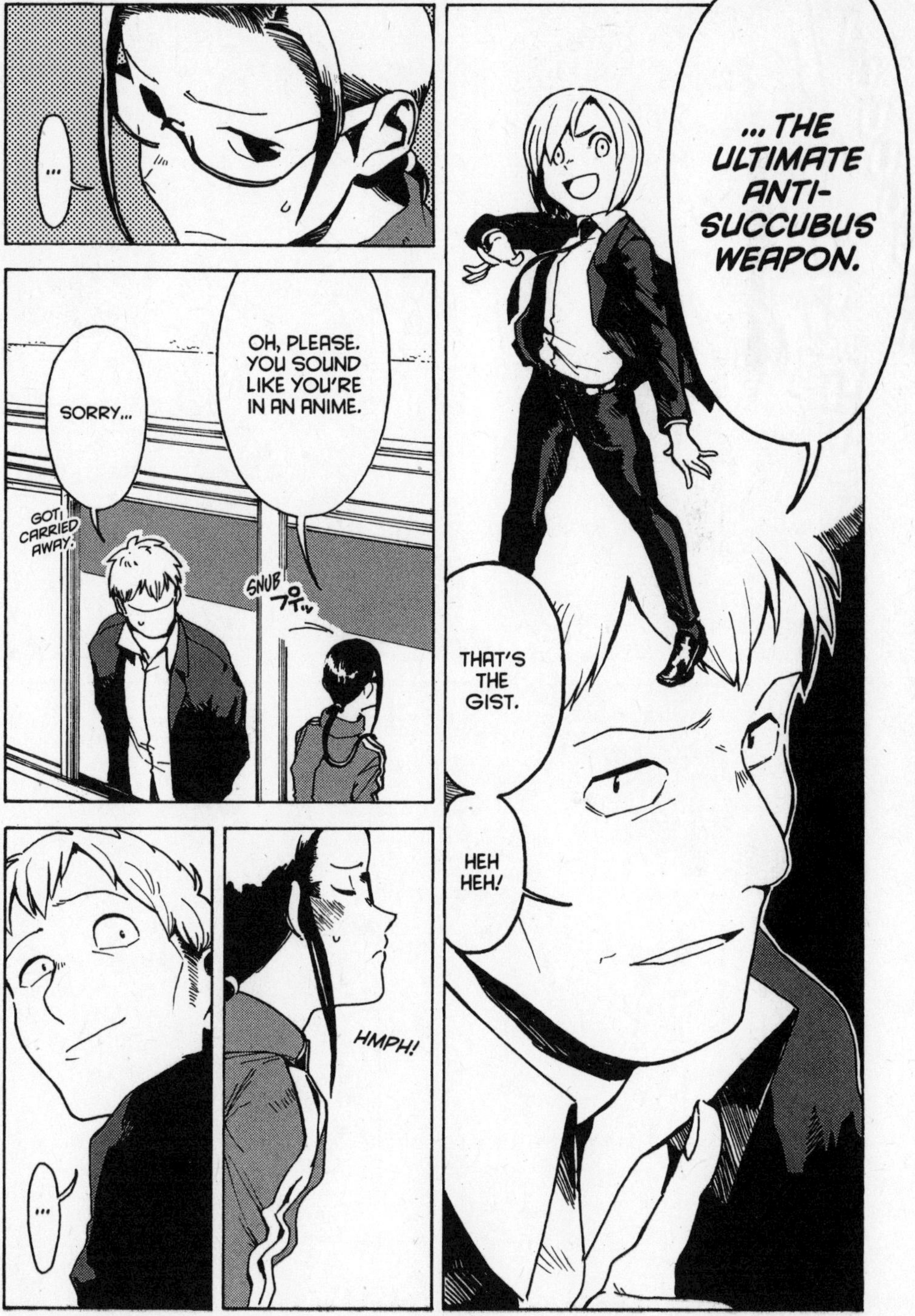
...THE ULTIMATE ANTI-SUCCUBUS WEAPON.
THAT'S THE GIST.
HEH HEH!
...
OH, PLEASE. YOU SOUND LIKE YOU'RE IN AN ANIME.
SORRY...
GOT CARRIED AWAY.
SNUB
プイッ
HMPH!
...

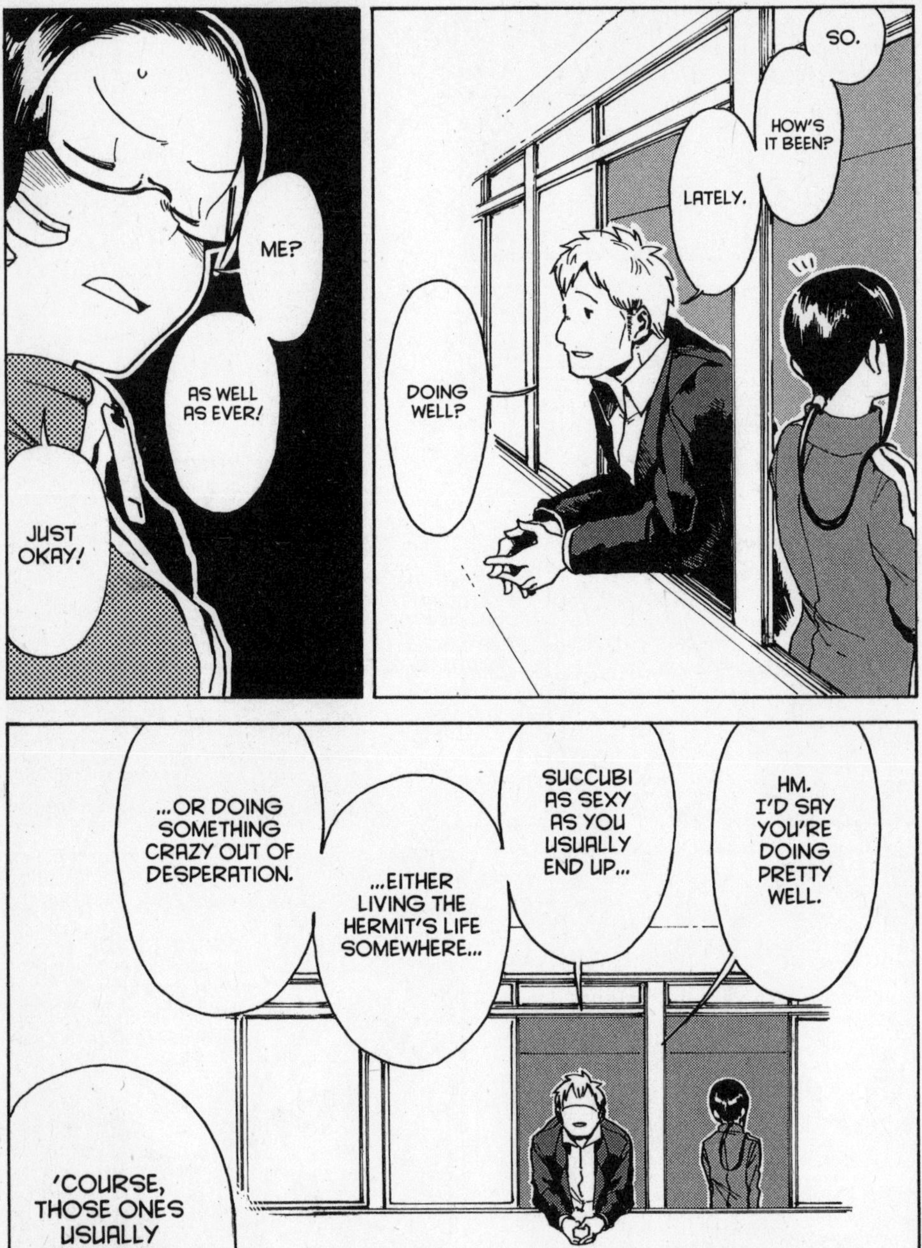
SO.
HOW'S IT BEEN?
LATELY.
DOING WELL?
ME?
AS WELL AS EVER!
JUST OKAY!
HM. I'D SAY YOU'RE DOING PRETTY WELL.
SUCCUBI AS SEXY AS YOU USUALLY END UP...
...EITHER LIVING THE HERMIT'S LIFE SOMEWHERE...
...OR DOING SOMETHING CRAZY OUT OF DESPERATION.
'COURSE, THOSE ONES USUALLY END UP AT THE STATION WITH US.

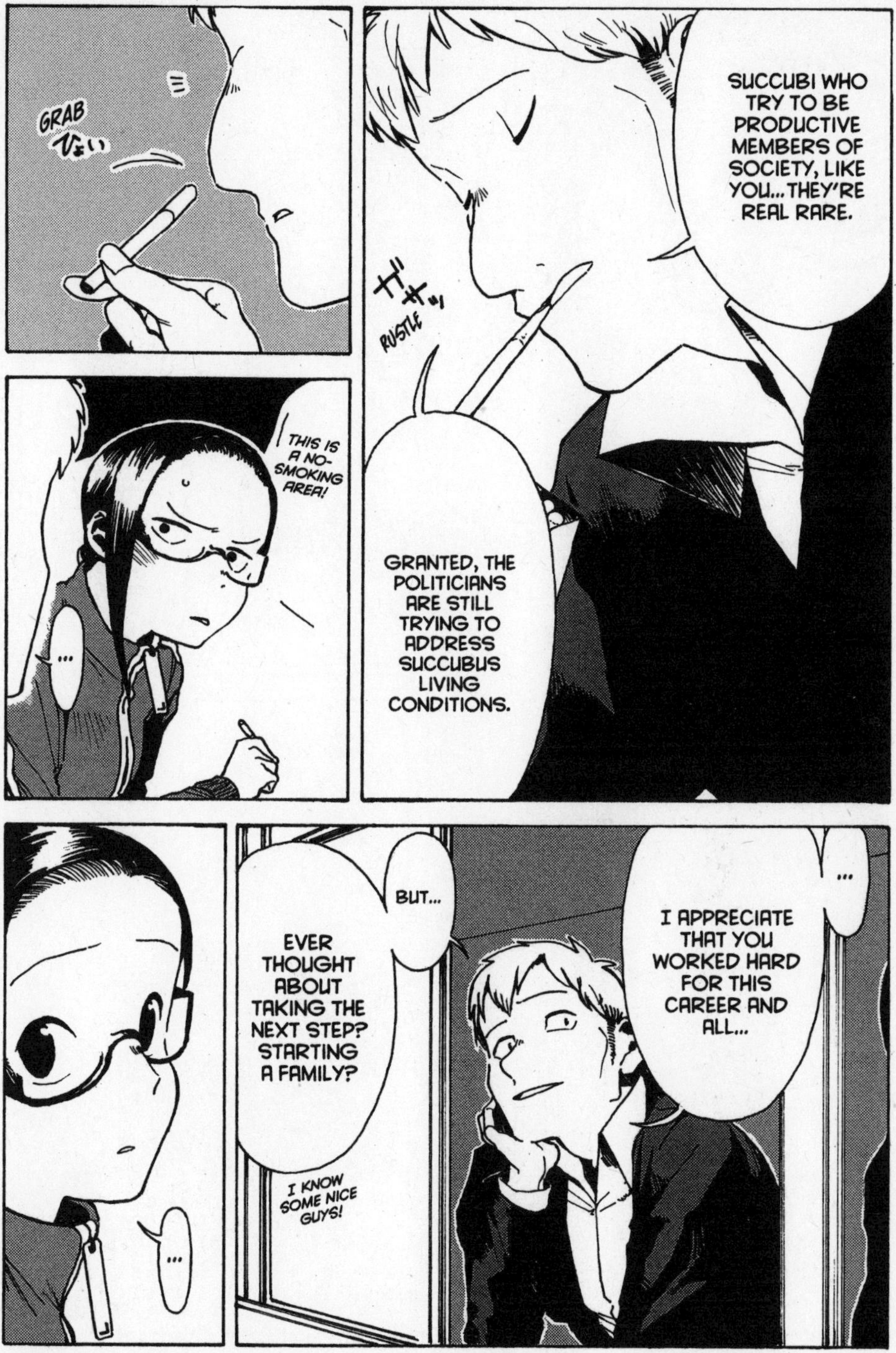
SUCCUBI WHO TRY TO BE PRODUCTIVE MEMBERS OF SOCIETY, LIKE YOU...THEY'RE REAL RARE.
RUSTLE
GRANTED, THE POLITICIANS ARE STILL TRYING TO ADDRESS SUCCUBUS LIVING CONDITIONS.
GRAB
THIS IS A NO-SMOKING AREA!
...
...
I APPRECIATE THAT YOU WORKED HARD FOR THIS CAREER AND ALL...
BUT...
EVER THOUGHT ABOUT TAKING THE NEXT STEP? STARTING A FAMILY?
I KNOW SOME NICE GUYS!
...

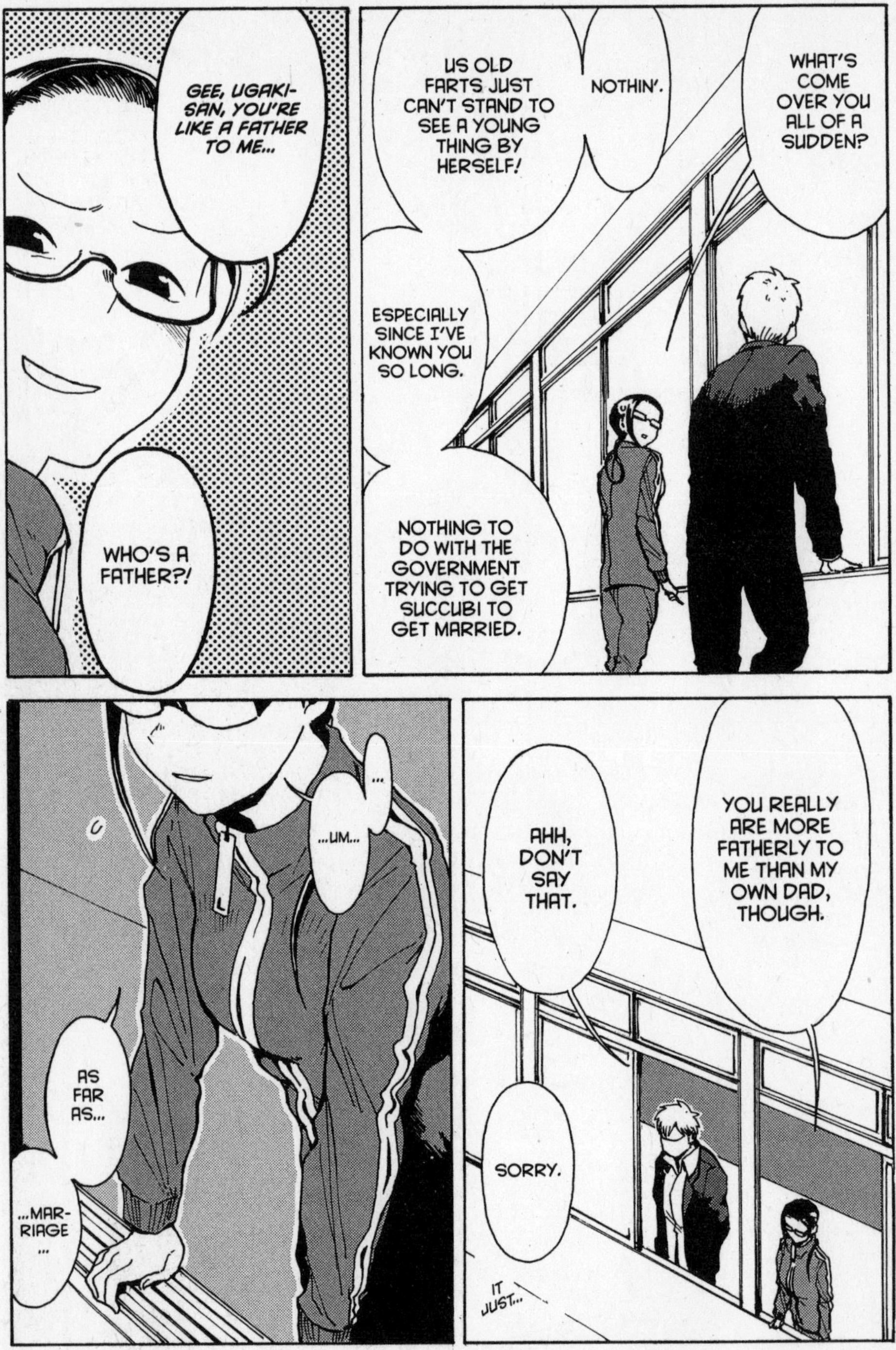
WHAT'S COME OVER YOU ALL OF A SUDDEN?
NOTHIN'.
US OLD FARTS JUST CAN'T STAND TO SEE A YOUNG THING BY HERSELF!
ESPECIALLY SINCE I'VE KNOWN YOU SO LONG.
NOTHING TO DO WITH THE GOVERNMENT TRYING TO GET SUCCUBI TO GET MARRIED.
GEE, UGAKI-SAN, YOU'RE LIKE A FATHER TO ME...
WHO'S A FATHER?!
YOU REALLY ARE MORE FATHERLY TO ME THAN MY OWN DAD, THOUGH.
AHH, DON'T SAY THAT.
SORRY.
IT JUST...
...
...UM...
AS FAR AS...
...MARRIAGE...

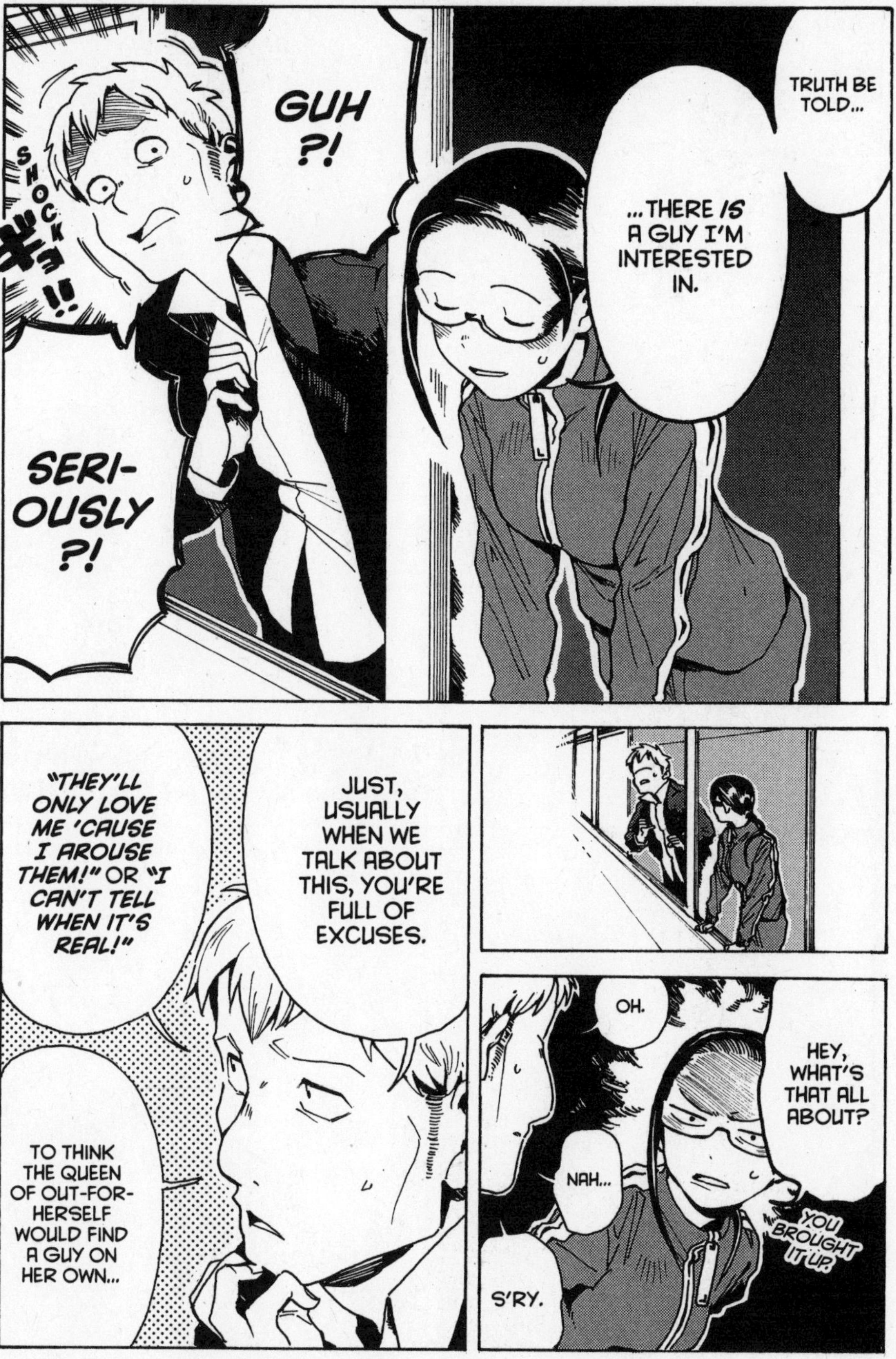
TRUTH BE TOLD...
...THERE *IS* A GUY I'M INTERESTED IN.
GUH ?!
SHOCK
ギョ!!
SERI-OUSLY ?!
OH.
HEY, WHAT'S THAT ALL ABOUT?
YOU BROUGHT IT UP.
NAH...
S'RY.
JUST, USUALLY WHEN WE TALK ABOUT THIS, YOU'RE FULL OF EXCUSES.
"THEY'LL ONLY LOVE ME 'CAUSE I AROUSE THEM!" OR *"I CAN'T TELL WHEN IT'S REAL!"*
TO THINK THE QUEEN OF OUT-FOR-HERSELF WOULD FIND A GUY ON HER OWN...

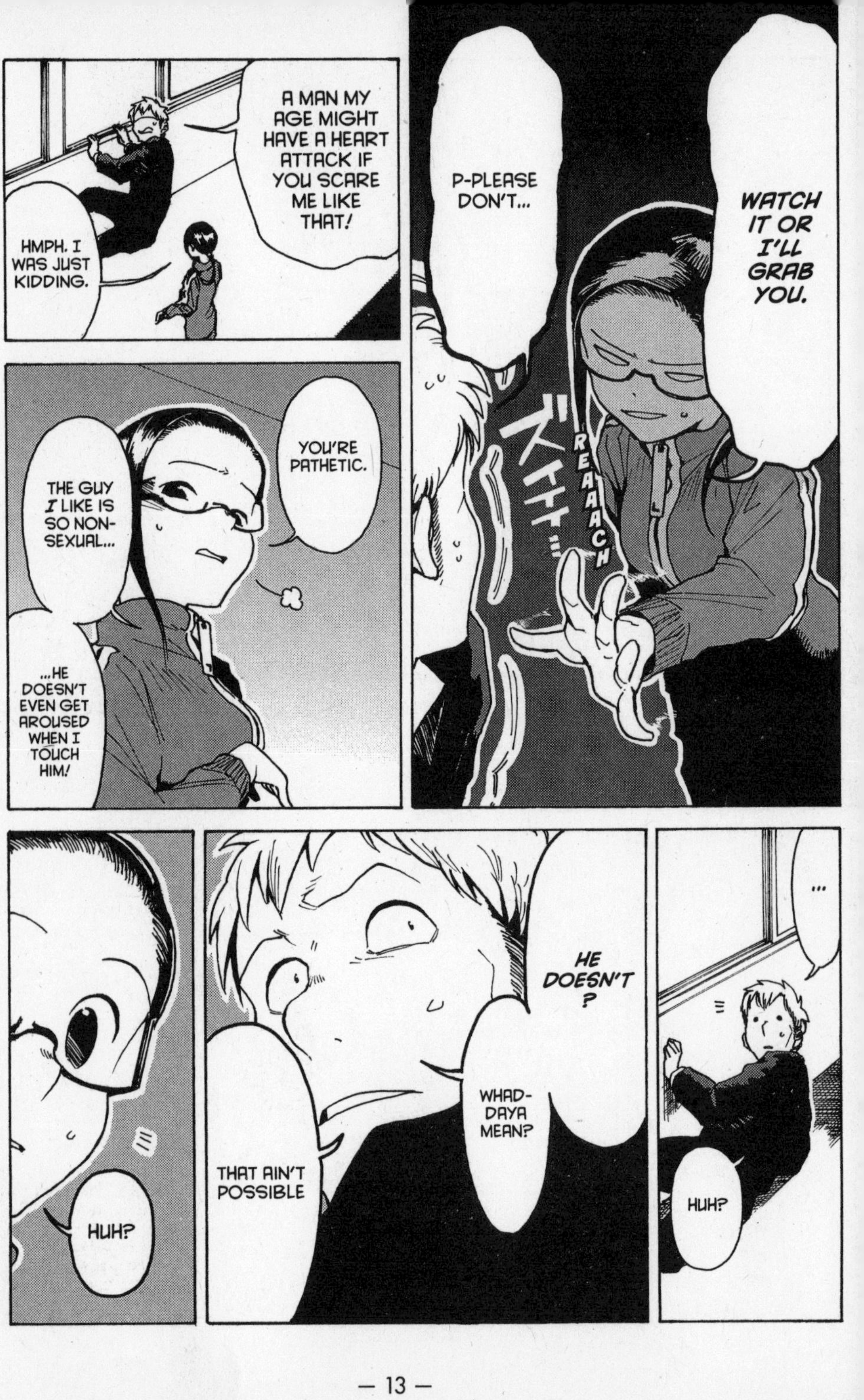

WATCH IT OR I'LL GRAB YOU.
P-PLEASE DON'T...
REAAACH
A MAN MY AGE MIGHT HAVE A HEART ATTACK IF YOU SCARE ME LIKE THAT!
HMPH. I WAS JUST KIDDING.
YOU'RE PATHETIC.
THE GUY I LIKE IS SO NON-SEXUAL...
...HE DOESN'T EVEN GET AROUSED WHEN I TOUCH HIM!
...
HUH?
HE DOESN'T?
WHAD-DAYA MEAN?
THAT AIN'T POSSIBLE
HUH?

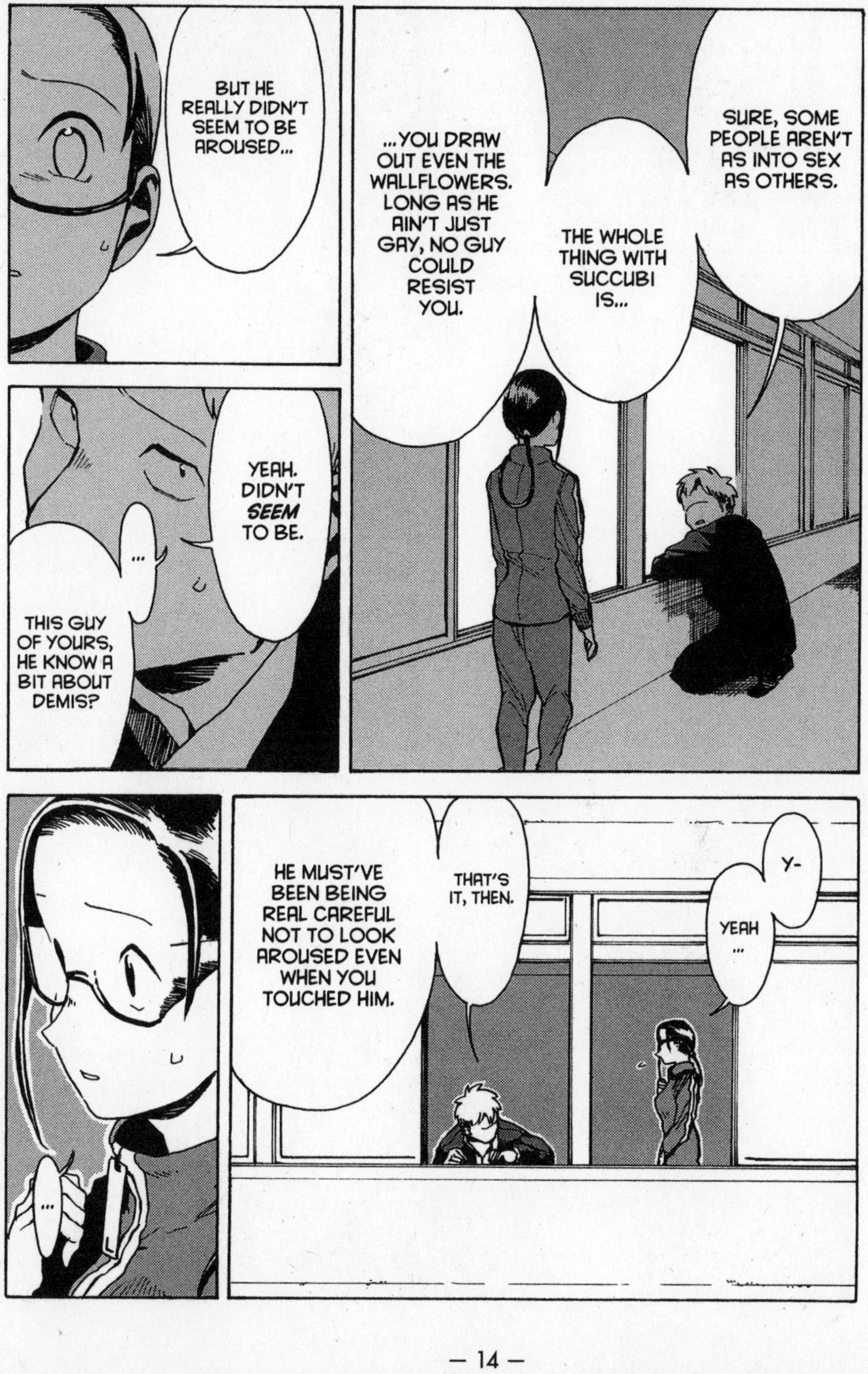
SURE, SOME PEOPLE AREN'T AS INTO SEX AS OTHERS.
THE WHOLE THING WITH SUCCUBI IS...
...YOU DRAW OUT EVEN THE WALLFLOWERS. LONG AS HE AIN'T JUST GAY, NO GUY COULD RESIST YOU.
BUT HE REALLY DIDN'T SEEM TO BE AROUSED...
YEAH. DIDN'T *SEEM* TO BE.
...
THIS GUY OF YOURS, HE KNOW A BIT ABOUT DEMIS?
Y-
YEAH ...
THAT'S IT, THEN.
HE MUST'VE BEEN BEING REAL CAREFUL NOT TO LOOK AROUSED EVEN WHEN YOU TOUCHED HIM.
...

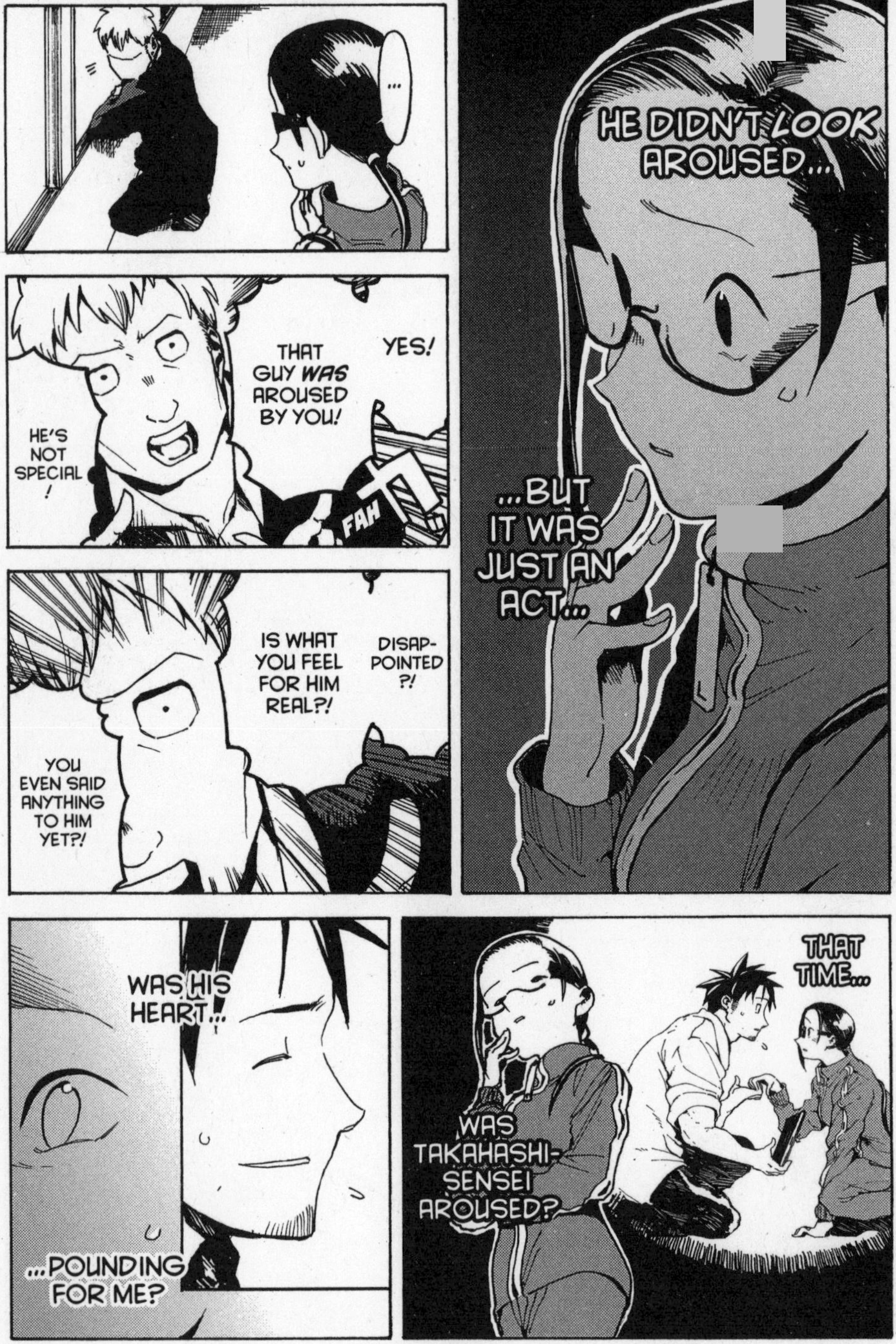
HE DIDN'T LOOK AROUSED...
...BUT IT WAS JUST AN ACT...
...
YES!
THAT GUY WAS AROUSED BY YOU!
HE'S NOT SPECIAL!
FAH
DISAP-POINTED?!
IS WHAT YOU FEEL FOR HIM REAL?!
YOU EVEN SAID ANYTHING TO HIM YET?!
THAT TIME...
WAS TAKAHASHI-SENSEI AROUSED?
WAS HIS HEART...
...POUNDING FOR ME?

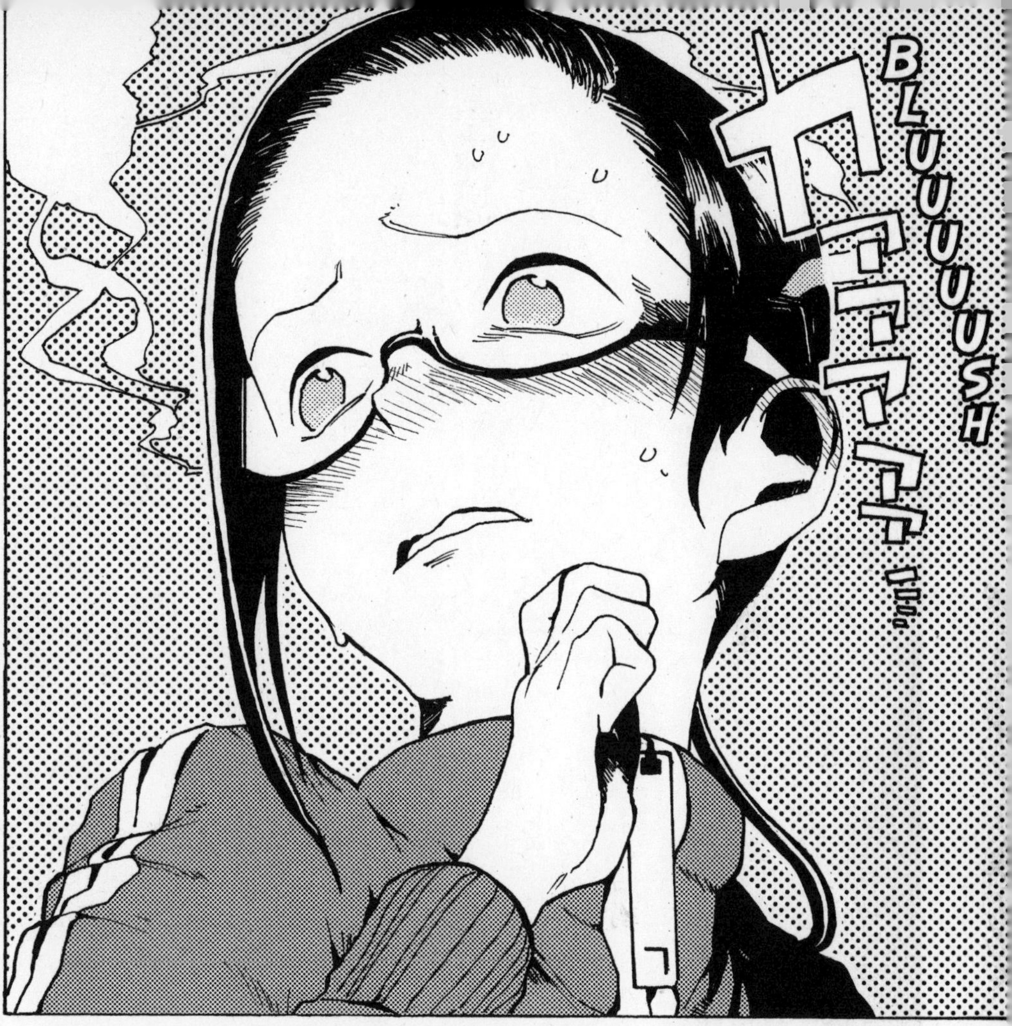
BLUUUUUSH
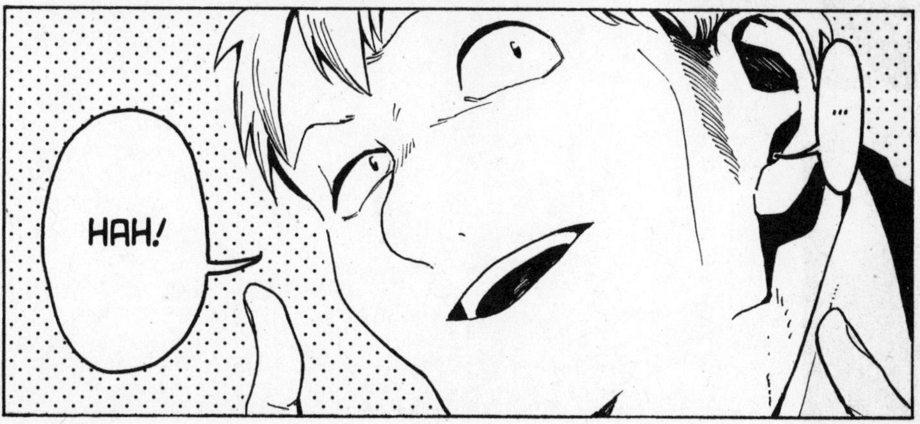
...
HAH!

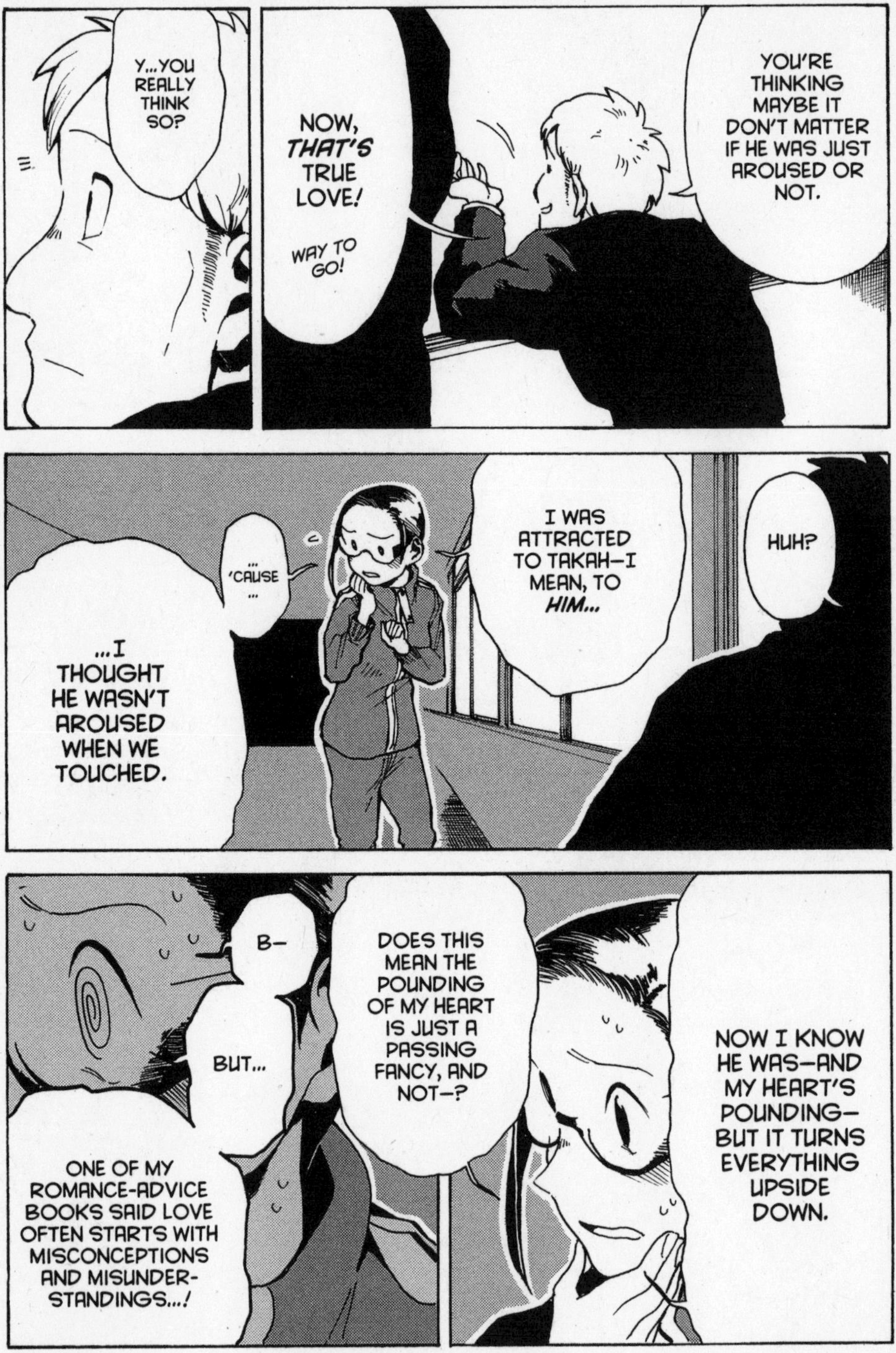

YOU'RE THINKING MAYBE IT DON'T MATTER IF HE WAS JUST AROUSED OR NOT.
NOW, *THAT'S* TRUE LOVE!
WAY TO GO!
Y...YOU REALLY THINK SO?
HUH?
I WAS ATTRACTED TO TAKAH—I MEAN, TO *HIM*...
...'CAUSE...
...I THOUGHT HE WASN'T AROUSED WHEN WE TOUCHED.
NOW I KNOW HE WAS—AND MY HEART'S POUNDING—BUT IT TURNS EVERYTHING UPSIDE DOWN.
DOES THIS MEAN THE POUNDING OF MY HEART IS JUST A PASSING FANCY, AND NOT—?
B—
BUT...
ONE OF MY ROMANCE-ADVICE BOOKS SAID LOVE OFTEN STARTS WITH MISCONCEPTIONS AND MISUNDER-STANDINGS...!

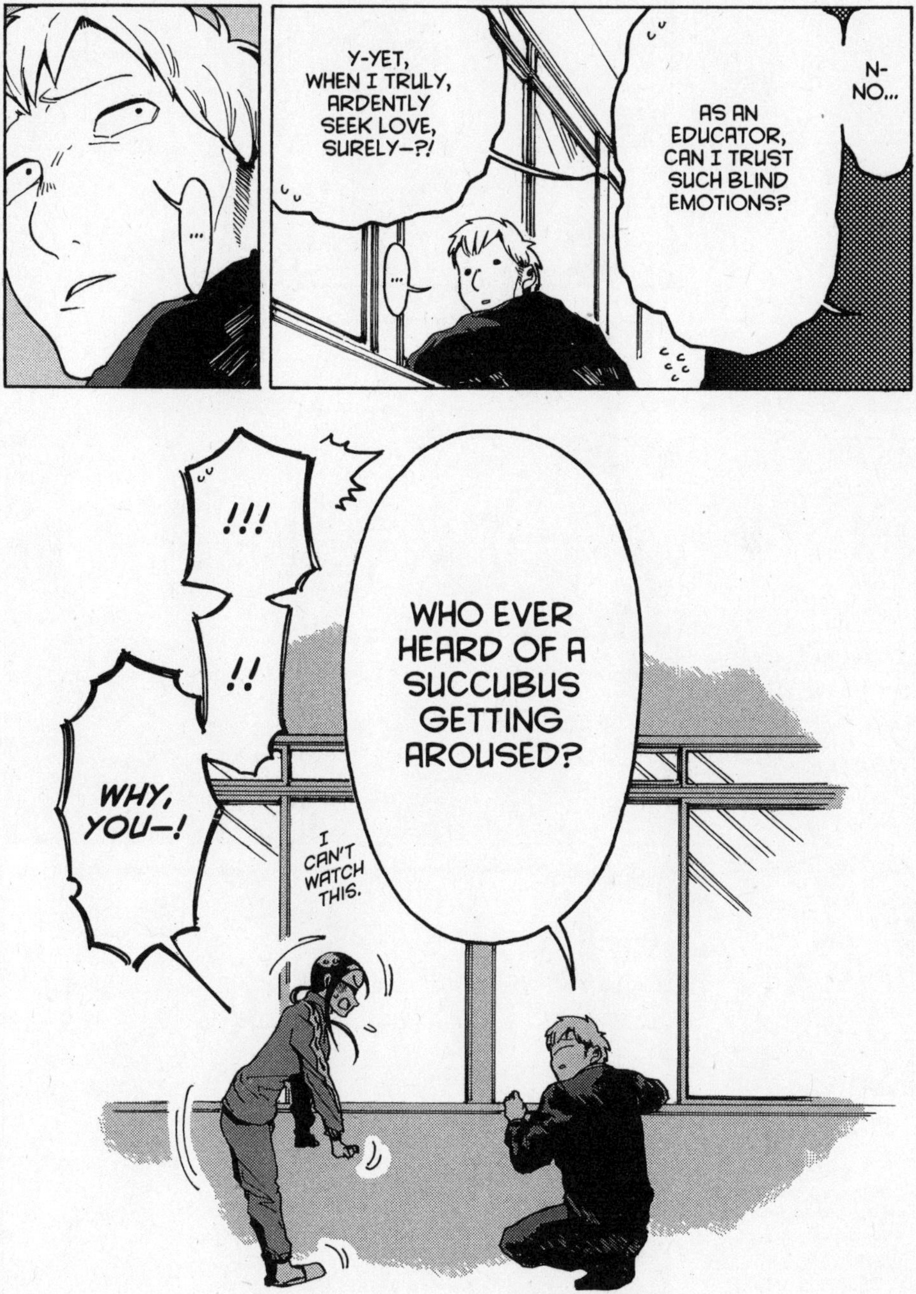

N-NO...
AS AN EDUCATOR, CAN I TRUST SUCH BLIND EMOTIONS?
Y-YET, WHEN I TRULY, ARDENTLY SEEK LOVE, SURELY—?!
...
...
WHO EVER HEARD OF A SUCCUBUS GETTING AROUSED?
!!!
!!
I CAN'T WATCH THIS.
WHY, YOU—!

EARLIER...
YOU'LL NEED TO WRITE YOUR NAME IN THE VISITOR REGISTER...
HUH?
OH YEAH?
SORRY 'BOUT THAT.
OKAY, KURTZ, YOU HANDLE IT.
DON'T GIMMIE THAT FACE.
HE'S A DETECTIVE TOO, HUH...?
HE'S SO YOUNG. AND A FOREIGNER, TO BOOT.
GUESS THE POLICE TAKE ALL KINDS.
I'LL DO IT IF YOU BUY ME TAKOYAKI ON THE WAY HOME.
HRK!
YOU...
ALL KINDS ...
SNUB

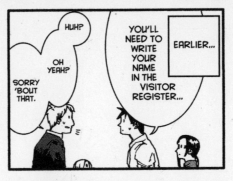

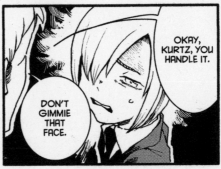

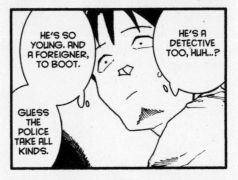

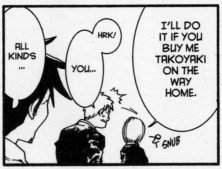

INTERVIEWS WITH MONSTER GIRLS

Chapter 18: Adults Want to Smoke

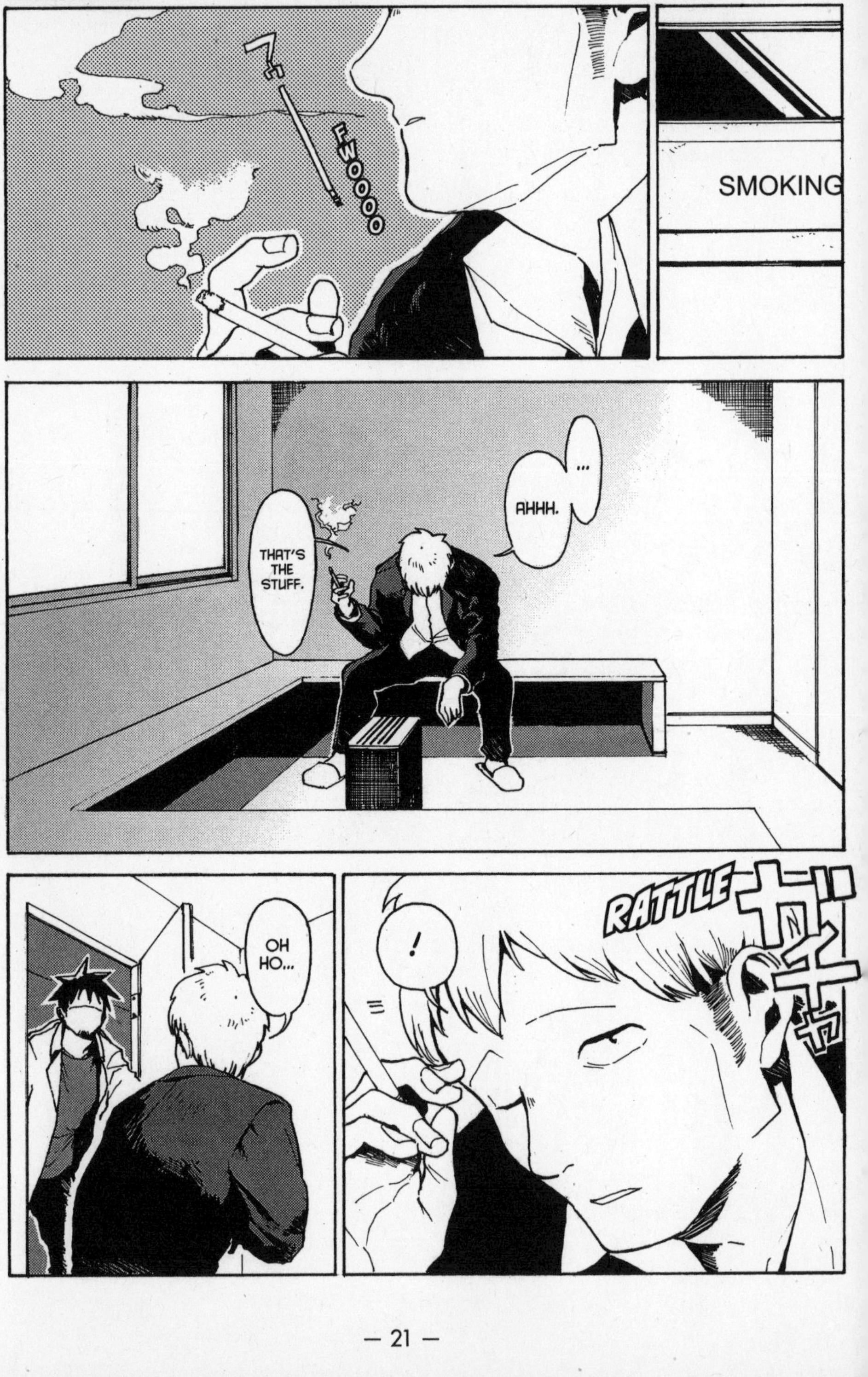
SMOKING
フー
FWOOOO
...
AHHH.
THAT'S THE STUFF.
RATTLE
ガチャ
!
OH HO...

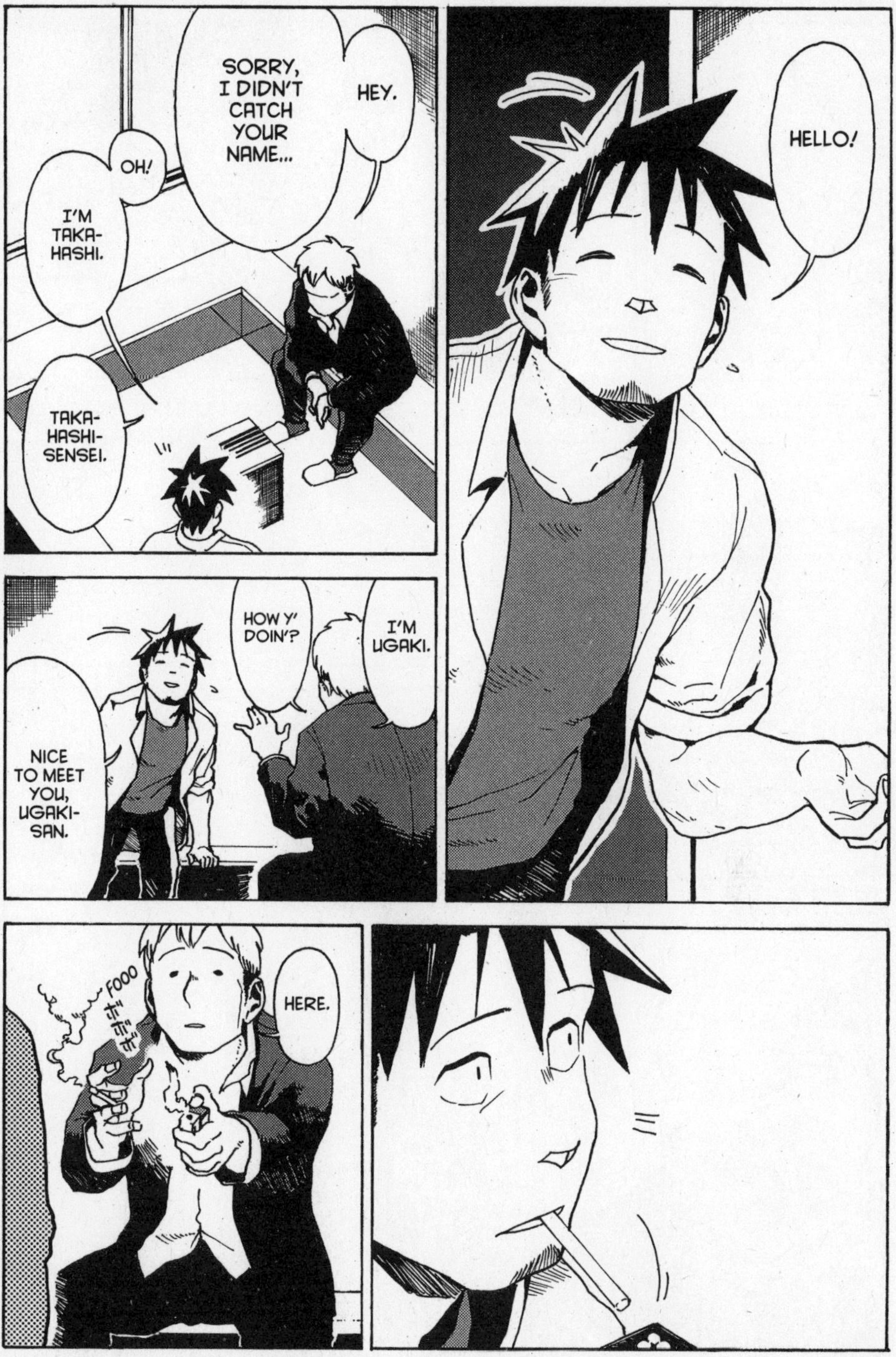
HELLO!
HEY.
SORRY, I DIDN'T CATCH YOUR NAME...
OH!
I'M TAKA-HASHI.
TAKA-HASHI-SENSEI.
I'M UGAKI.
HOW Y' DOIN'?
NICE TO MEET YOU, UGAKI-SAN.
HERE.
FOOO

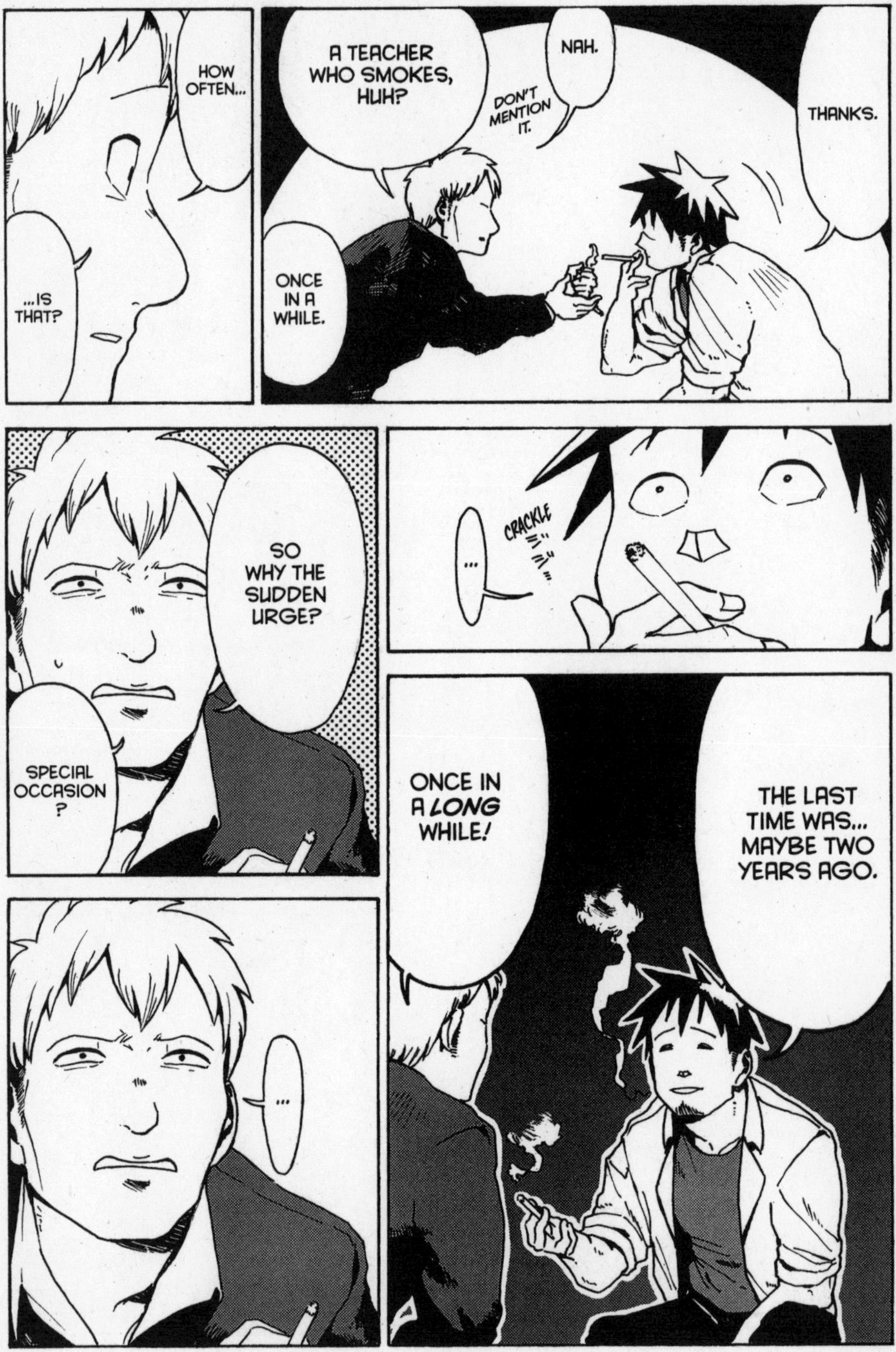
THANKS.
NAH.
DON'T MENTION IT.
A TEACHER WHO SMOKES, HUH?
ONCE IN A WHILE.
HOW OFTEN...
...IS THAT?
...
CRACKLE
SO WHY THE SUDDEN URGE?
SPECIAL OCCASION?
THE LAST TIME WAS... MAYBE TWO YEARS AGO.
ONCE IN A *LONG* WHILE!
...

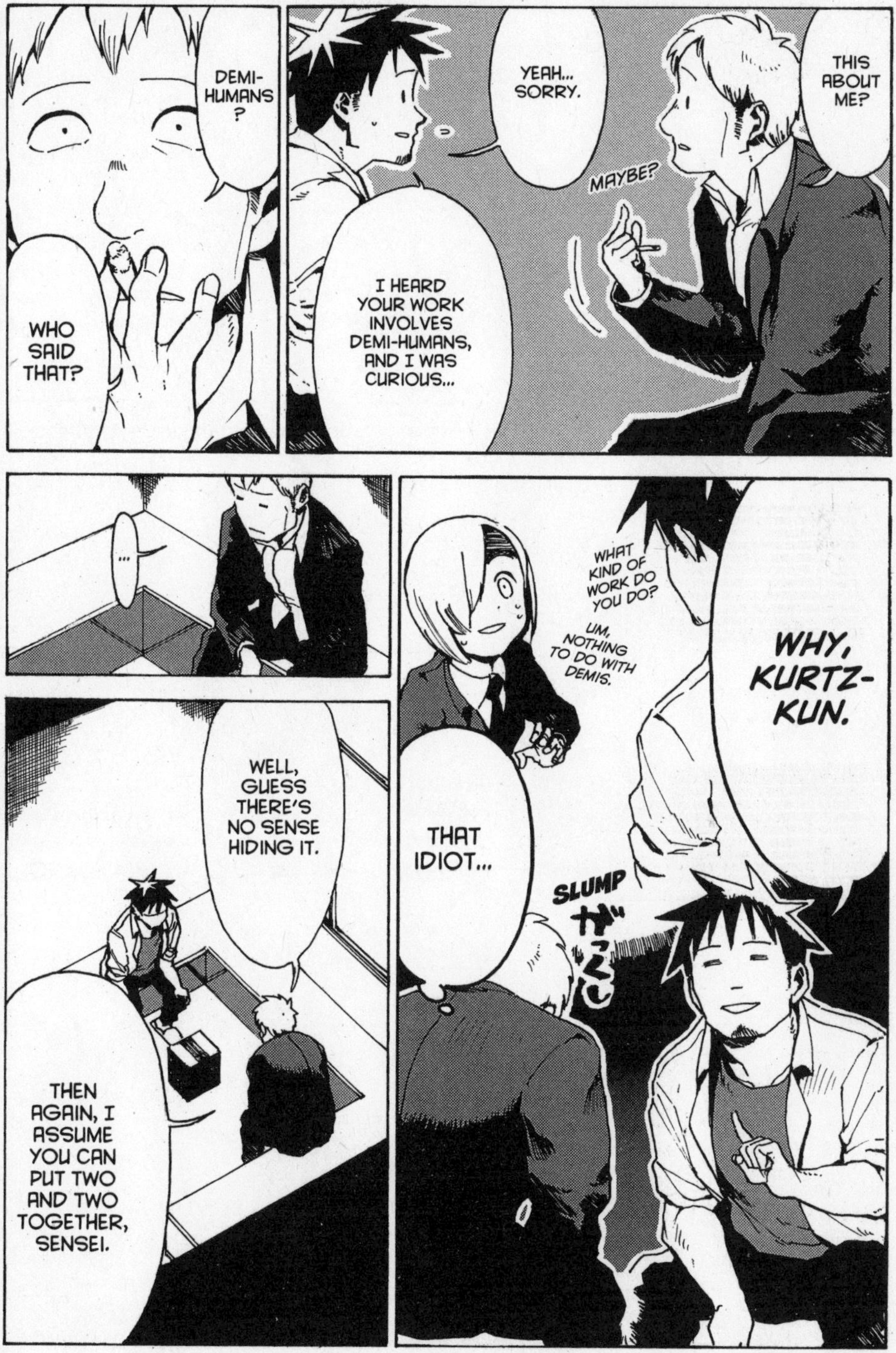
THIS ABOUT ME?
MAYBE?
YEAH... SORRY.
I HEARD YOUR WORK INVOLVES DEMI-HUMANS, AND I WAS CURIOUS...
DEMI-HUMANS?
WHO SAID THAT?
WHY, KURTZ-KUN.
WHAT KIND OF WORK DO YOU DO?
UM, NOTHING TO DO WITH DEMIS.
SLUMP
がっくし
THAT IDIOT...
...
WELL, GUESS THERE'S NO SENSE HIDING IT.
THEN AGAIN, I ASSUME YOU CAN PUT TWO AND TWO TOGETHER, SENSEI.

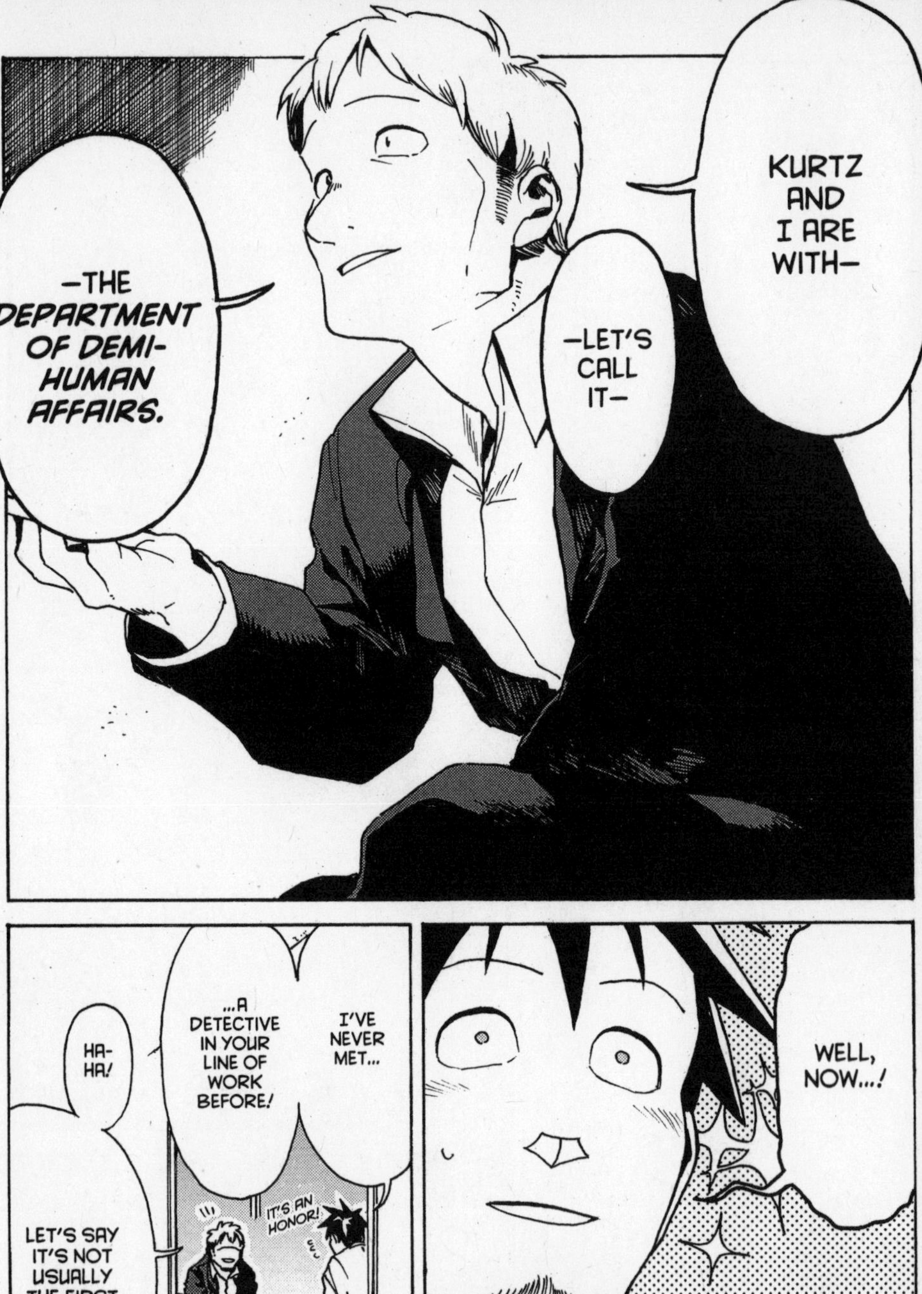
KURTZ AND I ARE WITH—
—LET'S CALL IT—
—THE DEPARTMENT OF DEMI-HUMAN AFFAIRS.
WELL, NOW...!
I'VE NEVER MET...
...A DETECTIVE IN YOUR LINE OF WORK BEFORE!
IT'S AN HONOR!
HA-HA!
LET'S SAY IT'S NOT USUALLY THE FIRST THING I MENTION.

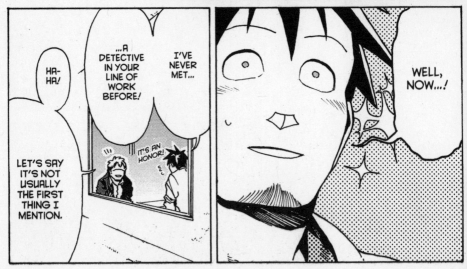

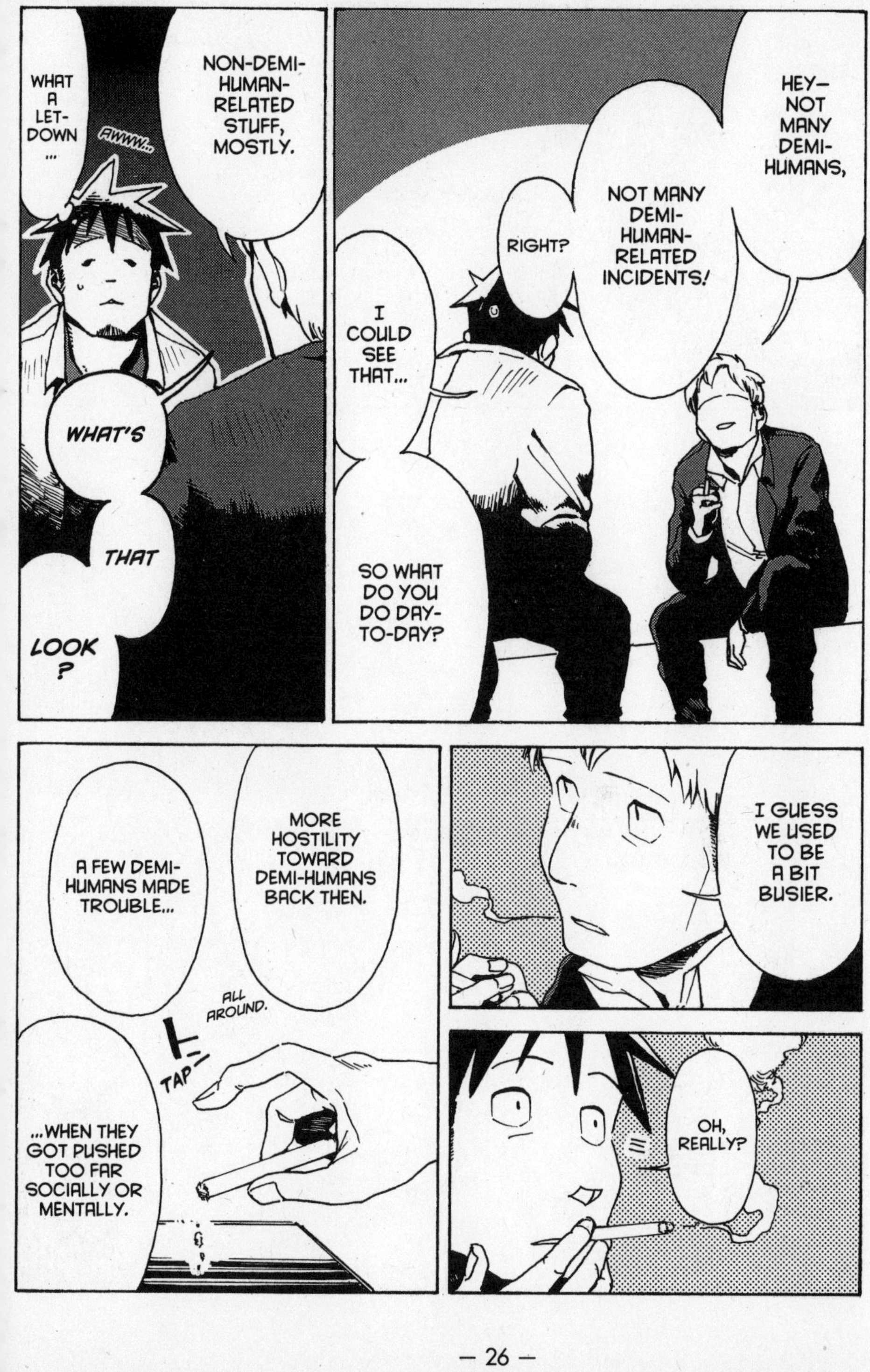
HEY— NOT MANY DEMI-HUMANS,
NOT MANY DEMI-HUMAN-RELATED INCIDENTS!
RIGHT?
I COULD SEE THAT...
SO WHAT DO YOU DO DAY-TO-DAY?
NON-DEMI-HUMAN-RELATED STUFF, MOSTLY.
AWWW...
WHAT A LET-DOWN...
WHAT'S
THAT
LOOK?
I GUESS WE USED TO BE A BIT BUSIER.
OH, REALLY?
MORE HOSTILITY TOWARD DEMI-HUMANS BACK THEN.
A FEW DEMI-HUMANS MADE TROUBLE...
ALL AROUND.
TAP
...WHEN THEY GOT PUSHED TOO FAR SOCIALLY OR MENTALLY.

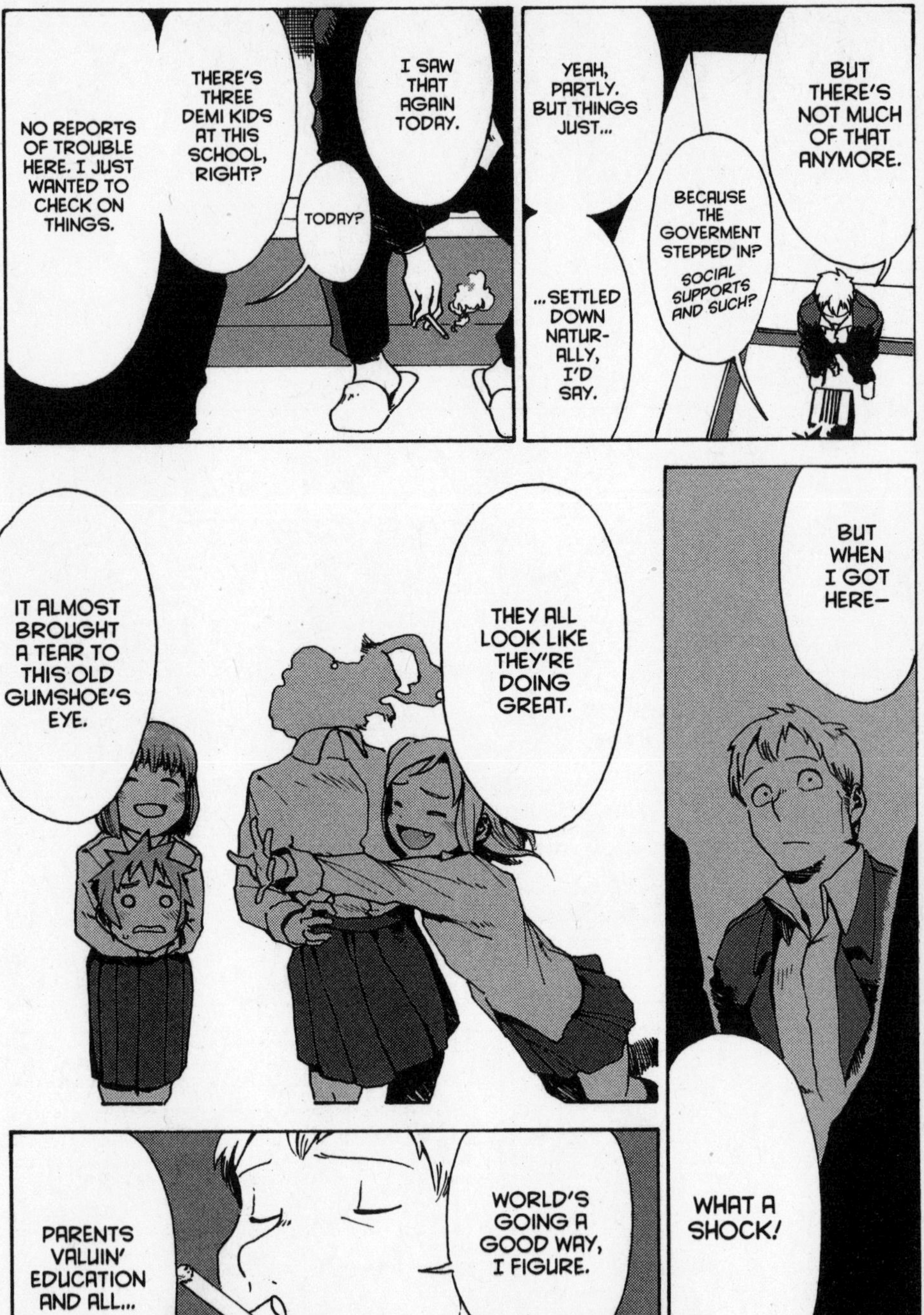
BUT THERE'S NOT MUCH OF THAT ANYMORE.
BECAUSE THE GOVERMENT STEPPED IN?
SOCIAL SUPPORTS AND SUCH?
YEAH, PARTLY. BUT THINGS JUST...
...SETTLED DOWN NATURALLY, I'D SAY.
I SAW THAT AGAIN TODAY.
TODAY?
THERE'S THREE DEMI KIDS AT THIS SCHOOL, RIGHT?
NO REPORTS OF TROUBLE HERE. I JUST WANTED TO CHECK ON THINGS.
BUT WHEN I GOT HERE—
WHAT A SHOCK!
THEY ALL LOOK LIKE THEY'RE DOING GREAT.
IT ALMOST BROUGHT A TEAR TO THIS OLD GUMSHOE'S EYE.
WORLD'S GOING A GOOD WAY, I FIGURE.
PARENTS VALUIN' EDUCATION AND ALL...

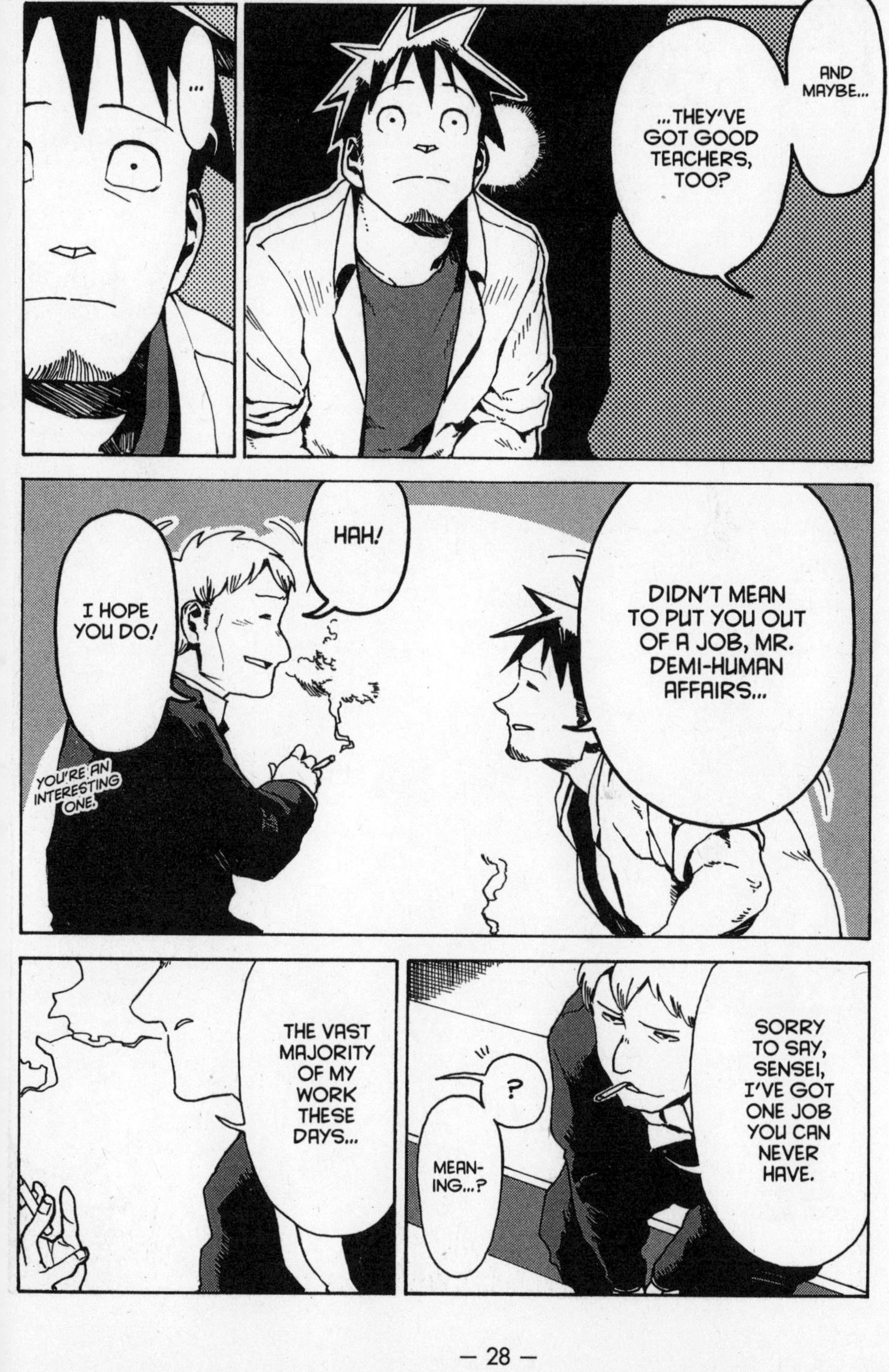
AND MAYBE...
...THEY'VE GOT GOOD TEACHERS, TOO?
...
DIDN'T MEAN TO PUT YOU OUT OF A JOB, MR. DEMI-HUMAN AFFAIRS...
HAH!
I HOPE YOU DO!
YOU'RE AN INTERESTING ONE.
SORRY TO SAY, SENSEI, I'VE GOT ONE JOB YOU CAN NEVER HAVE.
?
MEAN-ING...?
THE VAST MAJORITY OF MY WORK THESE DAYS...

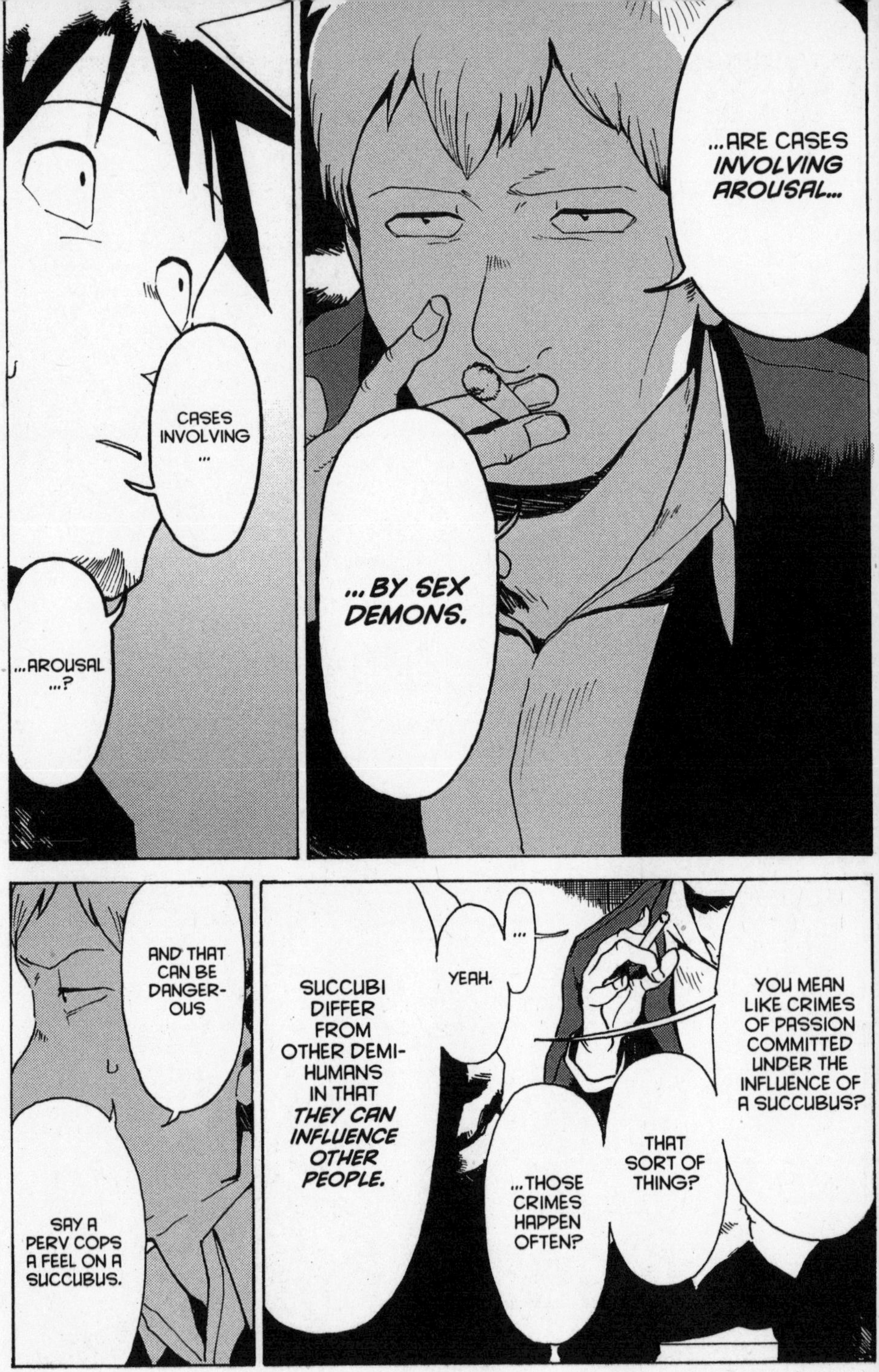
...ARE CASES INVOLVING AROUSAL...
...BY SEX DEMONS.
CASES INVOLVING ...
...AROUSAL ...?
YOU MEAN LIKE CRIMES OF PASSION COMMITTED UNDER THE INFLUENCE OF A SUCCUBUS?
THAT SORT OF THING?
...THOSE CRIMES HAPPEN OFTEN?
...
YEAH.
SUCCUBI DIFFER FROM OTHER DEMI-HUMANS IN THAT THEY CAN INFLUENCE OTHER PEOPLE.
AND THAT CAN BE DANGER-OUS
SAY A PERV COPS A FEEL ON A SUCCUBUS.

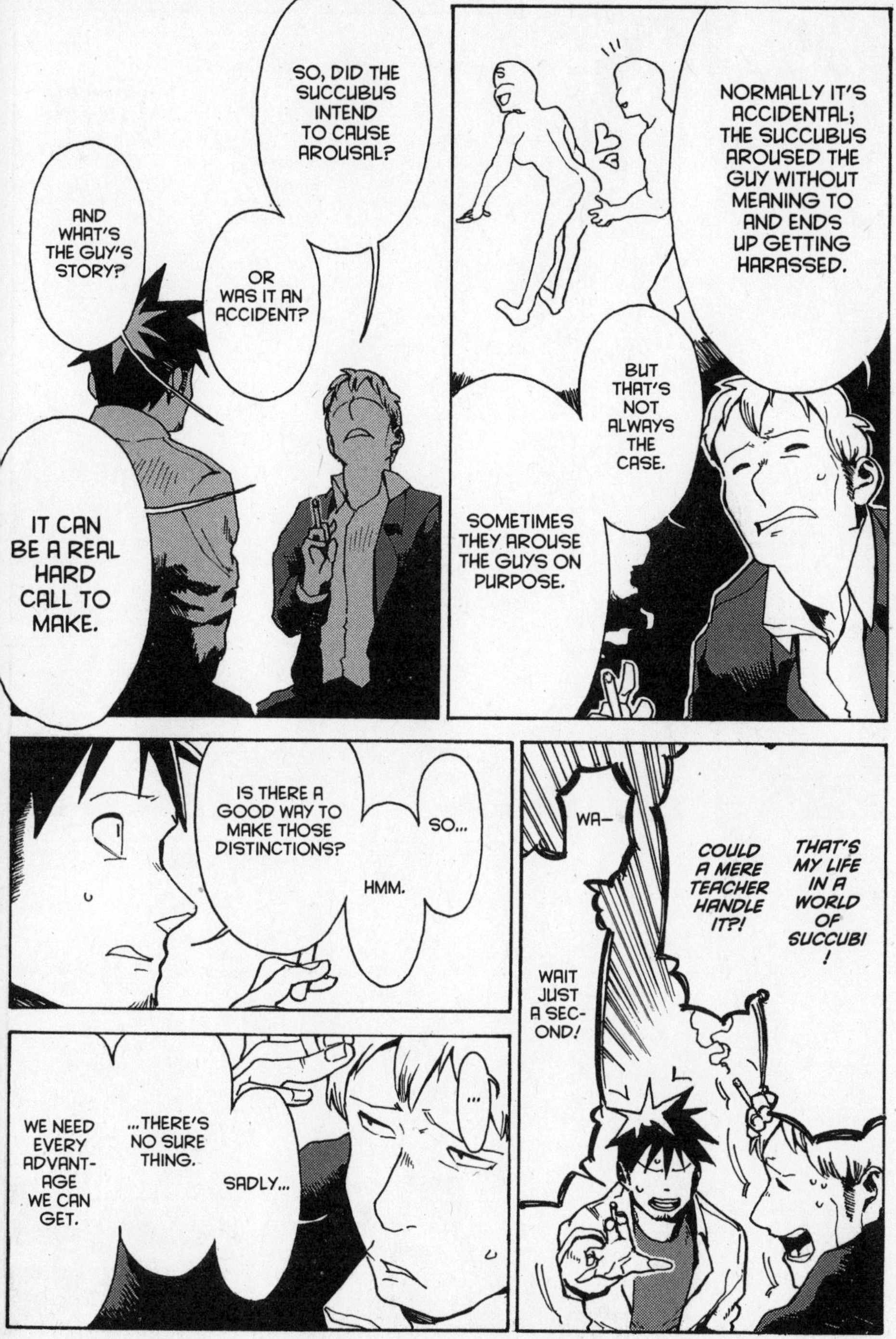

NORMALLY IT'S ACCIDENTAL; THE SUCCUBUS AROUSED THE GUY WITHOUT MEANING TO AND ENDS UP GETTING HARASSED.
BUT THAT'S NOT ALWAYS THE CASE.
SOMETIMES THEY AROUSE THE GUYS ON PURPOSE.
SO, DID THE SUCCUBUS INTEND TO CAUSE AROUSAL?
OR WAS IT AN ACCIDENT?
AND WHAT'S THE GUY'S STORY?
IT CAN BE A REAL HARD CALL TO MAKE.
THAT'S MY LIFE IN A WORLD OF SUCCUBI!
COULD A MERE TEACHER HANDLE IT?!
WA-
WAIT JUST A SEC-OND!
SO...
HMM.
IS THERE A GOOD WAY TO MAKE THOSE DISTINCTIONS?
...
SADLY...
...THERE'S NO SURE THING.
WE NEED EVERY ADVANT-AGE WE CAN GET.

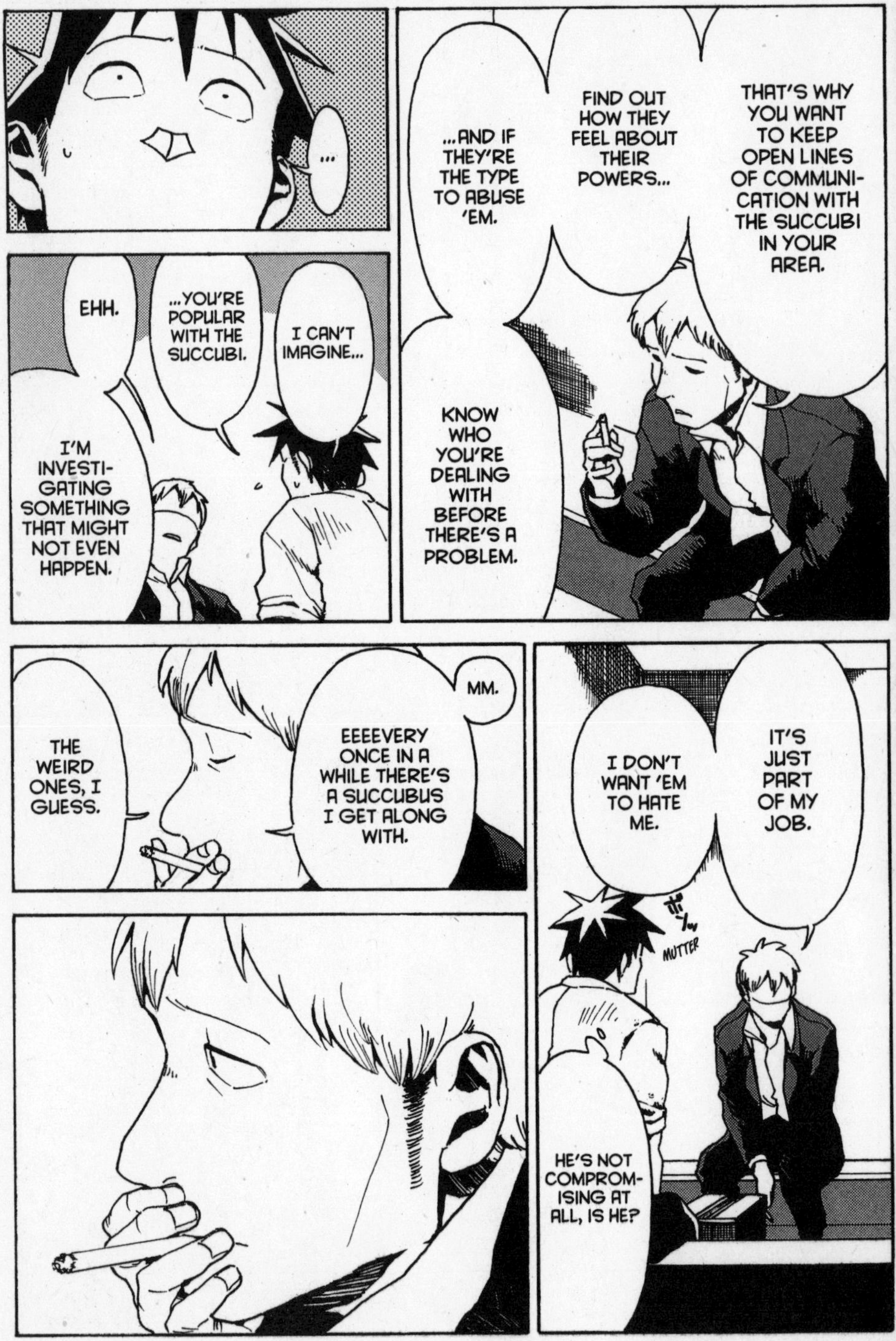
THAT'S WHY YOU WANT TO KEEP OPEN LINES OF COMMUNICATION WITH THE SUCCUBI IN YOUR AREA.
FIND OUT HOW THEY FEEL ABOUT THEIR POWERS...
...AND IF THEY'RE THE TYPE TO ABUSE 'EM.
KNOW WHO YOU'RE DEALING WITH BEFORE THERE'S A PROBLEM.
...
I CAN'T IMAGINE...
...YOU'RE POPULAR WITH THE SUCCUBI.
EHH.
I'M INVESTIGATING SOMETHING THAT MIGHT NOT EVEN HAPPEN.
IT'S JUST PART OF MY JOB.
I DON'T WANT 'EM TO HATE ME.
MUTTER
HE'S NOT COMPROMISING AT ALL, IS HE?
MM.
EEEEVERY ONCE IN A WHILE THERE'S A SUCCUBUS I GET ALONG WITH.
THE WEIRD ONES, I GUESS.

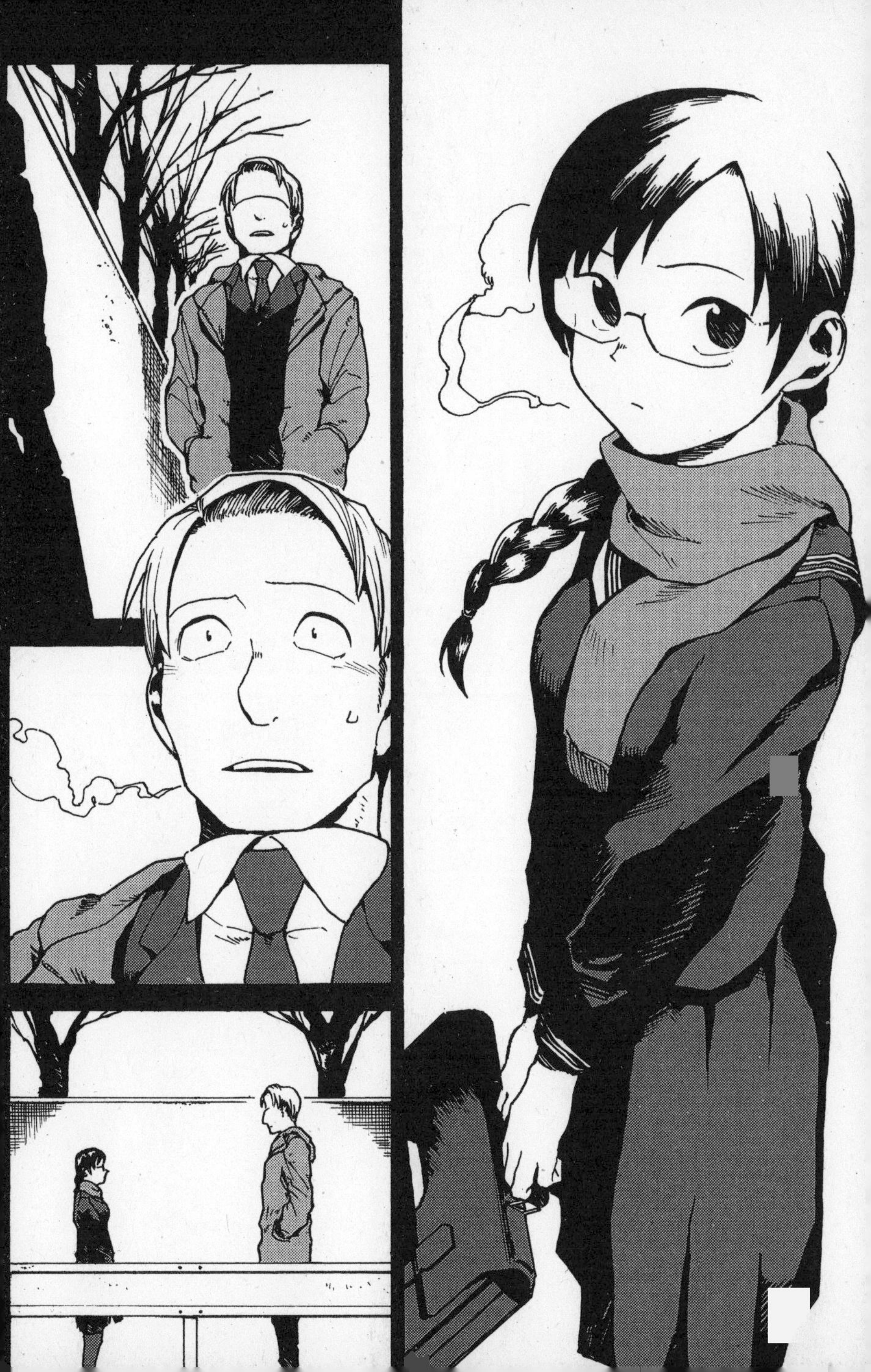

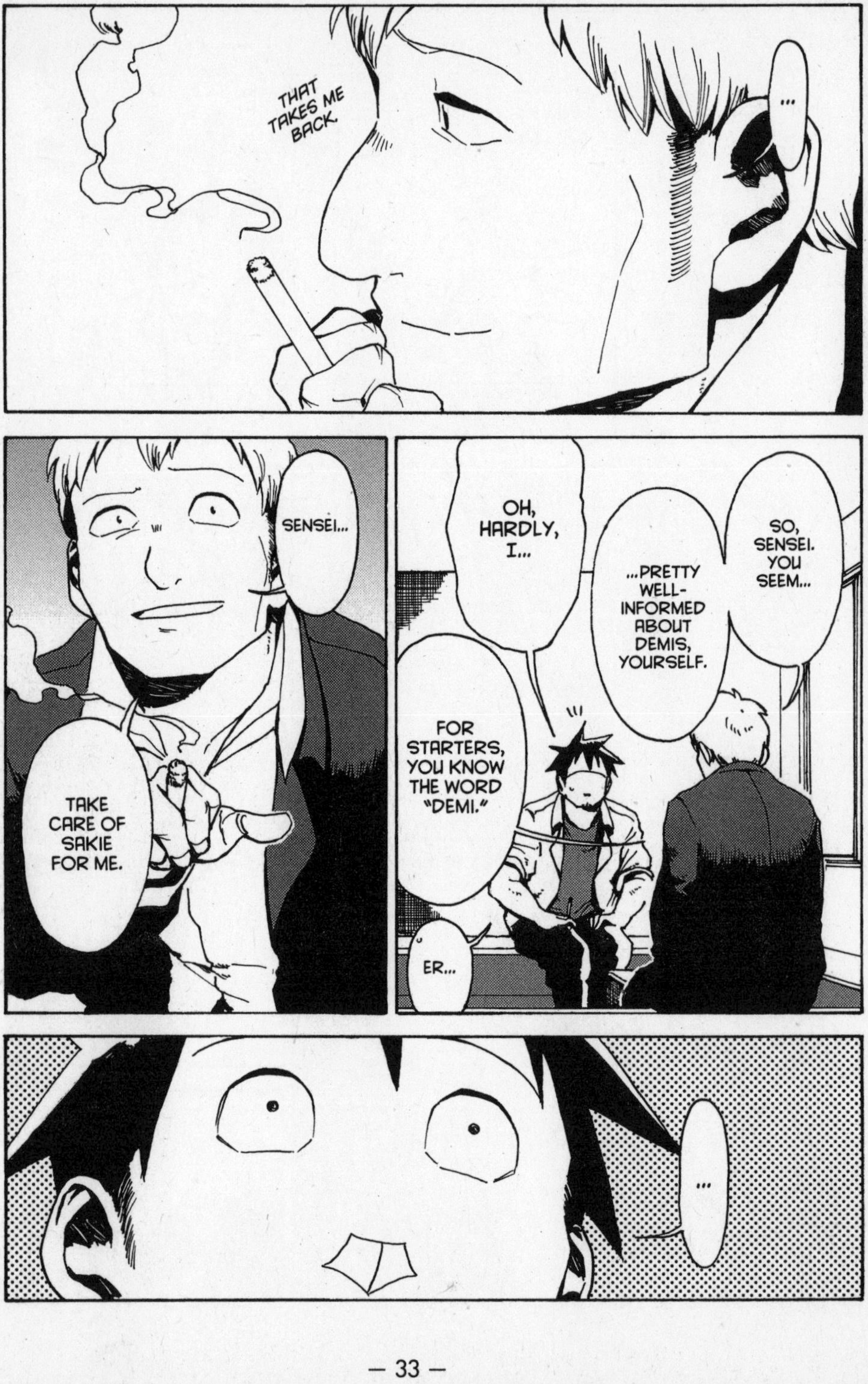
...
THAT TAKES ME BACK.
SO, SENSEI. YOU SEEM...
...PRETTY WELL-INFORMED ABOUT DEMIS, YOURSELF.
OH, HARDLY, I...
FOR STARTERS, YOU KNOW THE WORD "DEMI."
ER...
SENSEI...
TAKE CARE OF SAKIE FOR ME.
...

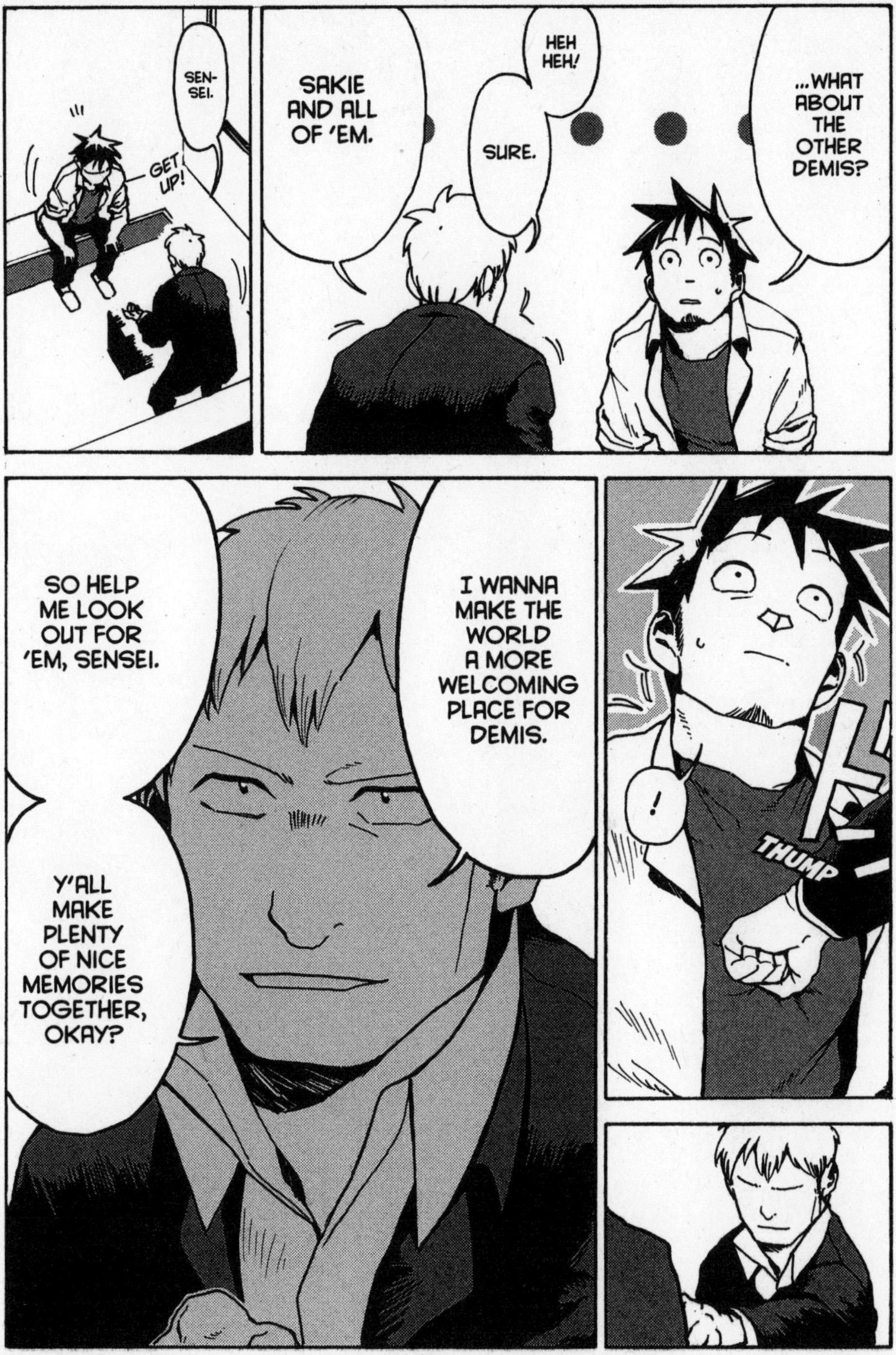
...WHAT ABOUT THE OTHER DEMIS?
HEH HEH!
SURE.
SAKIE AND ALL OF 'EM.
SEN-SEI.
GET UP!
!
THUMP
I WANNA MAKE THE WORLD A MORE WELCOMING PLACE FOR DEMIS.
SO HELP ME LOOK OUT FOR 'EM, SENSEI.
Y'ALL MAKE PLENTY OF NICE MEMORIES TOGETHER, OKAY?

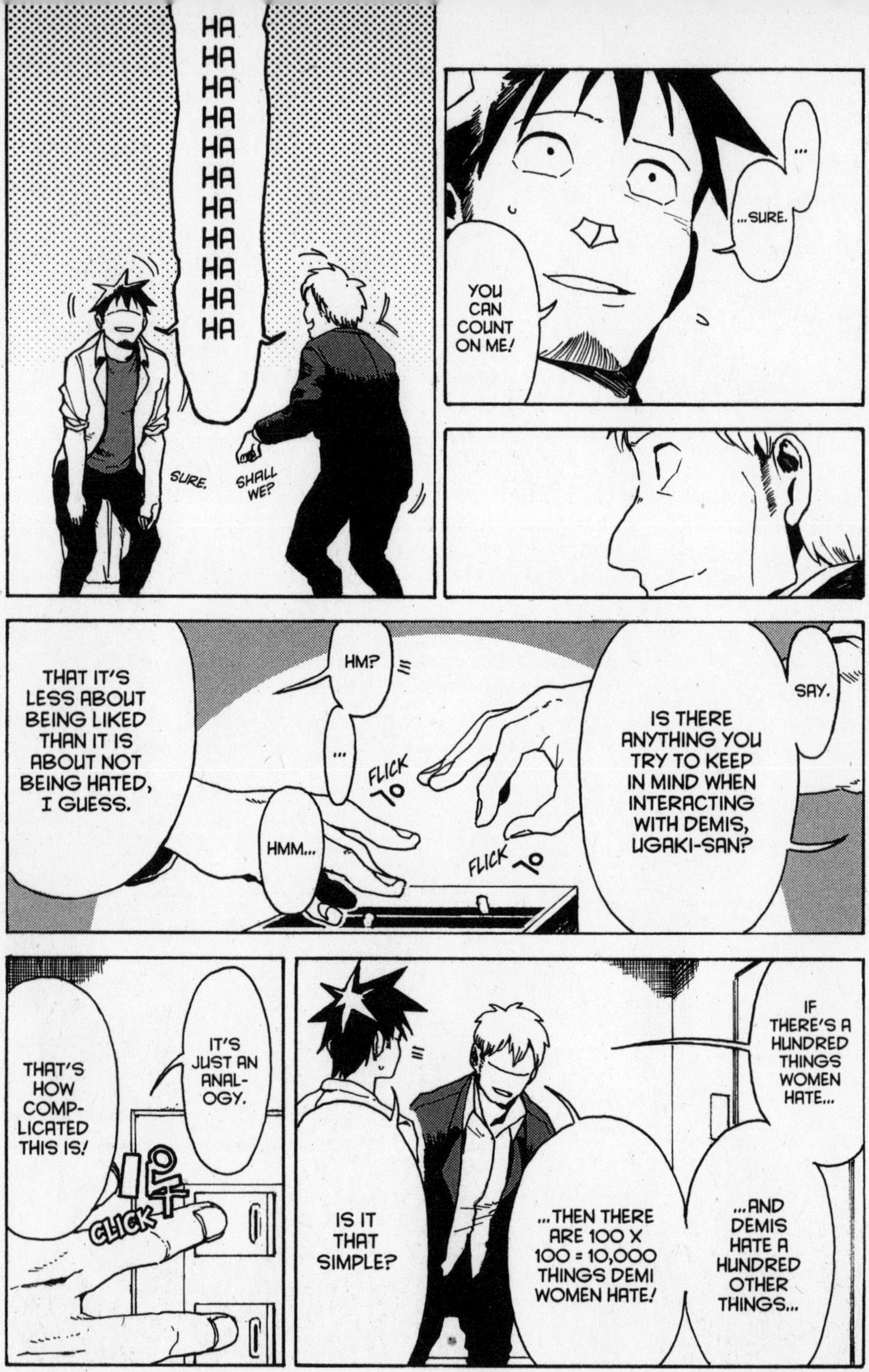
...
...SURE.
YOU CAN COUNT ON ME!
HA HA HA HA HA HA HA HA HA HA HA
SHALL WE?
SURE.
SAY.
IS THERE ANYTHING YOU TRY TO KEEP IN MIND WHEN INTERACTING WITH DEMIS, UGAKI-SAN?
FLICK
FLICK
HM?
...
HMM...
THAT IT'S LESS ABOUT BEING LIKED THAN IT IS ABOUT NOT BEING HATED, I GUESS.
IF THERE'S A HUNDRED THINGS WOMEN HATE...
...AND DEMIS HATE A HUNDRED OTHER THINGS...
...THEN THERE ARE 100 X 100 = 10,000 THINGS DEMI WOMEN HATE!
IS IT THAT SIMPLE?
IT'S JUST AN ANALOGY.
CLICK
THAT'S HOW COMPLICATED THIS IS!

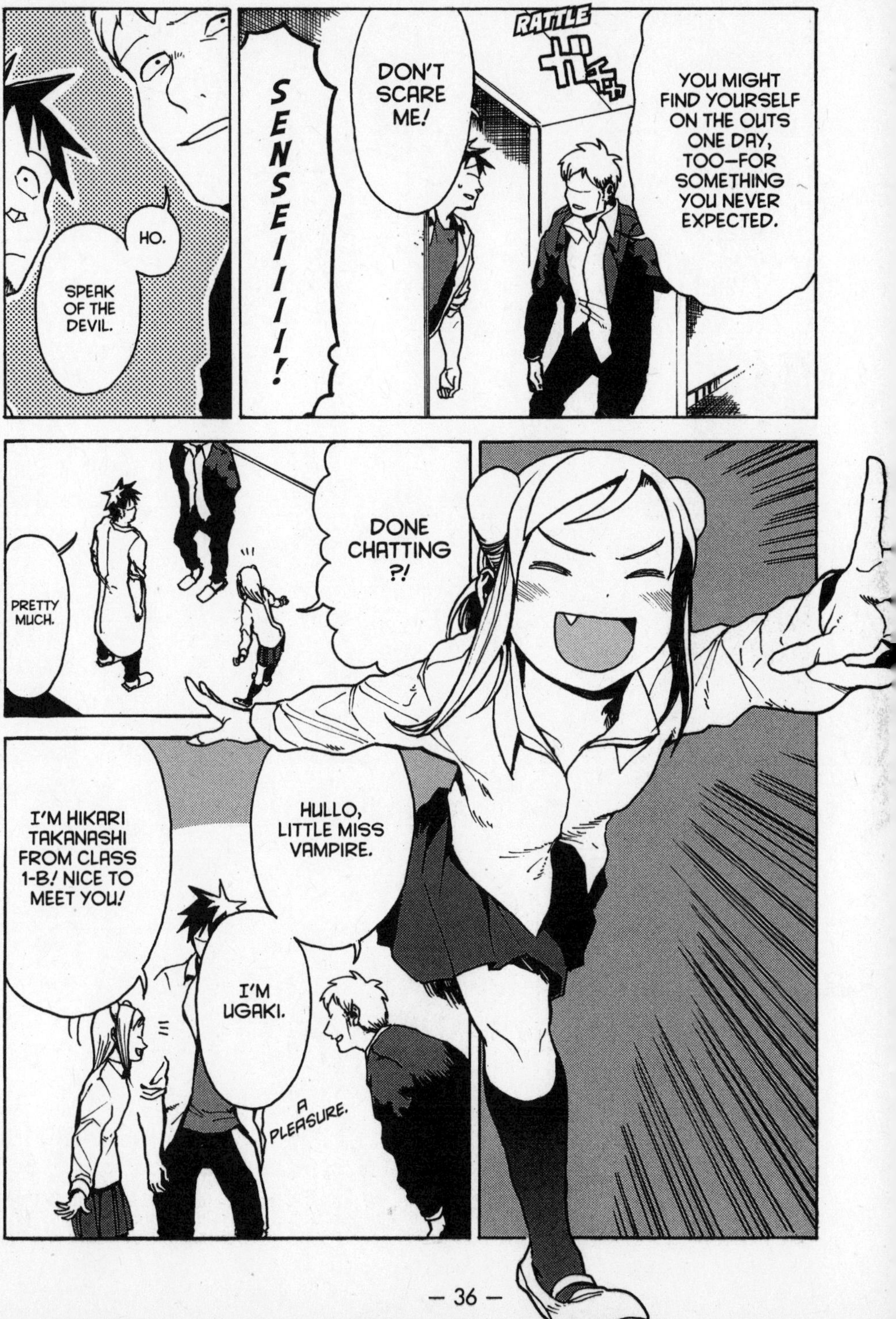
RATTLE
YOU MIGHT FIND YOURSELF ON THE OUTS ONE DAY, TOO—FOR SOMETHING YOU NEVER EXPECTED.
DON'T SCARE ME!
SENSEIIIII!
HO.
SPEAK OF THE DEVIL.
DONE CHATTING?!
PRETTY MUCH.
HULLO, LITTLE MISS VAMPIRE.
I'M HIKARI TAKANASHI FROM CLASS 1-B! NICE TO MEET YOU!
I'M UGAKI.
A PLEASURE.

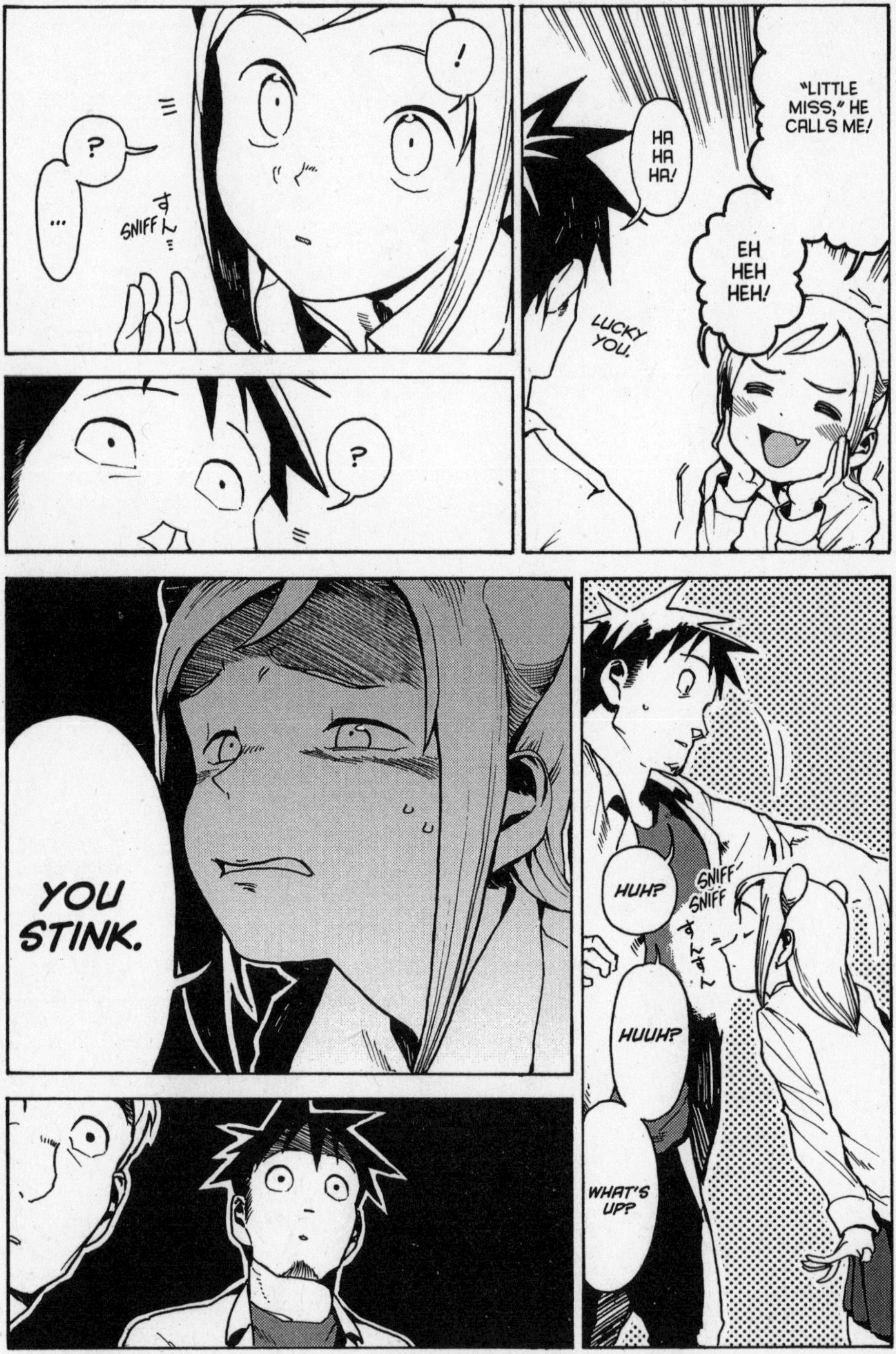
"LITTLE MISS," HE CALLS ME!
HA HA HA!
EH HEH HEH!
LUCKY YOU.
!
?
...
SNIFF すん
?
SNIFF SNIFF
すんすん
HUH?
HUUH?
WHAT'S UP?
YOU STINK.

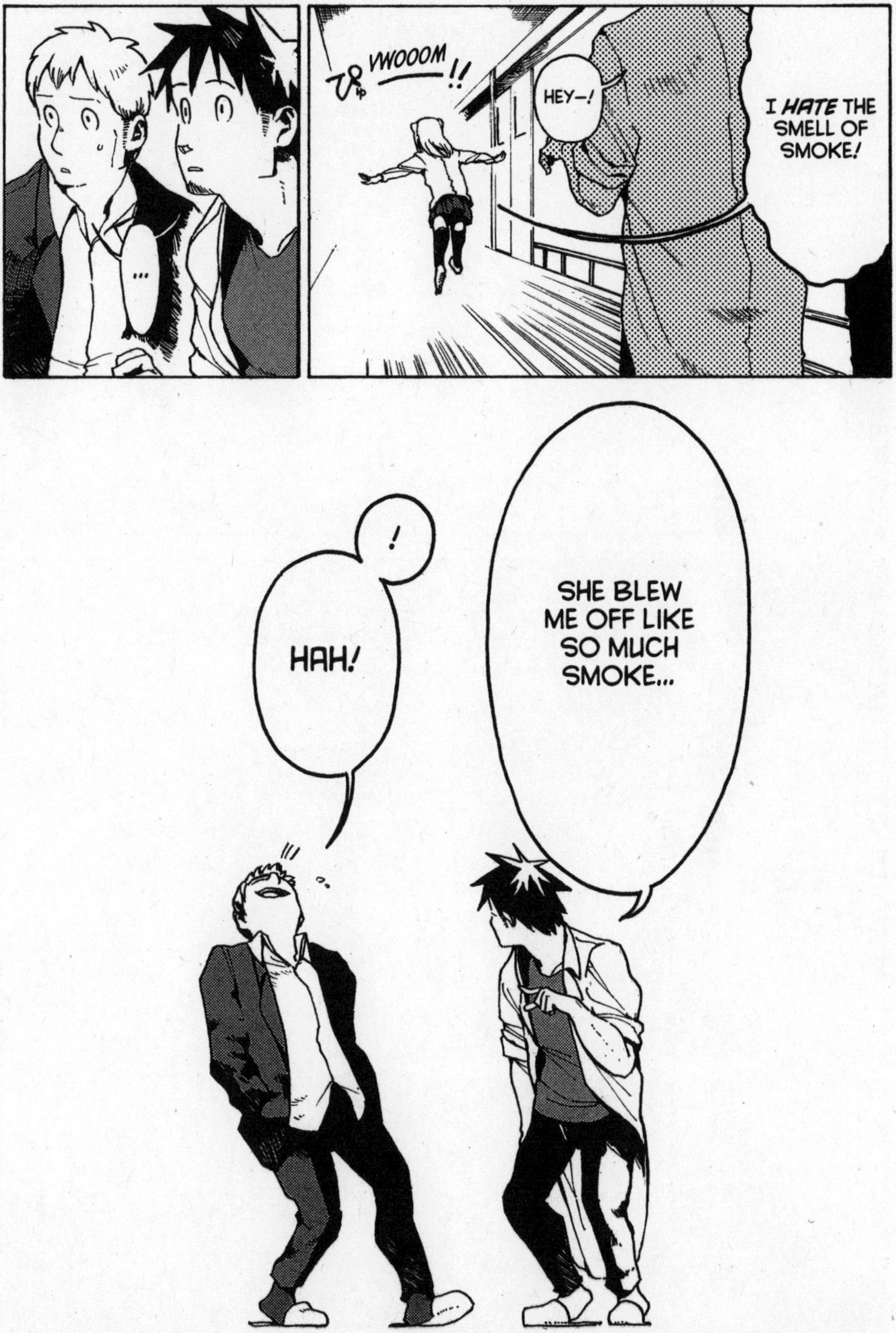

I HATE THE SMELL OF SMOKE!
HEY—!
ぴゅ
VWOOOM!!
...
SHE BLEW ME OFF LIKE SO MUCH SMOKE...
!
HAH!

SO, THAT'S LIFE IN OUR DEPARTMENT.
VRRRM
GOTTA CHECK ON THE DEMIS AROUND TOWN PERIODICALLY.
I GUESS MOST DEMIS AREN'T AN ISSUE FOR THE POLICE.
CREAK
MAINLY THE SUCCUBI.
ONE OF THESE DAYS, I'LL ASK YOU TO START PULLIN' YOUR WEIGHT...
SMIRK
THIS TAKOYAKI'S THE *BEST*...!
GOTTA SET HIM STRAIGHT LATER.

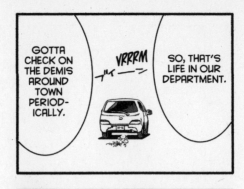

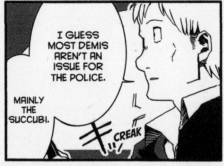

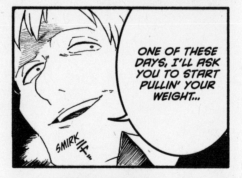

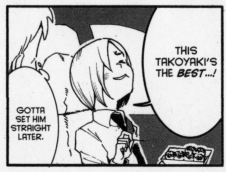

INTERVIEWS WITH MONSTER GIRLS

Chapter 19: Demis Want to Learn

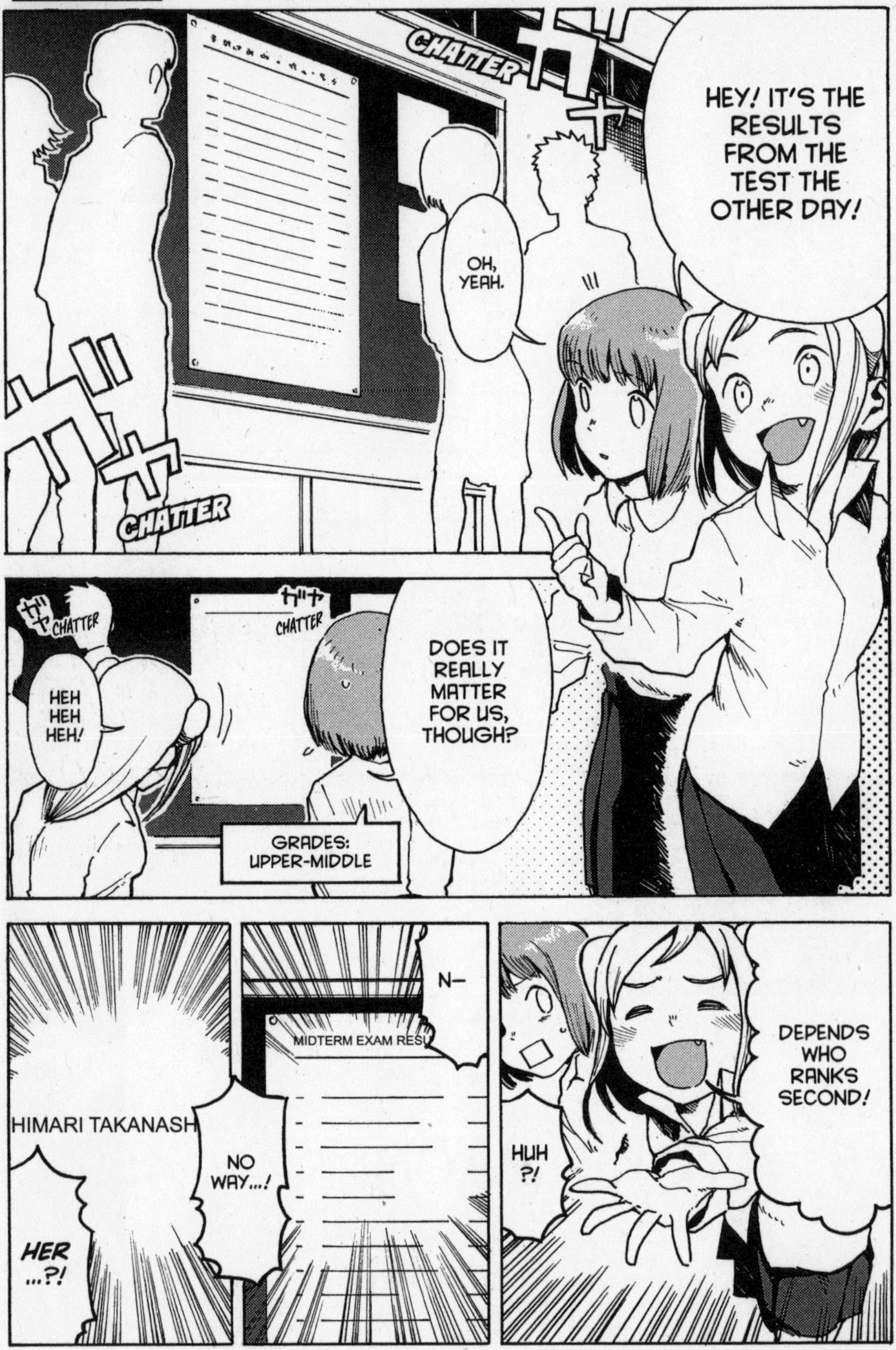
CHATTER
HEY! IT'S THE RESULTS FROM THE TEST THE OTHER DAY!
OH, YEAH.
CHATTER
DOES IT REALLY MATTER FOR US, THOUGH?
CHATTER
GRADES: UPPER-MIDDLE
CHATTER
HEH HEH HEH!
DEPENDS WHO RANKS SECOND!
HUH ?!
N—
MIDTERM EXAM RESU
NO WAY...!
HIMARI TAKANASH
HER ...?!

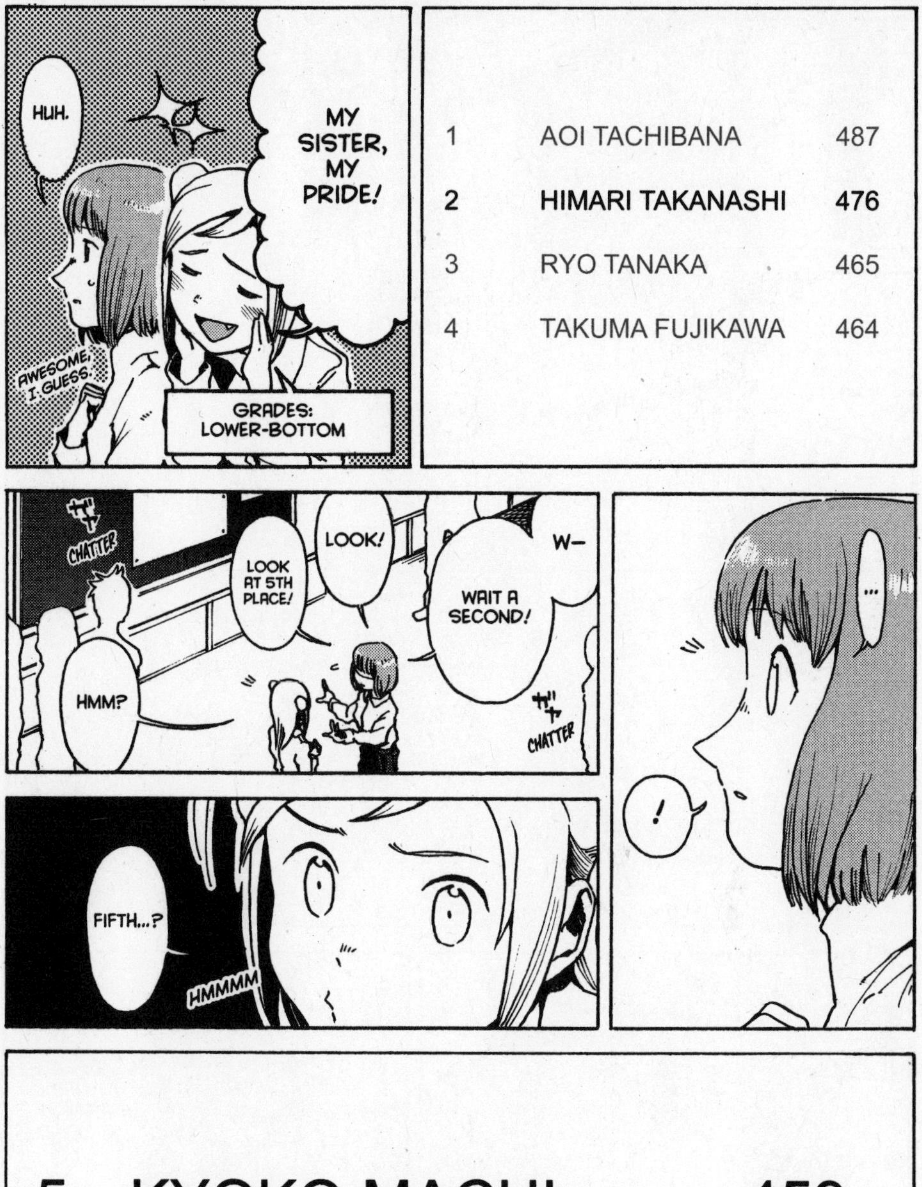
1 AOI TACHIBANA 487
2 HIMARI TAKANASHI 476
3 RYO TANAKA 465
4 TAKUMA FUJIKAWA 464
MY SISTER, MY PRIDE!
HUH.
AWESOME, I GUESS.
GRADES: LOWER-BOTTOM
...
!
W-
WAIT A SECOND!
CHATTER
LOOK!
LOOK AT 5TH PLACE!
HMM?
CHATTER
HMMMM
FIFTH...?
5 KYOKO MACHI 459

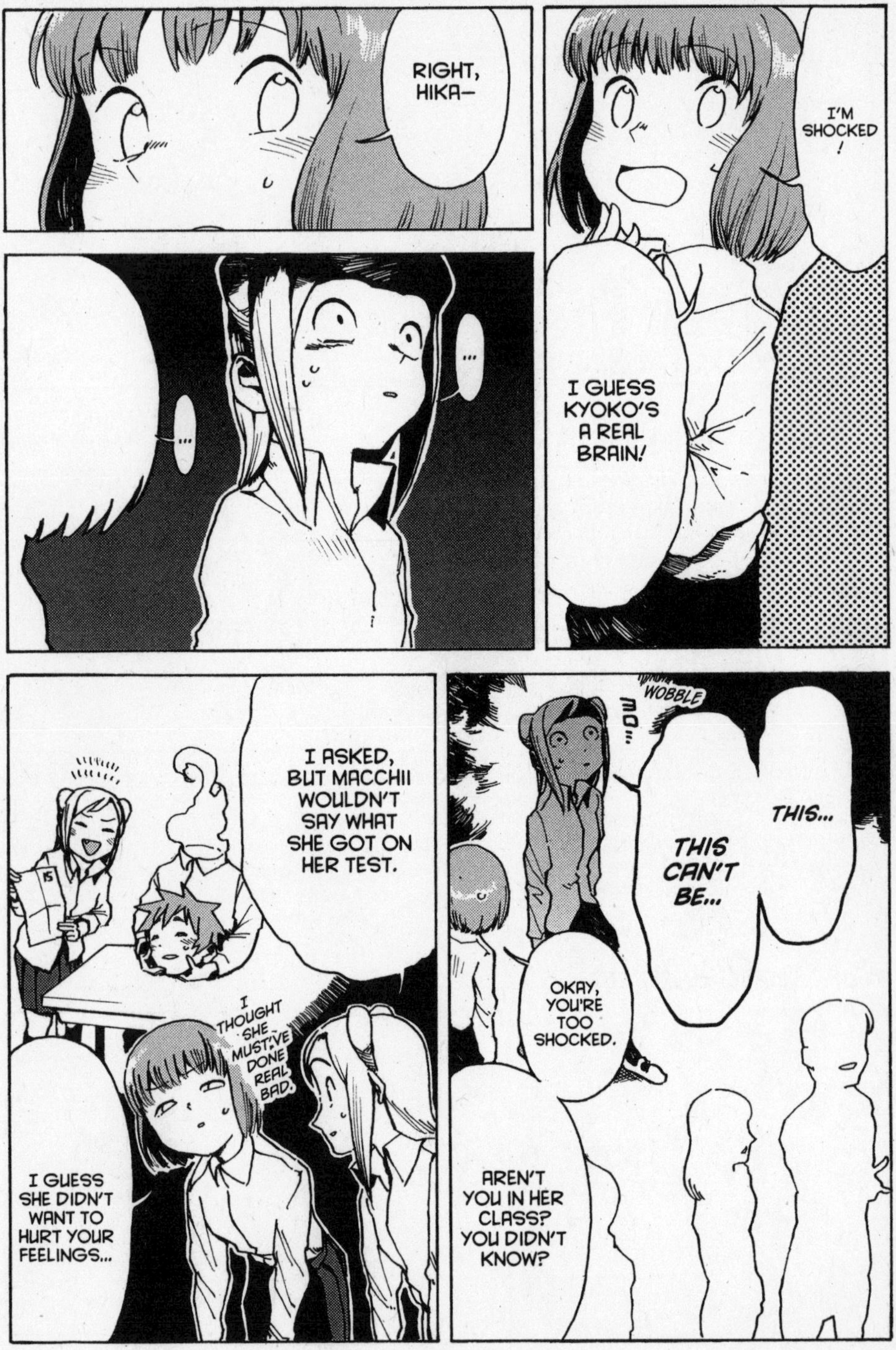
I'M SHOCKED!
I GUESS KYOKO'S A REAL BRAIN!
RIGHT, HIKA—
...
...
WOBBLE
MO...
THIS...
THIS CAN'T BE...
OKAY, YOU'RE TOO SHOCKED.
AREN'T YOU IN HER CLASS? YOU DIDN'T KNOW?
I ASKED, BUT MACCHII WOULDN'T SAY WHAT SHE GOT ON HER TEST.
15
I THOUGHT SHE MUST'VE DONE REAL BAD.
I GUESS SHE DIDN'T WANT TO HURT YOUR FEELINGS...

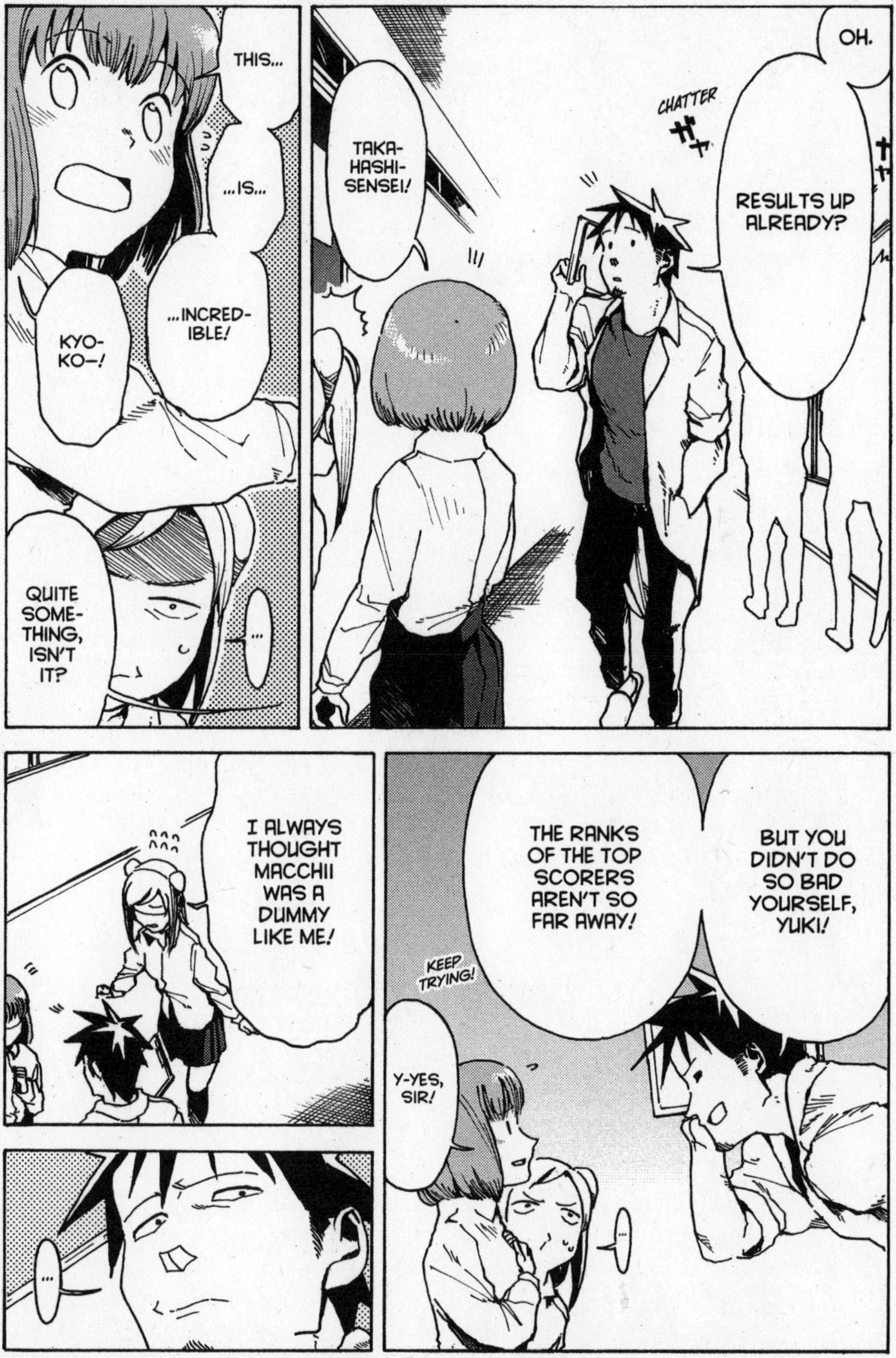
OH.
RESULTS UP ALREADY?
CHATTER
TAKA-HASHI-SENSEI!
THIS...
...IS...
...INCREDIBLE!
KYO-KO-!
...
QUITE SOMETHING, ISN'T IT?
BUT YOU DIDN'T DO SO BAD YOURSELF, YUKI!
THE RANKS OF THE TOP SCORERS AREN'T SO FAR AWAY!
KEEP TRYING!
Y-YES, SIR!
...
I ALWAYS THOUGHT MACCHII WAS A DUMMY LIKE ME!
...

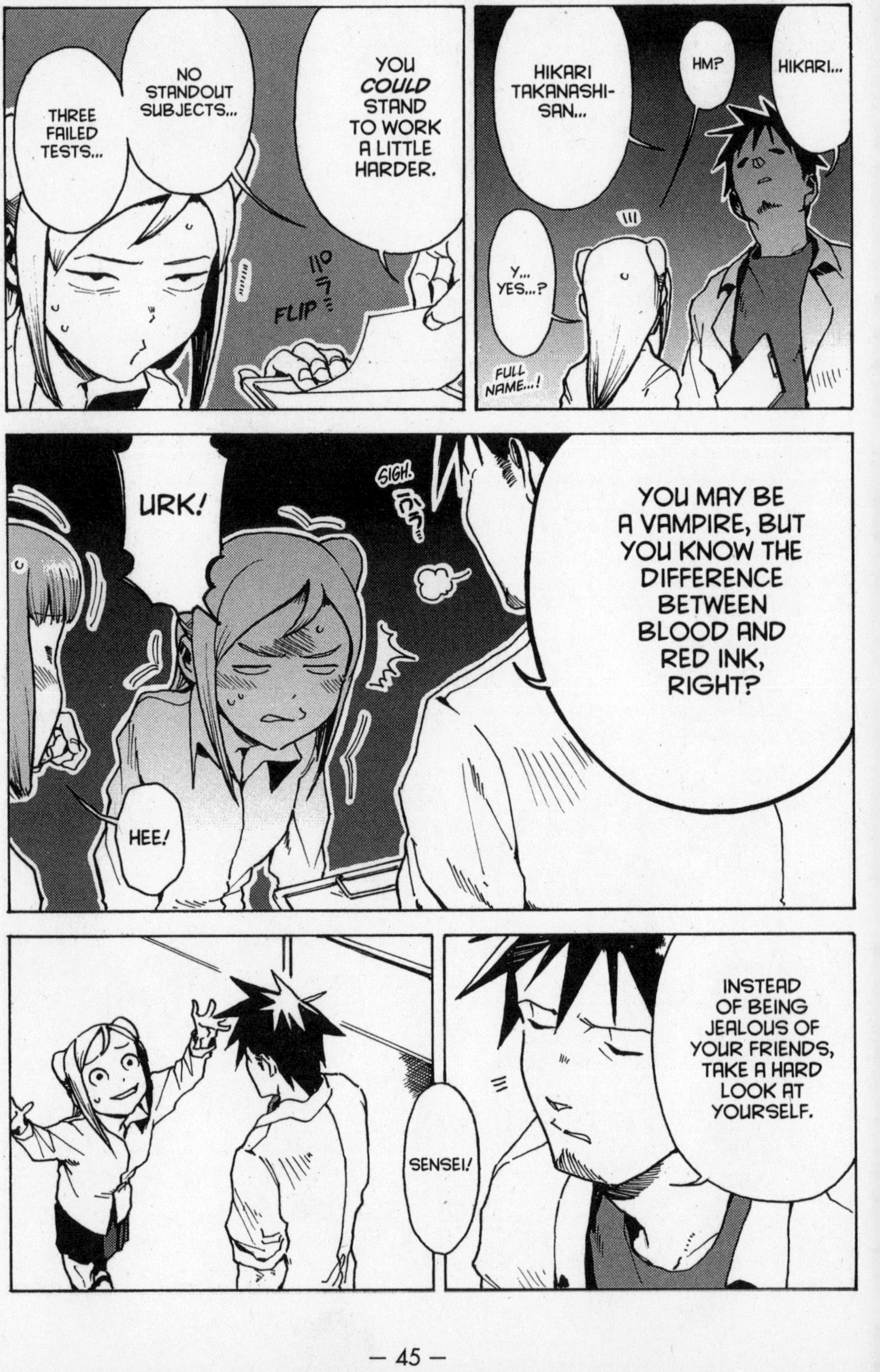
HIKARI...
HM?
HIKARI TAKANASHI-SAN...
Y... YES...?
FULL NAME...!
YOU *COULD* STAND TO WORK A LITTLE HARDER.
NO STANDOUT SUBJECTS...
THREE FAILED TESTS...
FLIP
YOU MAY BE A VAMPIRE, BUT YOU KNOW THE DIFFERENCE BETWEEN BLOOD AND RED INK, RIGHT?
SIGH.
URK!
HEE!
INSTEAD OF BEING JEALOUS OF YOUR FRIENDS, TAKE A HARD LOOK AT YOURSELF.
SENSEI!

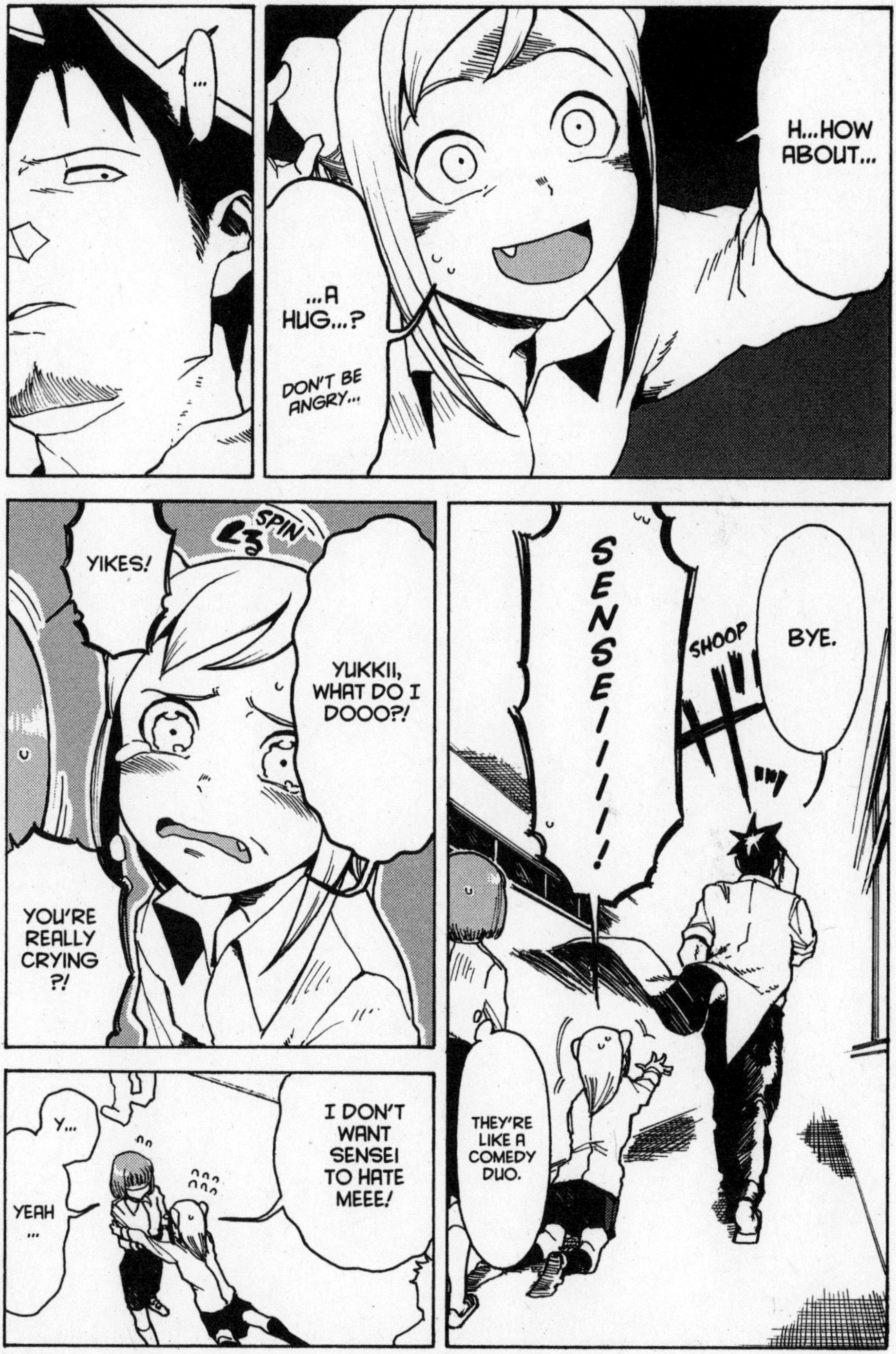

H...HOW ABOUT...
...A HUG...?
DON'T BE ANGRY...
...
BYE.
SHOOP
SENSEI!!!!!!!
THEY'RE LIKE A COMEDY DUO.
SPIN
YUKKII, WHAT DO I DOOO?!
YIKES!
YOU'RE REALLY CRYING ?!
I DON'T WANT SENSEI TO HATE MEEE!
Y...
YEAH ...

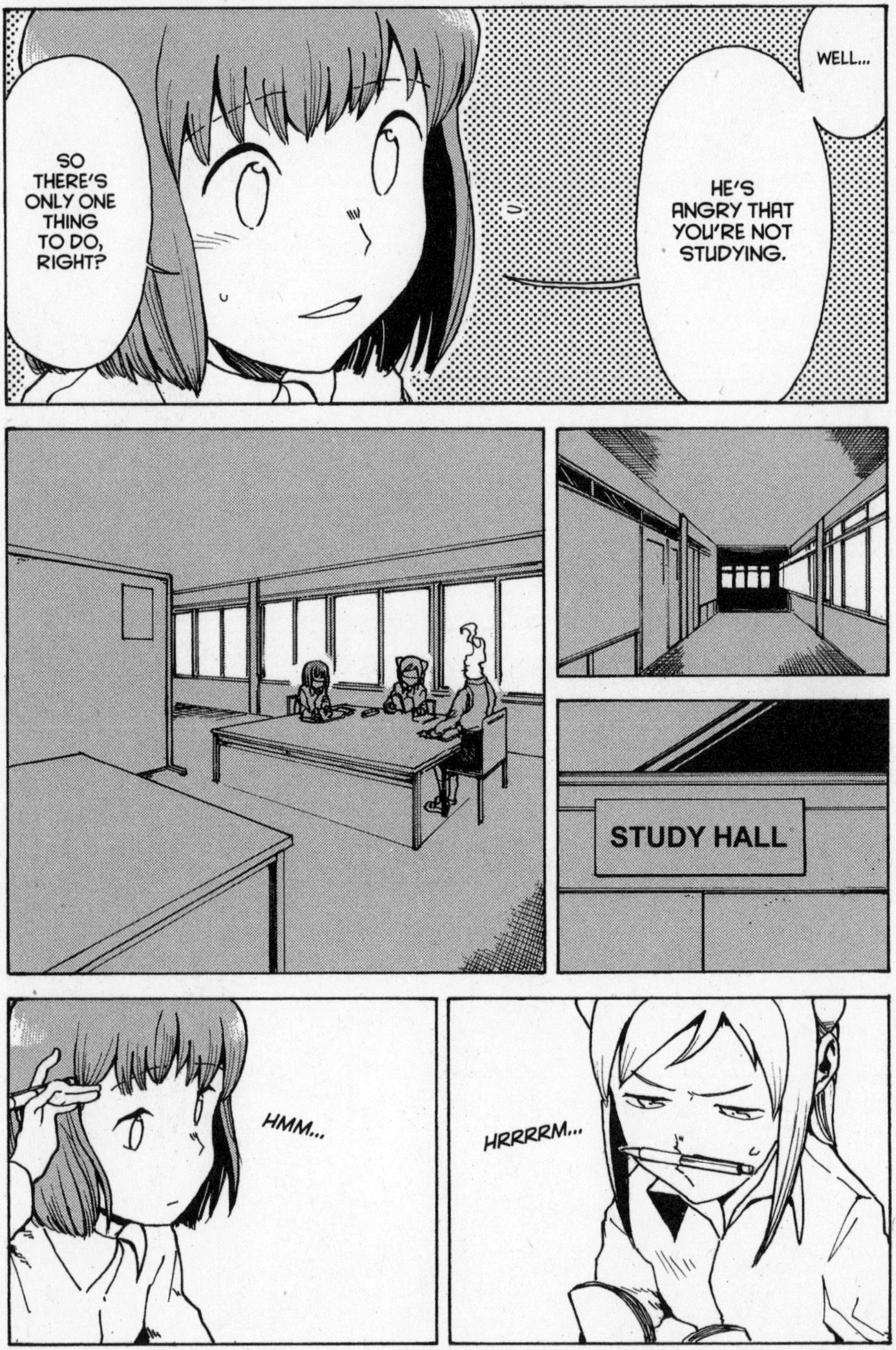
WELL...
HE'S ANGRY THAT YOU'RE NOT STUDYING.
SO THERE'S ONLY ONE THING TO DO, RIGHT?
STUDY HALL
HRRRRM...
HMM...

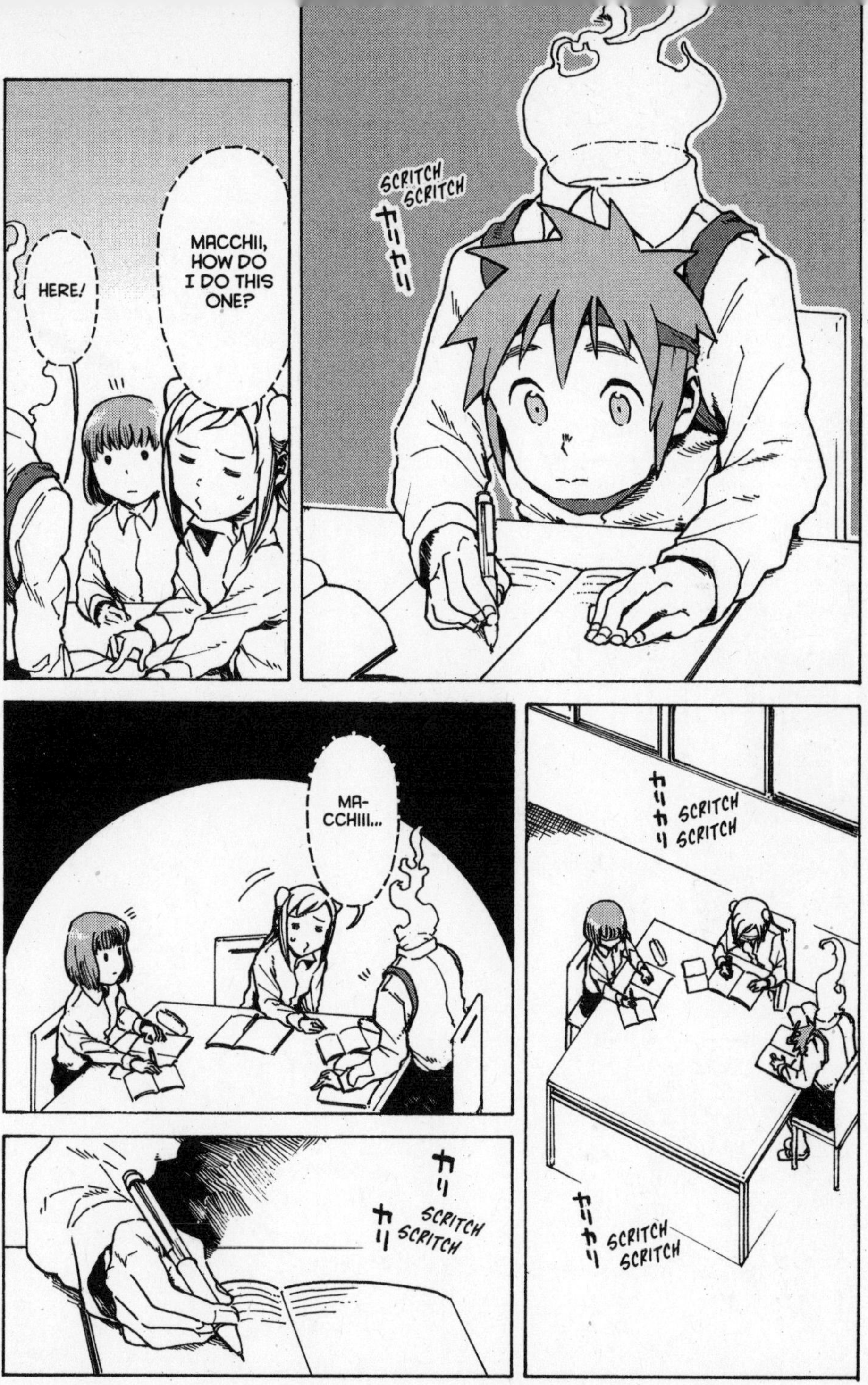
SCRITCH SCRITCH
カリカリ
MACCHII, HOW DO I DO THIS ONE?
HERE!
カリカリ
SCRITCH SCRITCH
カリカリ
SCRITCH SCRITCH
MA-CCHIII...
カリ
カリ
SCRITCH SCRITCH

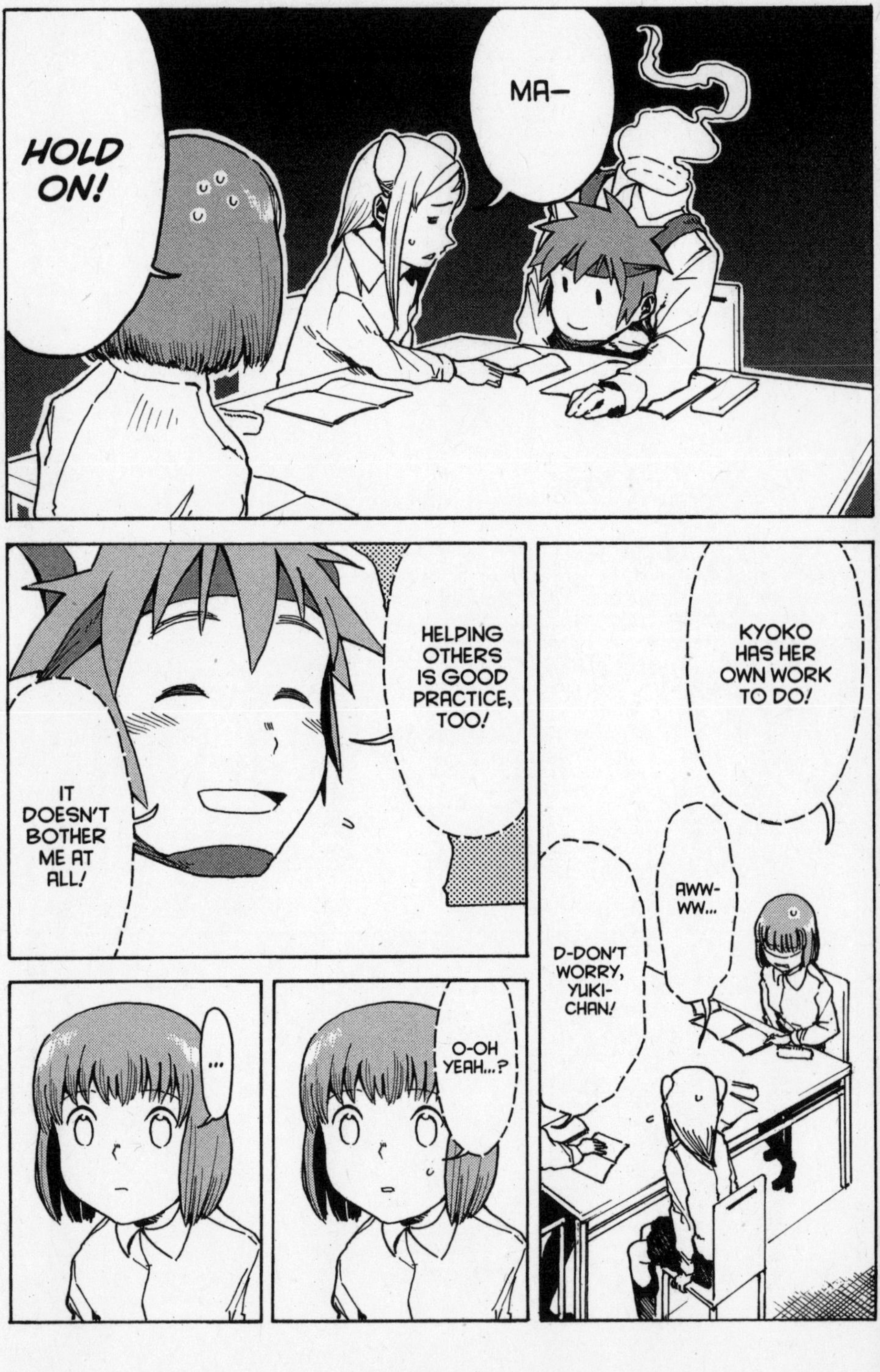
MA—
HOLD ON!
KYOKO HAS HER OWN WORK TO DO!
AWWW-WW...
D-DON'T WORRY, YUKI-CHAN!
HELPING OTHERS IS GOOD PRACTICE, TOO!
IT DOESN'T BOTHER ME AT ALL!
O-OH YEAH...?
...

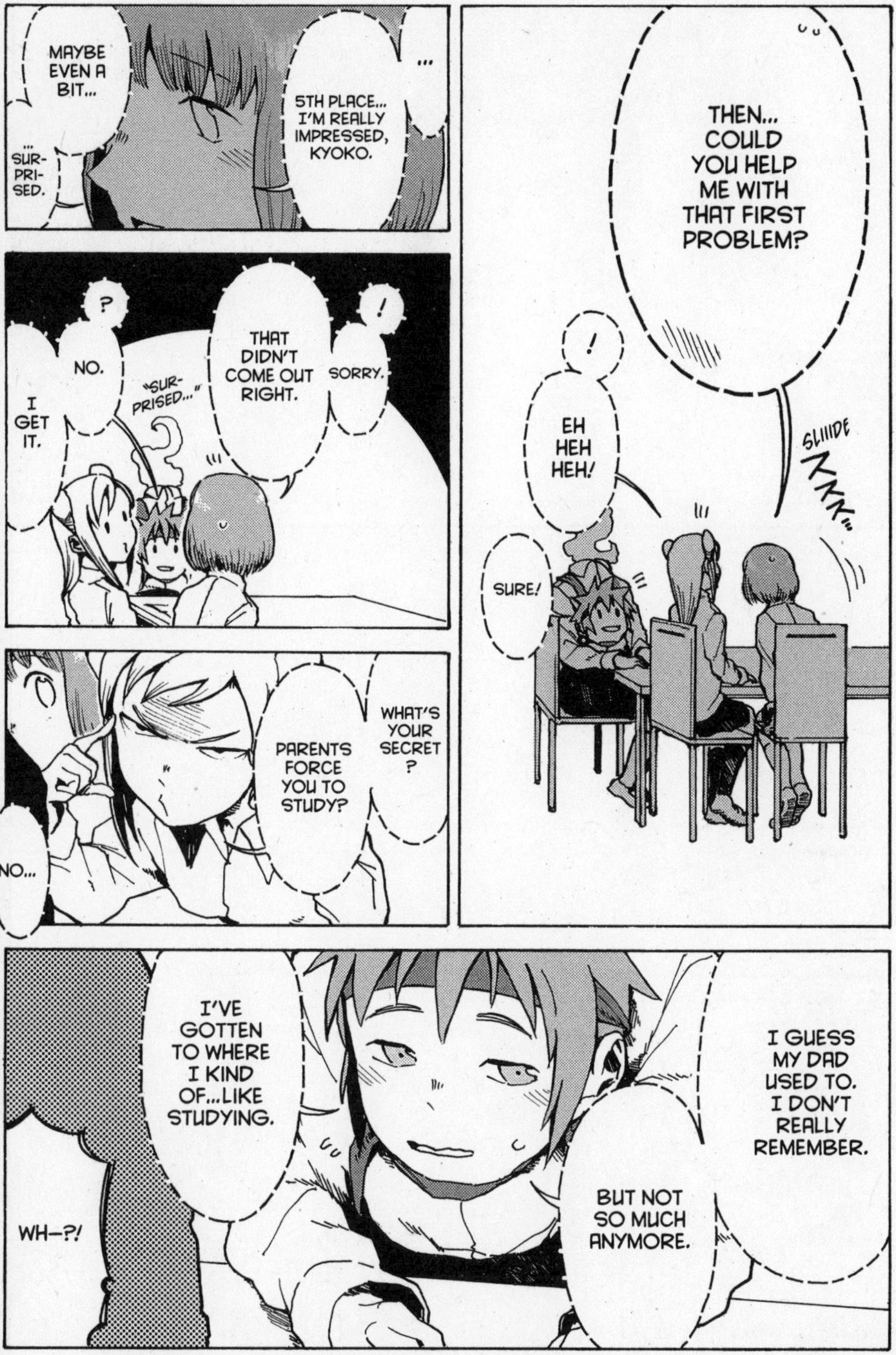
THEN... COULD YOU HELP ME WITH THAT FIRST PROBLEM?
!
EH HEH HEH!
SLIIIDE
SURE!
5TH PLACE... I'M REALLY IMPRESSED, KYOKO.
...
MAYBE EVEN A BIT...
... SUR-PRI-SED.
!
SORRY.
THAT DIDN'T COME OUT RIGHT.
"SUR-PRISED..."
?
NO.
I GET IT.
WHAT'S YOUR SECRET?
PARENTS FORCE YOU TO STUDY?
NO...
I GUESS MY DAD USED TO. I DON'T REALLY REMEMBER.
BUT NOT SO MUCH ANYMORE.
I'VE GOTTEN TO WHERE I KIND OF...LIKE STUDYING.
WH–?!

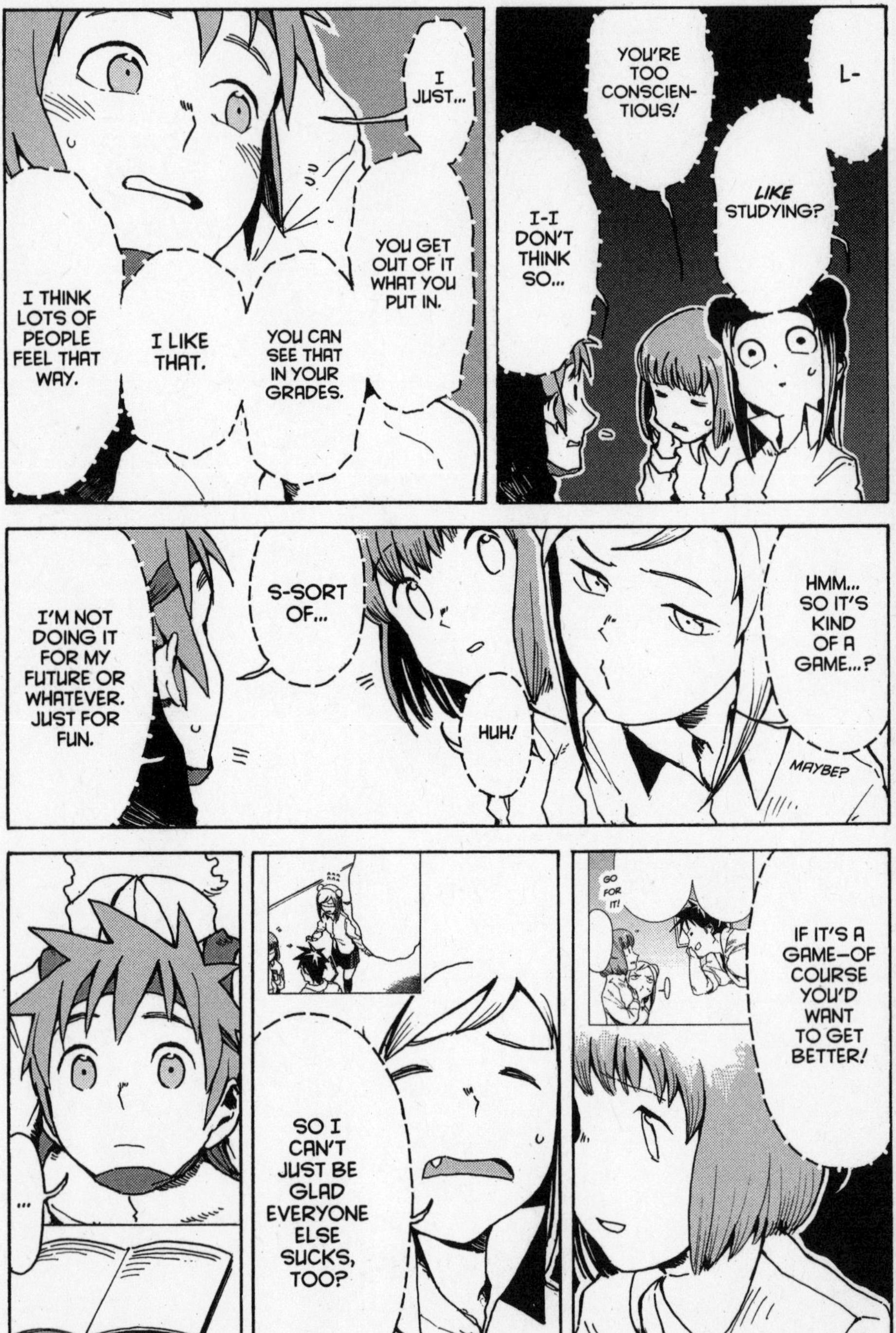
L-
LIKE STUDYING?
YOU'RE TOO CONSCIENTIOUS!
I-I DON'T THINK SO...
I JUST...
YOU GET OUT OF IT WHAT YOU PUT IN.
YOU CAN SEE THAT IN YOUR GRADES.
I LIKE THAT.
I THINK LOTS OF PEOPLE FEEL THAT WAY.
HMM... SO IT'S KIND OF A GAME...?
MAYBE?
HUH!
S-SORT OF...
I'M NOT DOING IT FOR MY FUTURE OR WHATEVER. JUST FOR FUN.
IF IT'S A GAME—OF COURSE YOU'D WANT TO GET BETTER!
GO FOR IT!
SO I CAN'T JUST BE GLAD EVERYONE ELSE SUCKS, TOO?
...

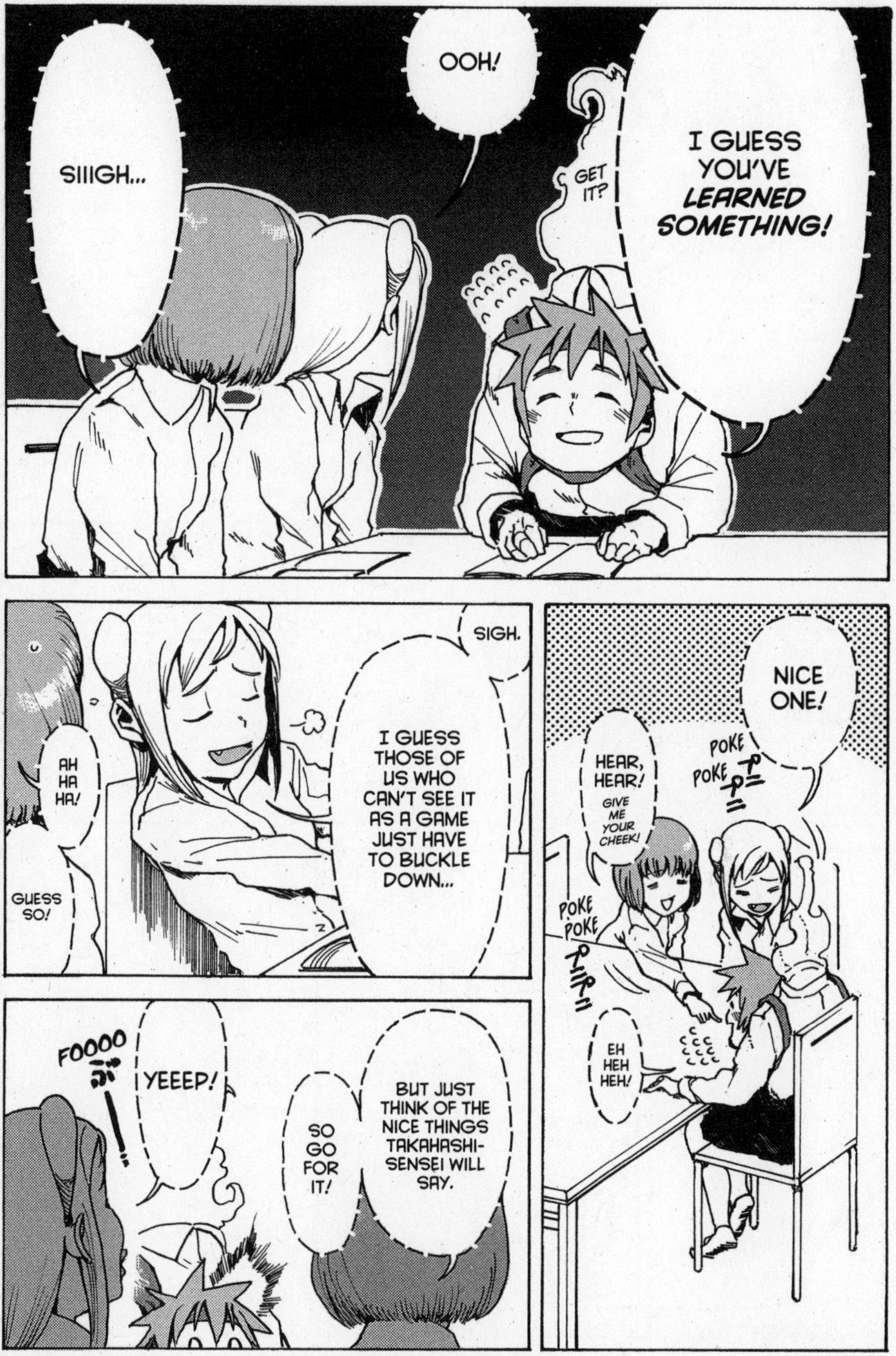
I GUESS YOU'VE *LEARNED* SOMETHING!
GET IT?
OOH!
SIIIGH...
NICE ONE!
POKE POKE
HEAR, HEAR!
GIVE ME YOUR CHEEK!
POKE POKE
EH HEH HEH!
SIGH.
I GUESS THOSE OF US WHO CAN'T SEE IT AS A GAME JUST HAVE TO BUCKLE DOWN...
AH HA HA!
GUESS SO!
BUT JUST THINK OF THE NICE THINGS TAKAHASHI-SENSEI WILL SAY.
SO GO FOR IT!
YEEEP!
FOOOO

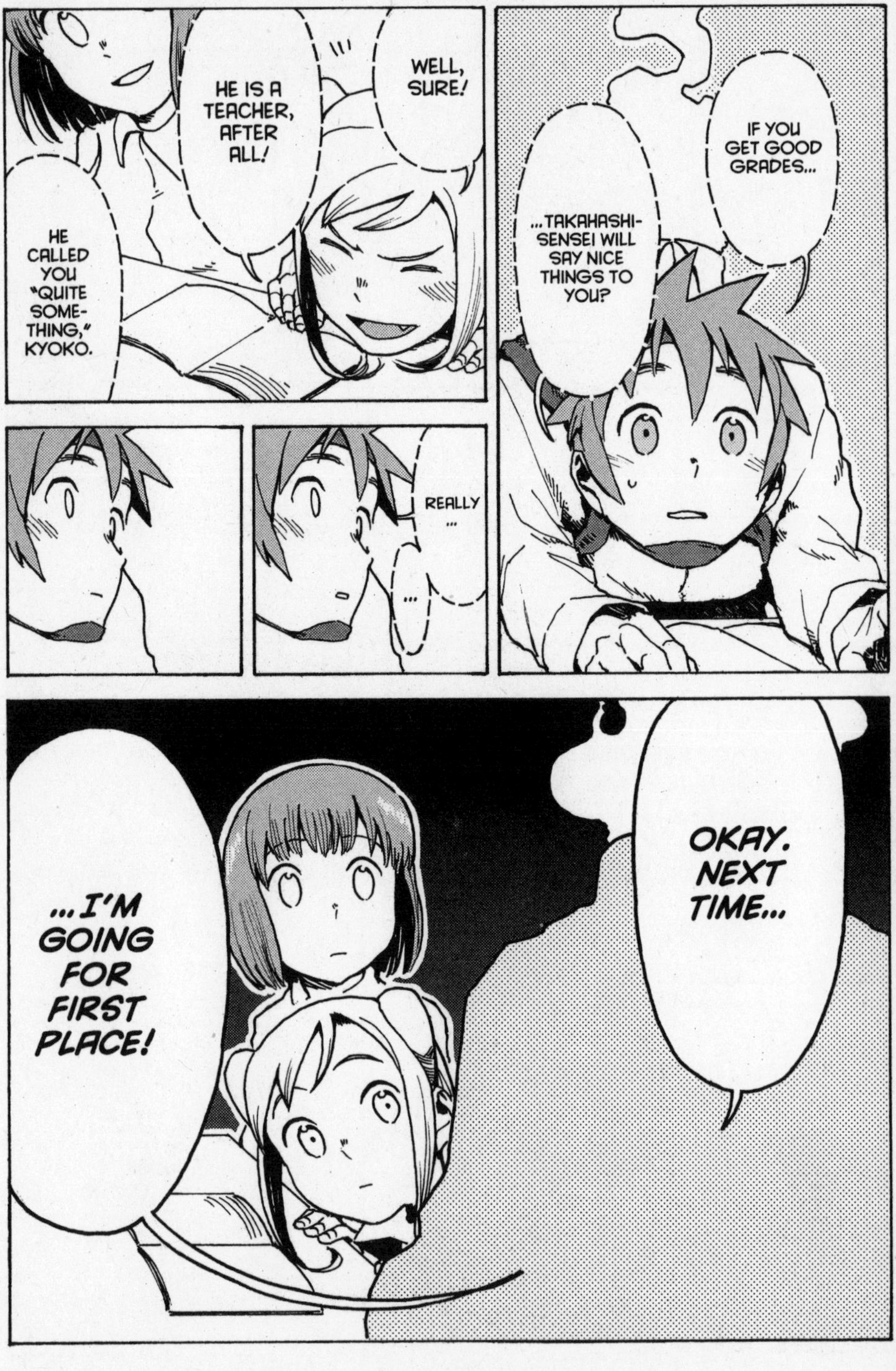
IF YOU GET GOOD GRADES...
...TAKAHASHI-SENSEI WILL SAY NICE THINGS TO YOU?
WELL, SURE!
HE IS A TEACHER, AFTER ALL!
HE CALLED YOU "QUITE SOME-THING," KYOKO.
REALLY ...
...
OKAY. NEXT TIME...
...I'M GOING FOR FIRST PLACE!

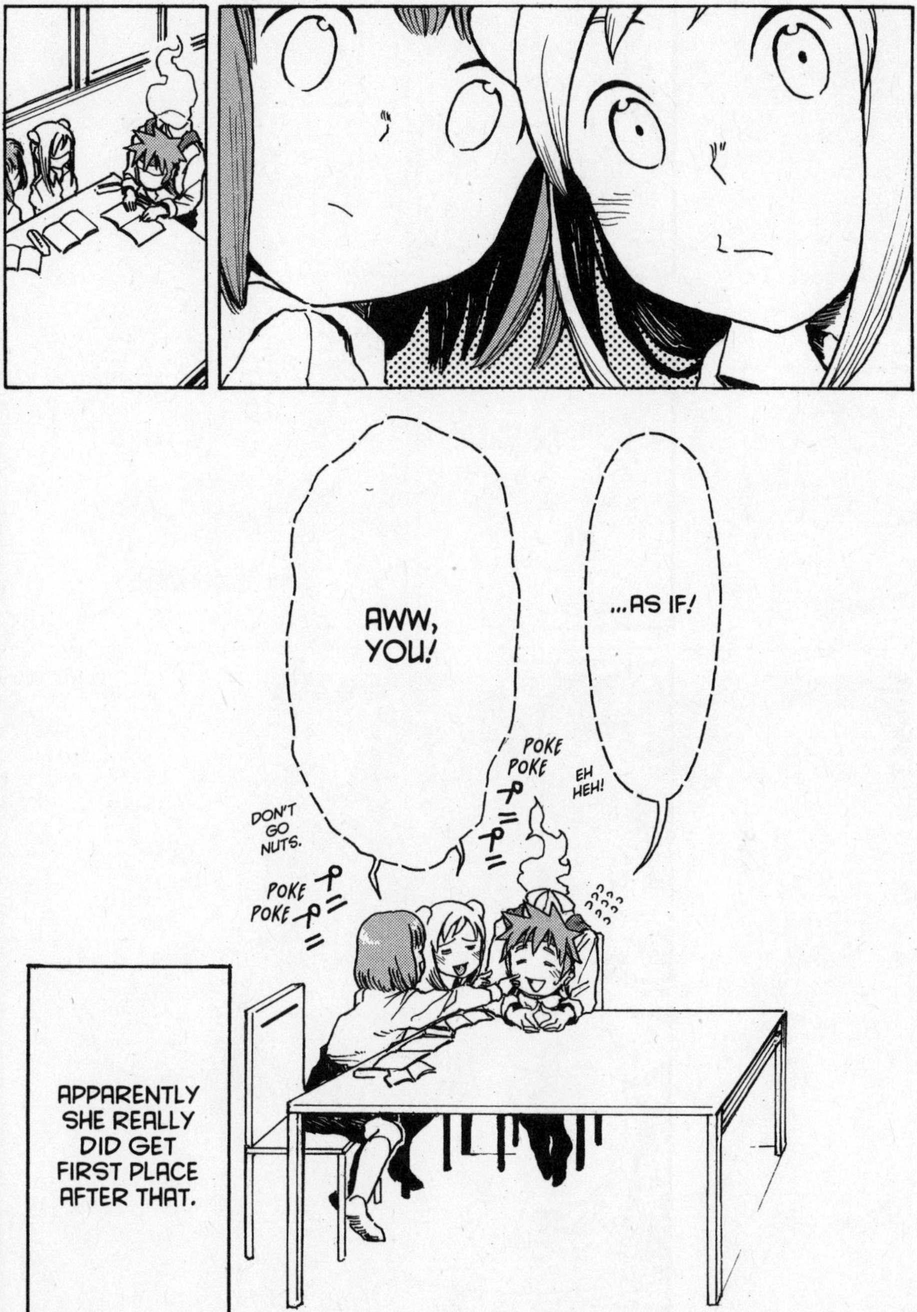
...AS IF!
EH HEH!
POKE POKE
AWW, YOU!
DON'T GO NUTS.
POKE POKE
APPARENTLY SHE REALLY DID GET FIRST PLACE AFTER THAT.

AFTER REVIEWING, HIKARI TAKES A RE-TEST
MM.
YEAH, THIS'LL DO.
SO.
GOOD WORK.
I'M IM-PRESSED.
I DO LOVE HEARING NICE THINGS!
YOU COULD'VE STUDIED FROM THE START, THEN...
GLOOOM

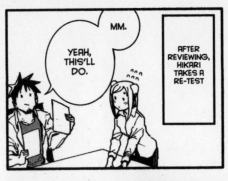

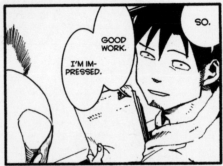

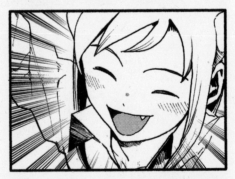

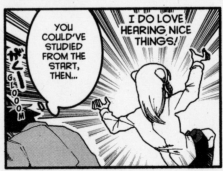

INTERVIEWS WITH MONSTER GIRLS

Chapter 20: Demis Want to Bite

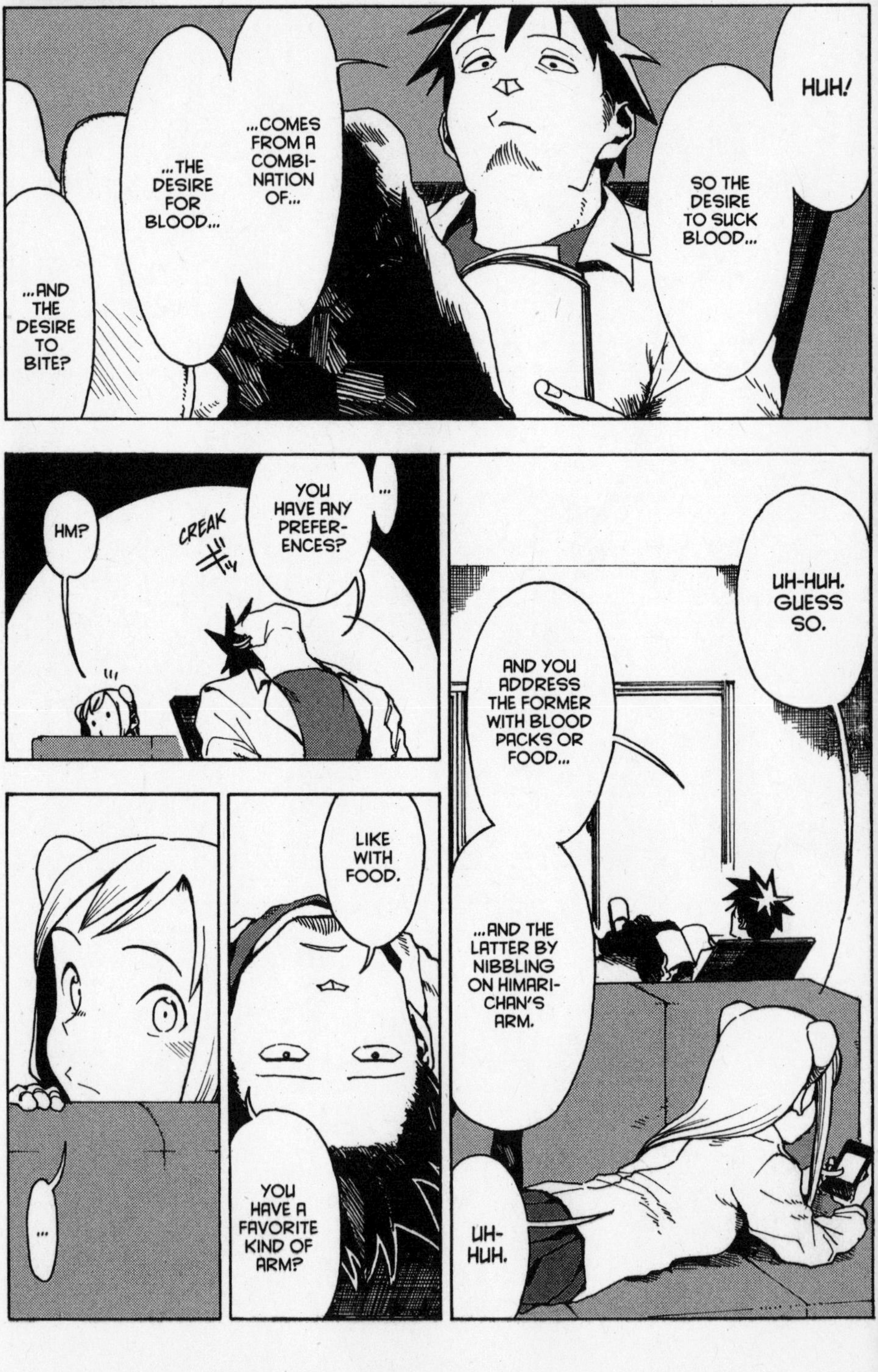
HUH!
SO THE DESIRE TO SUCK BLOOD...
...COMES FROM A COMBINATION OF...
...THE DESIRE FOR BLOOD...
...AND THE DESIRE TO BITE?
UH-HUH. GUESS SO.
AND YOU ADDRESS THE FORMER WITH BLOOD PACKS OR FOOD...
...AND THE LATTER BY NIBBLING ON HIMARI-CHAN'S ARM.
UH-HUH.
...
YOU HAVE ANY PREFERENCES?
CREAK
HM?
LIKE WITH FOOD.
YOU HAVE A FAVORITE KIND OF ARM?
...

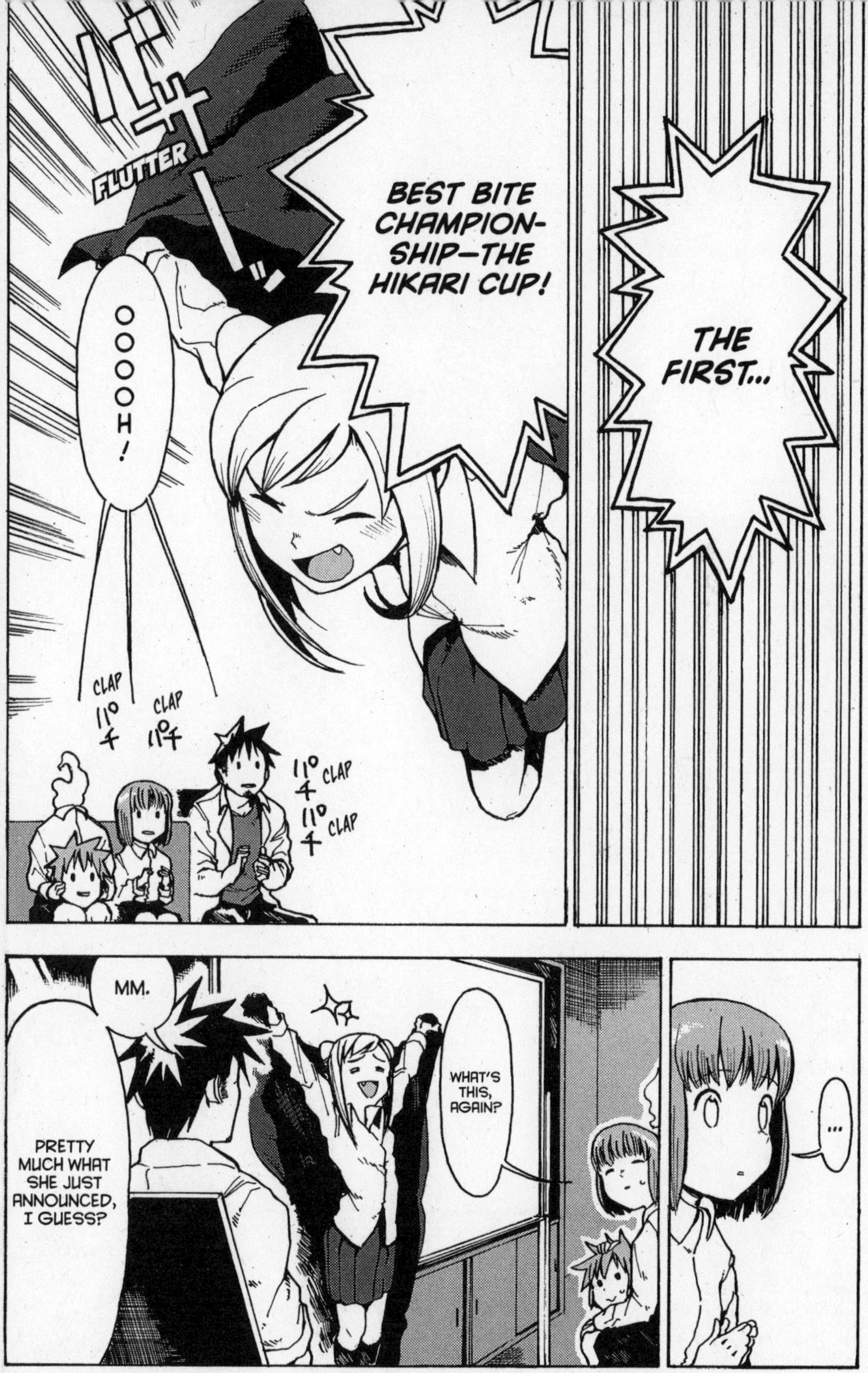
THE FIRST...
BEST BITE CHAMPION-SHIP—THE HIKARI CUP!
FLUTTER
OOOOOH!
CLAP
CLAP
CLAP
CLAP
...
WHAT'S THIS, AGAIN?
MM.
PRETTY MUCH WHAT SHE JUST ANNOUNCED, I GUESS?

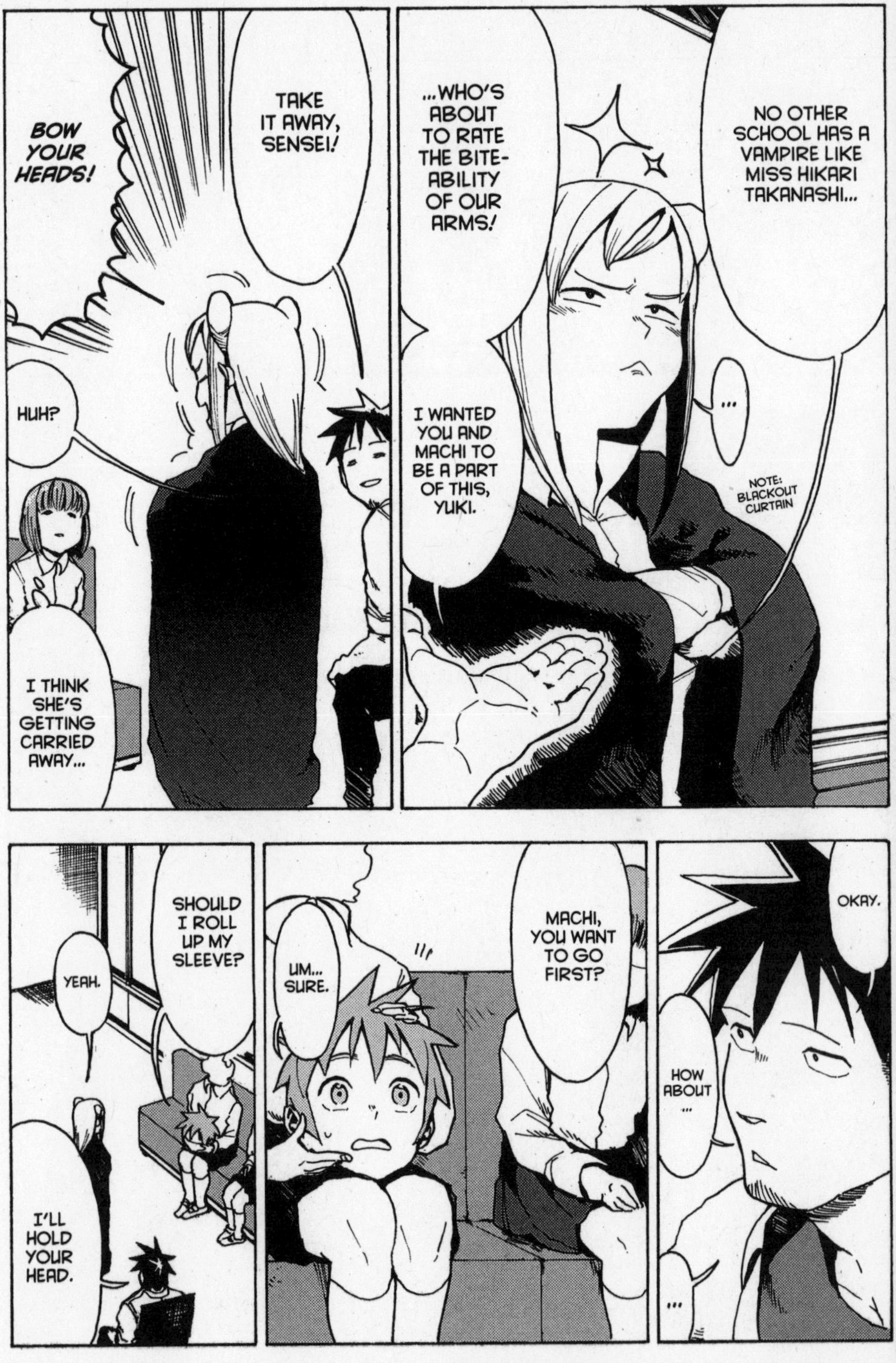
NO OTHER SCHOOL HAS A VAMPIRE LIKE MISS HIKARI TAKANASHI...
...WHO'S ABOUT TO RATE THE BITE-ABILITY OF OUR ARMS!
...
NOTE: BLACKOUT CURTAIN
I WANTED YOU AND MACHI TO BE A PART OF THIS, YUKI.
TAKE IT AWAY, SENSEI!
BOW YOUR HEADS!
HUH?
I THINK SHE'S GETTING CARRIED AWAY...
OKAY.
HOW ABOUT ...
...
MACHI, YOU WANT TO GO FIRST?
UM... SURE.
SHOULD I ROLL UP MY SLEEVE?
YEAH.
I'LL HOLD YOUR HEAD.

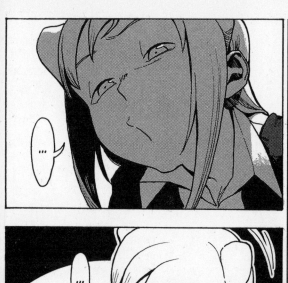

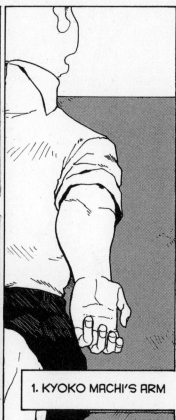

1. KYOKO MACHI'S ARM
...
...
HM-MM...
I LIKE THE SMOOTHNESS OF YOUR ARM, MACCHII...
POKE POKE
もにもに
LOTS OF MUSCLES, THOUGH.
'CAUSE YOU'RE SO ATHLETIC... AND CARRY YOUR HEAD EVERYWHERE.

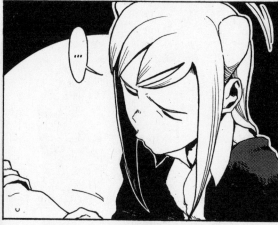

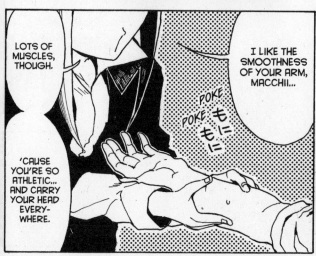

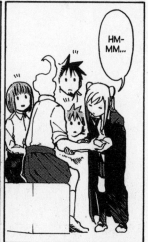

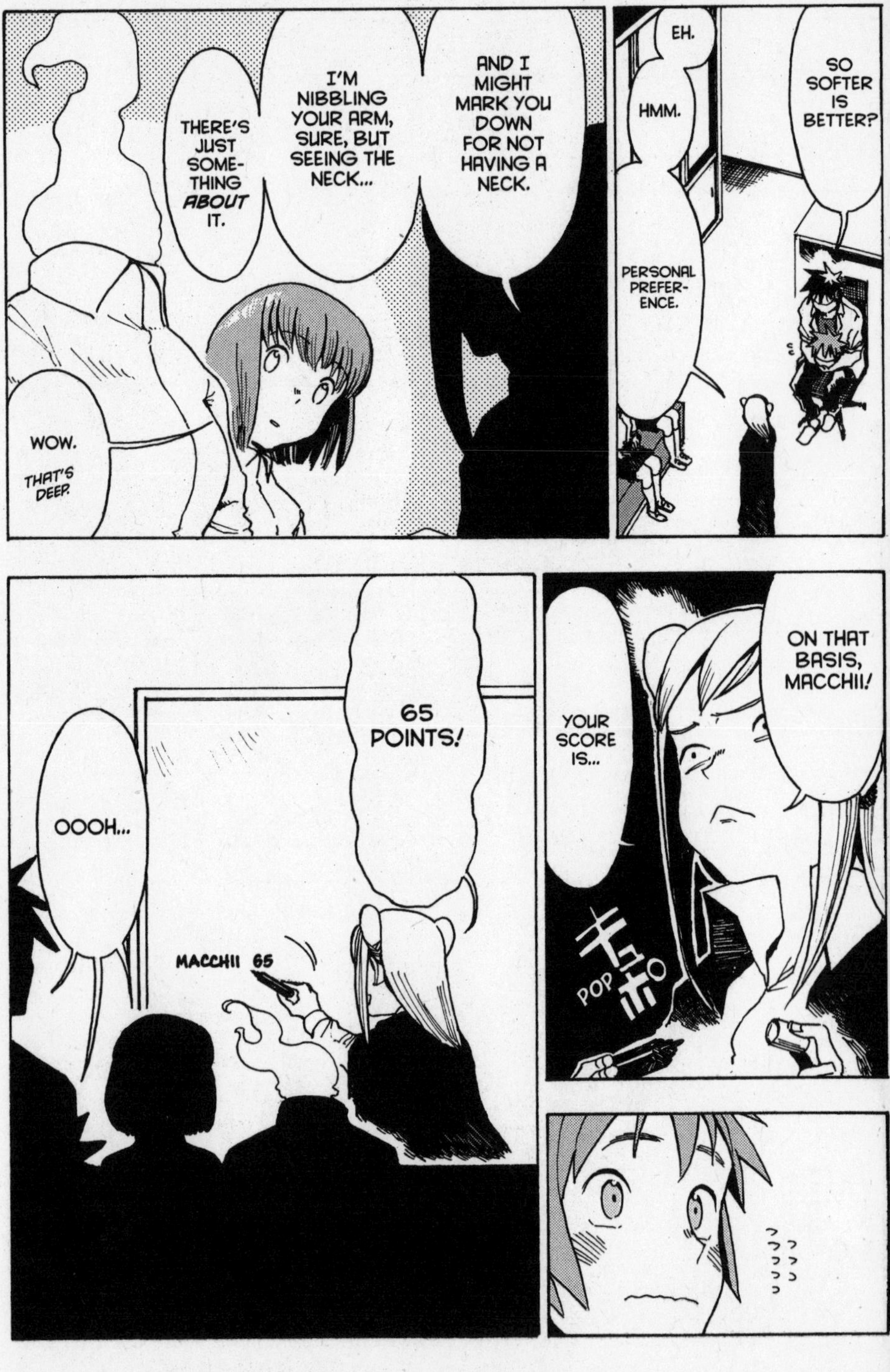
SO SOFTER IS BETTER?
EH.
HMM.
PERSONAL PREFERENCE.
AND I MIGHT MARK YOU DOWN FOR NOT HAVING A NECK.
I'M NIBBLING YOUR ARM, SURE, BUT SEEING THE NECK...
THERE'S JUST SOMETHING *ABOUT* IT.
WOW.
THAT'S DEEP.
ON THAT BASIS, MACCHII!
YOUR SCORE IS...
キュポ
POP
65 POINTS!
MACCHII 65
OOOH...

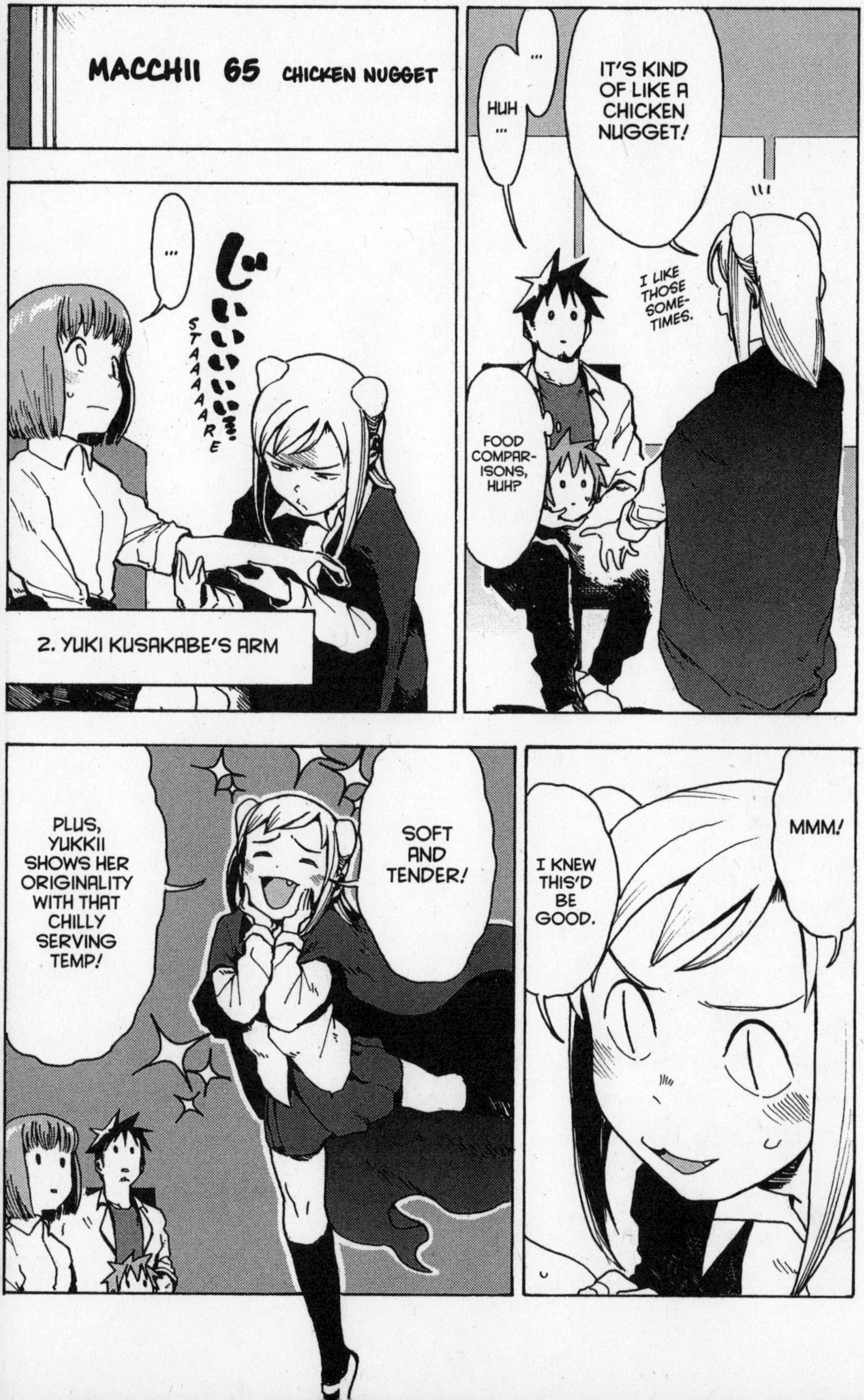
IT'S KIND OF LIKE A CHICKEN NUGGET!
...
HUH ...
I LIKE THOSE SOMETIMES.
FOOD COMPARISONS, HUH?
MACCHII 65 CHICKEN NUGGET
...
STAAAAARE
2. YUKI KUSAKABE'S ARM
MMM!
I KNEW THIS'D BE GOOD.
SOFT AND TENDER!
PLUS, YUKKII SHOWS HER ORIGINALITY WITH THAT CHILLY SERVING TEMP!

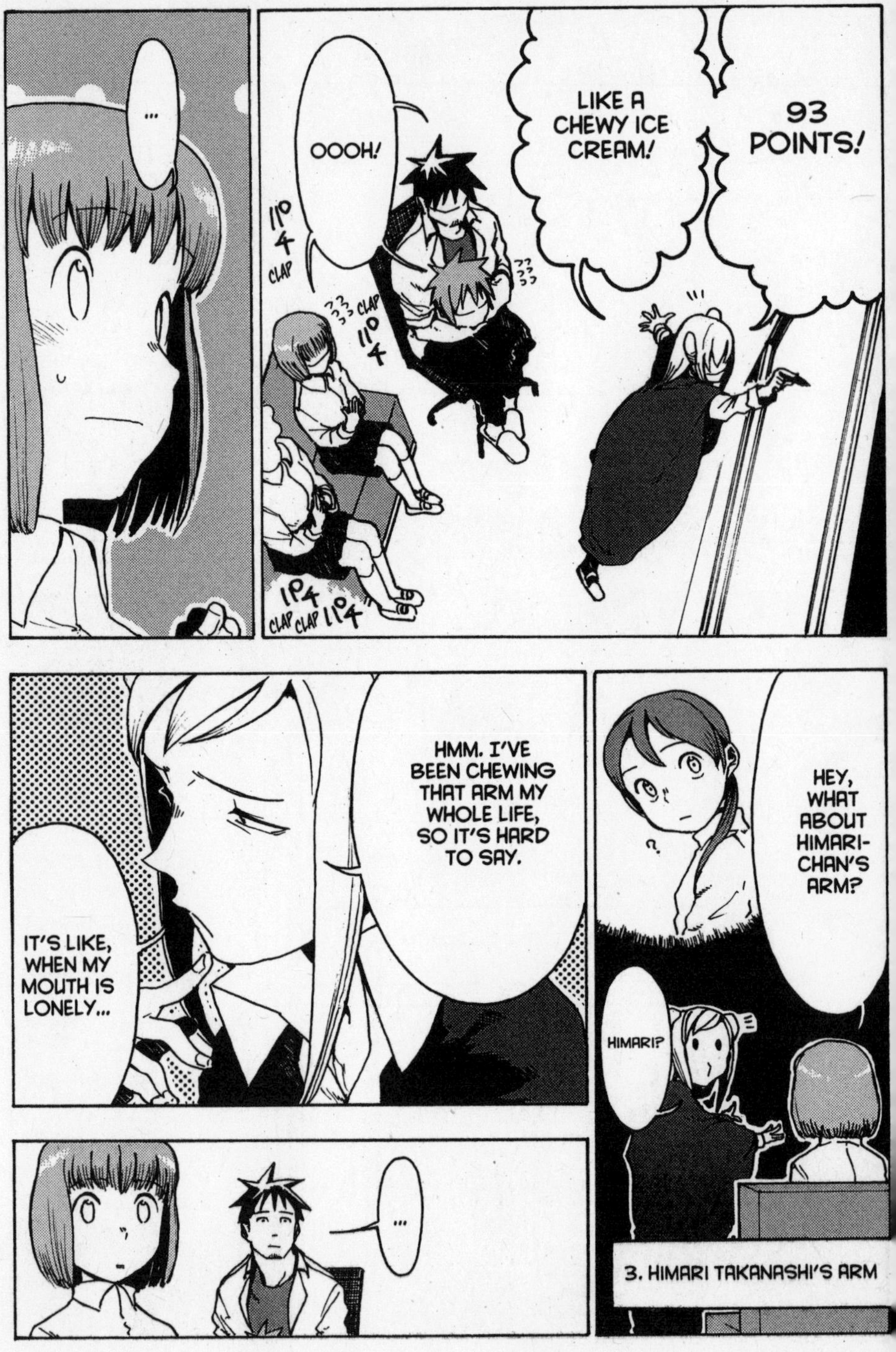
93 POINTS!
LIKE A CHEWY ICE CREAM!
OOOH!
CLAP
CLAP
CLAP
CLAP
...
HEY, WHAT ABOUT HIMARI-CHAN'S ARM?
HIMARI?
3. HIMARI TAKANASHI'S ARM
HMM. I'VE BEEN CHEWING THAT ARM MY WHOLE LIFE, SO IT'S HARD TO SAY.
IT'S LIKE, WHEN MY MOUTH IS LONELY...
...

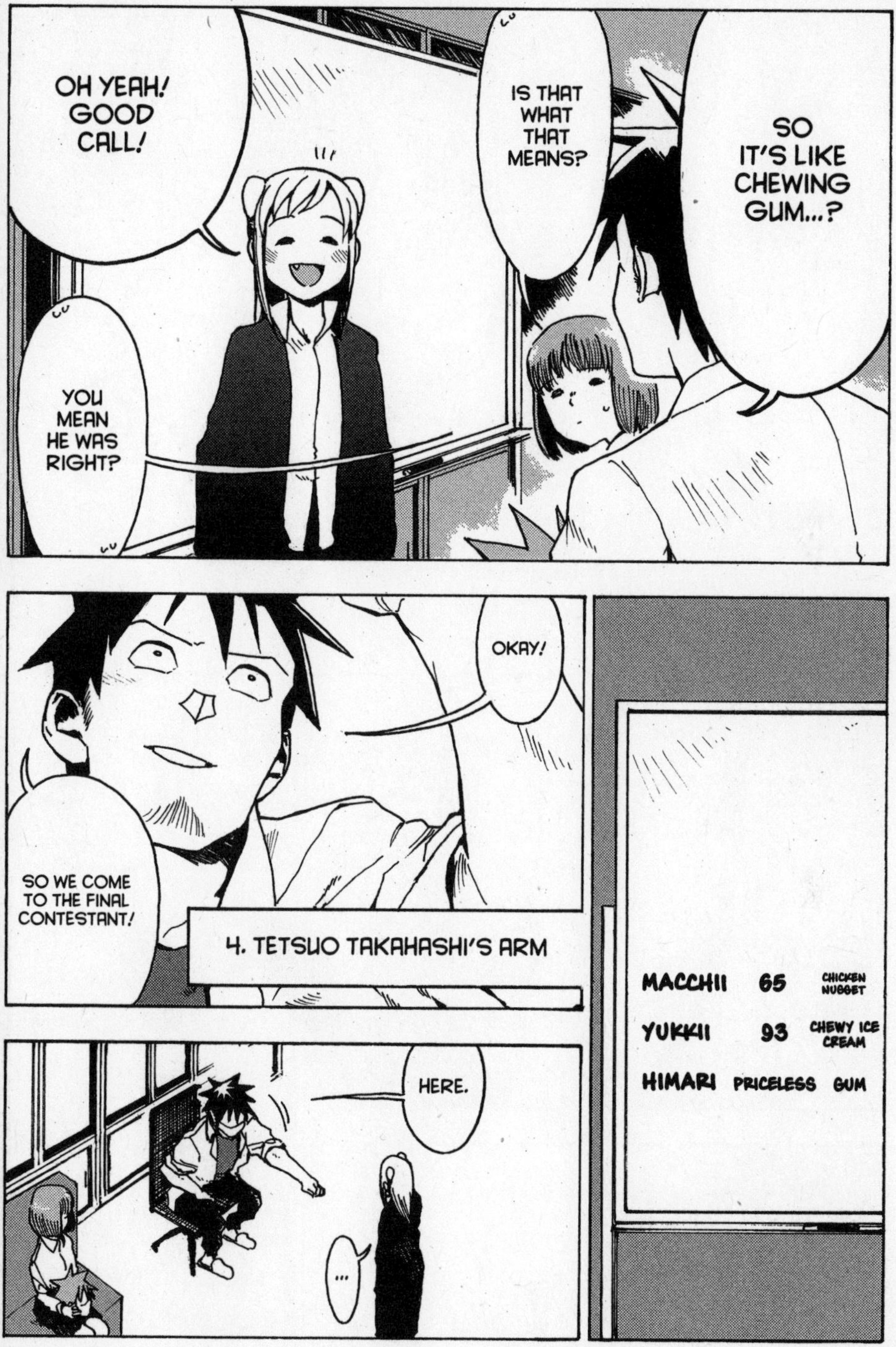
SO IT'S LIKE CHEWING GUM...?
IS THAT WHAT THAT MEANS?
OH YEAH! GOOD CALL!
YOU MEAN HE WAS RIGHT?
MACCHII 65 CHICKEN NUGGET
YUKKII 93 CHEWY ICE CREAM
HIMARI PRICELESS GUM
OKAY!
SO WE COME TO THE FINAL CONTESTANT!
4. TETSUO TAKAHASHI'S ARM
HERE.
...

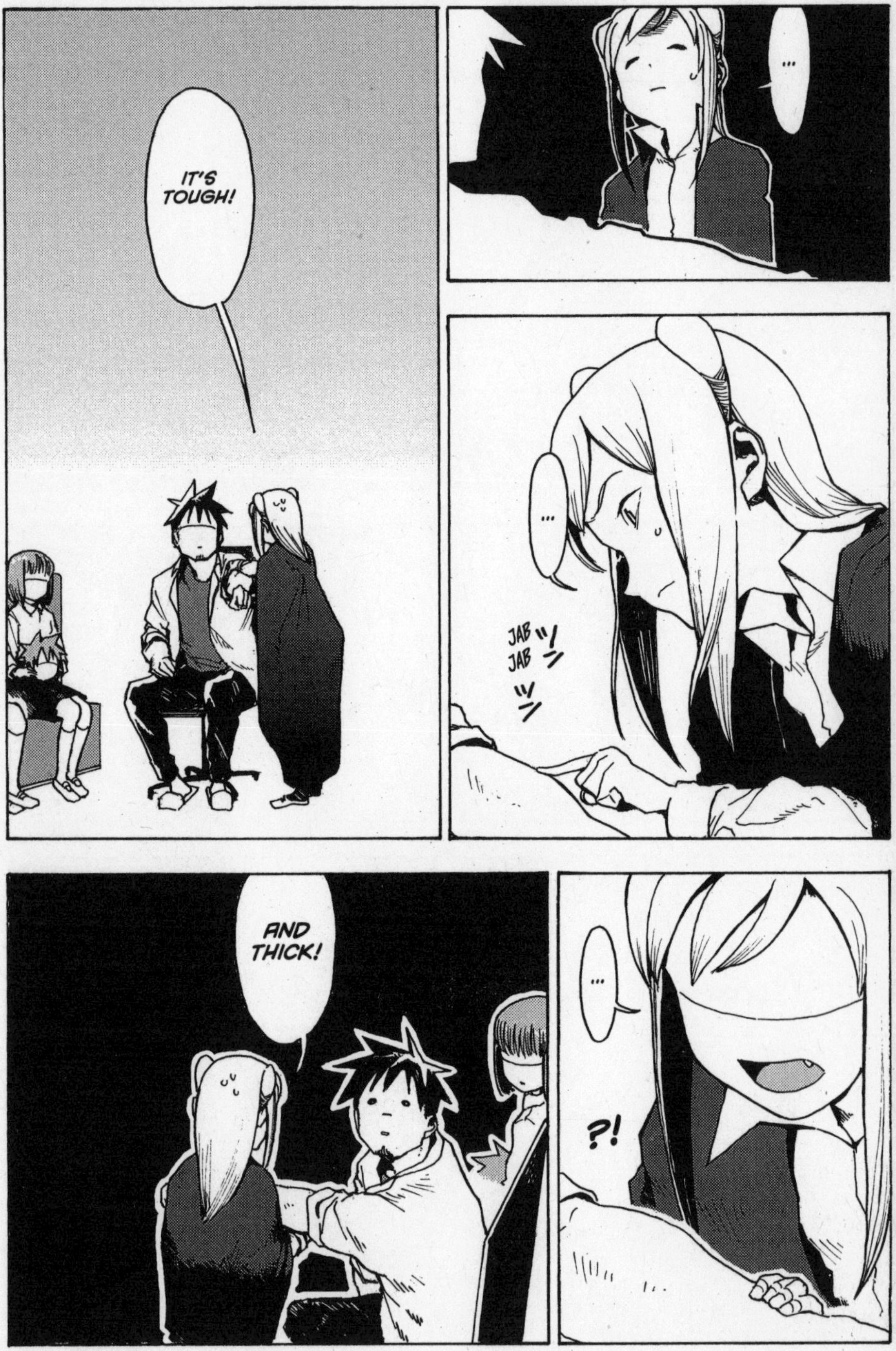
...
...
JAB JAB
IT'S TOUGH!
...
?!
AND THICK!

I THINK MY TEETH'D GET STUCK.
ALL THAT HAIR!
THAT'S NEVER LEAVING THIS ROOM, RIGHT?
...
...
SO?
MY SCORE?
...
POP
A BIG OL' ZERO! YOU FAIL!
OH, REALLY?
HA HA HA!
PAYBACK, HUH?

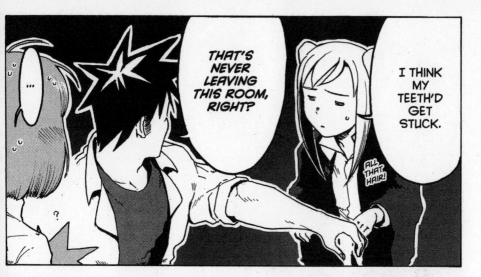

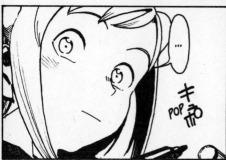

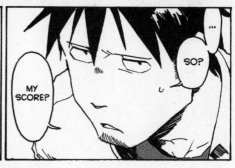

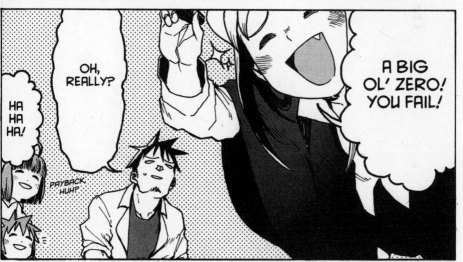

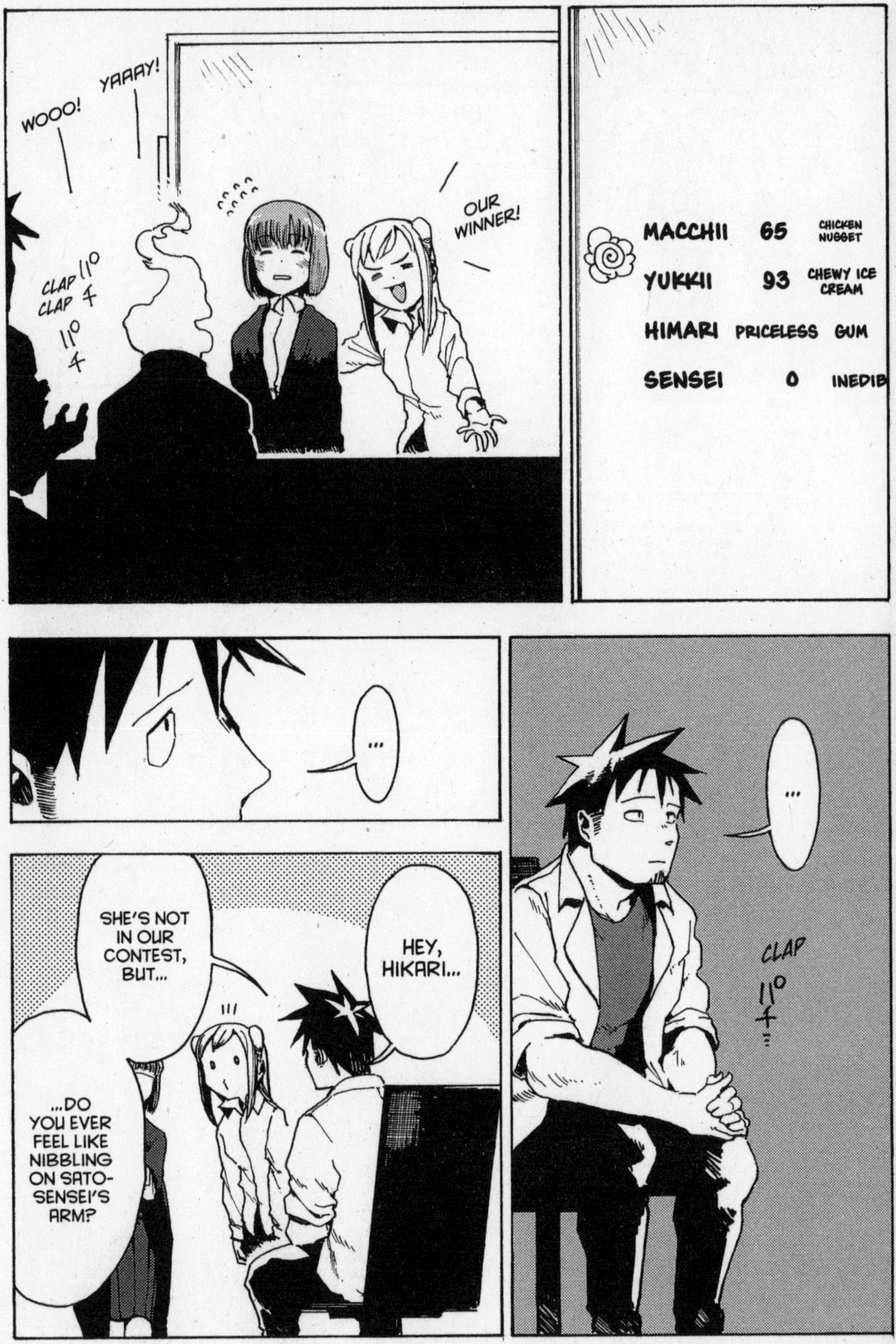
MACCHII 65 CHICKEN NUGGET
YUKKII 93 CHEWY ICE CREAM
HIMARI PRICELESS GUM
SENSEI 0 INEDIB
OUR WINNER!
YAAAY!
WOOO!
CLAP CLAP
...
CLAP
...
HEY, HIKARI...
SHE'S NOT IN OUR CONTEST, BUT...
...DO YOU EVER FEEL LIKE NIBBLING ON SATO-SENSEI'S ARM?

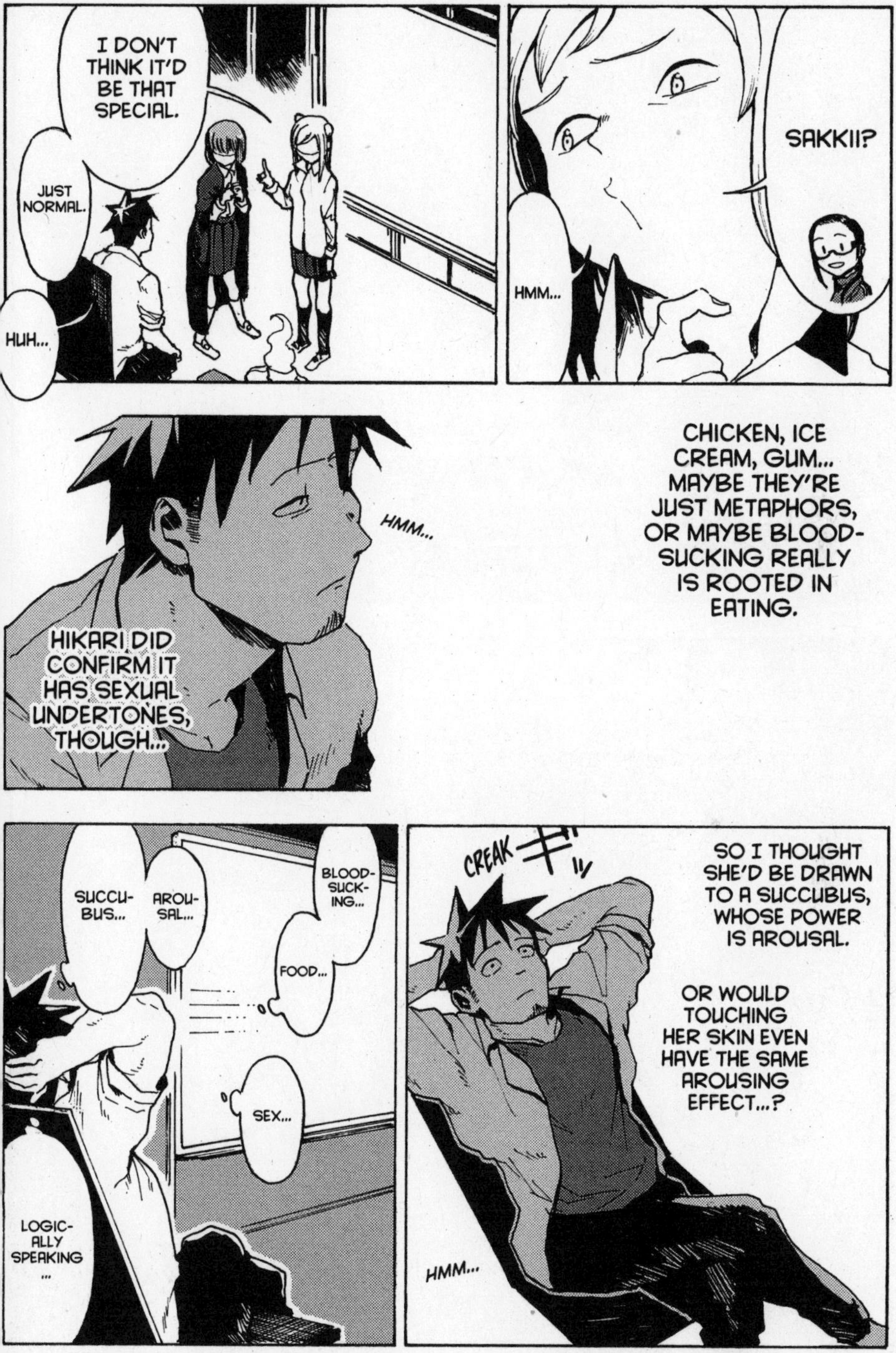
SAKKII?
HMM...
I DON'T THINK IT'D BE THAT SPECIAL.
JUST NORMAL.
HUH...
CHICKEN, ICE CREAM, GUM... MAYBE THEY'RE JUST METAPHORS, OR MAYBE BLOOD-SUCKING REALLY IS ROOTED IN EATING.
HMM...
HIKARI DID CONFIRM IT HAS SEXUAL UNDERTONES, THOUGH...
CREAK
SO I THOUGHT SHE'D BE DRAWN TO A SUCCUBUS, WHOSE POWER IS AROUSAL.
OR WOULD TOUCHING HER SKIN EVEN HAVE THE SAME AROUSING EFFECT...?
HMM...
BLOOD-SUCKING...
AROUSAL...
SUCCUBUS...
FOOD...
SEX...
LOGICALLY SPEAKING...

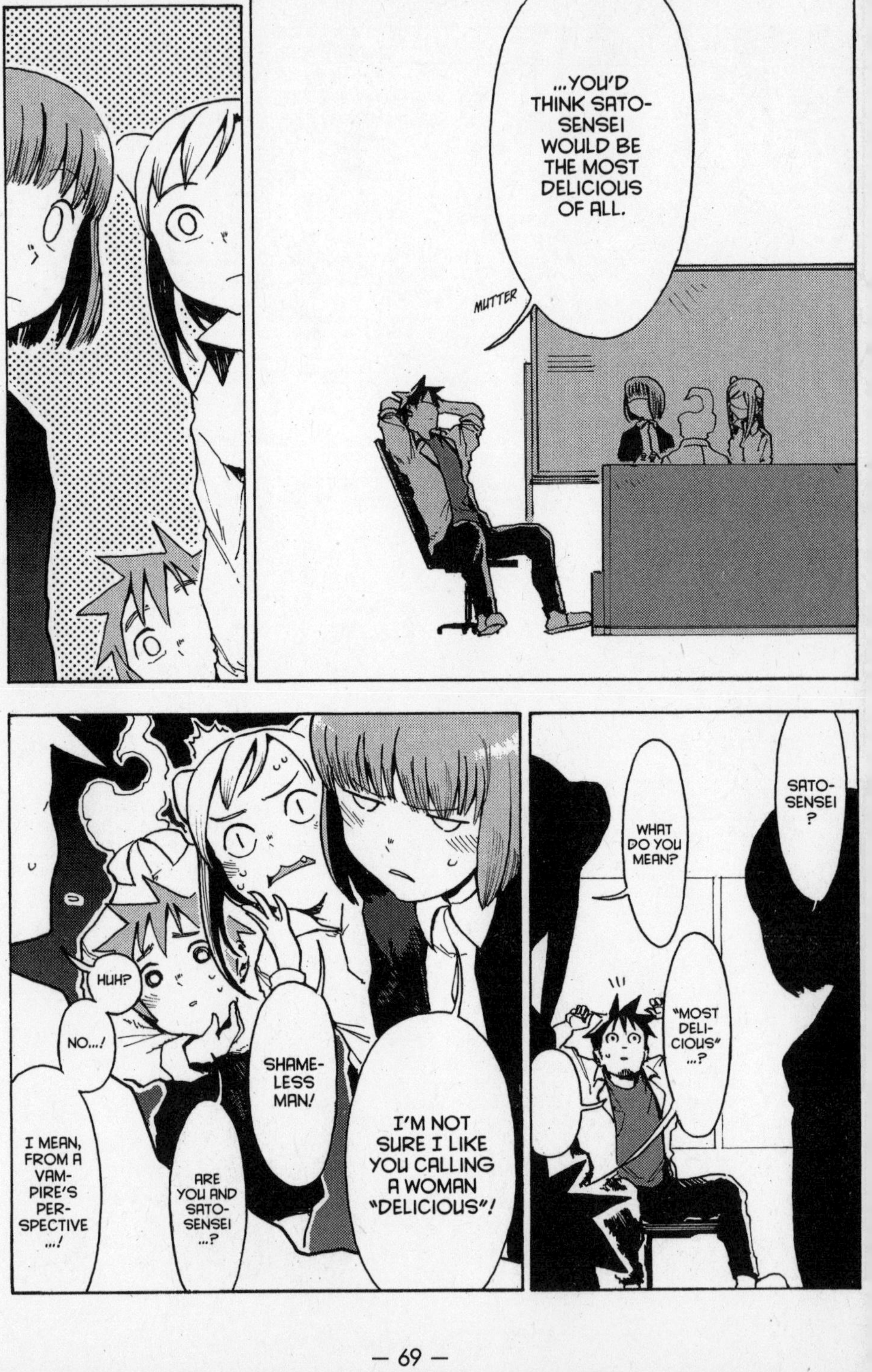
...YOU'D THINK SATO-SENSEI WOULD BE THE MOST DELICIOUS OF ALL.
MUTTER
SATO-SENSEI?
WHAT DO YOU MEAN?
"MOST DELICIOUS"...?
SHAMELESS MAN!
I'M NOT SURE I LIKE YOU CALLING A WOMAN "DELICIOUS"!
HUH?
NO...!
ARE YOU AND SATO-SENSEI...?
I MEAN, FROM A VAMPIRE'S PERSPECTIVE...!

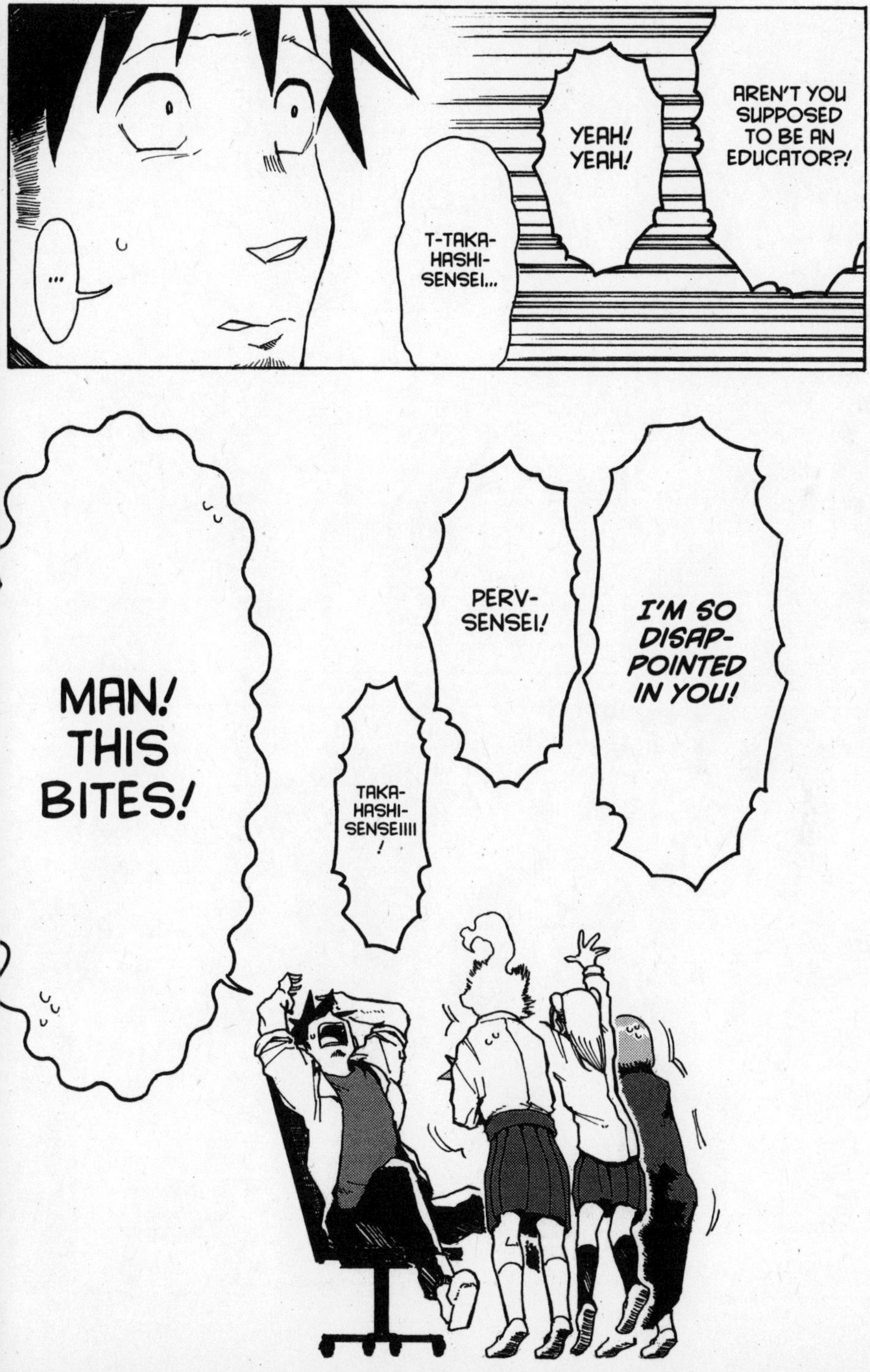
ARE N'T YOU SUPPOSED TO BE AN EDUCATOR?!
YEAH! YEAH!
T-TAKA-HASHI-SENSEI...
...
I'M SO DISAP-POINTED IN YOU!
PERV-SENSEI!
TAKA-HASHI-SENSEIIII!
MAN! THIS BITES!

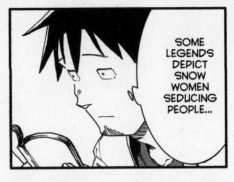

SOME LEGENDS DEPICT SNOW WOMEN SEDUCING PEOPLE...

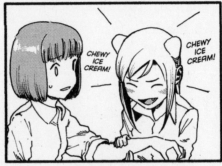

CHEWY ICE CREAM!

CHEWY ICE CREAM!

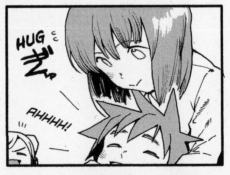

HUG

AHHHH!

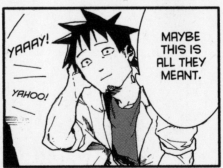

YAAAY!

YAHOO!

MAYBE THIS IS ALL THEY MEANT.

INTERVIEWS WITH MONSTER GIRLS

Chapter 21: Impatience is its Own Rebuke

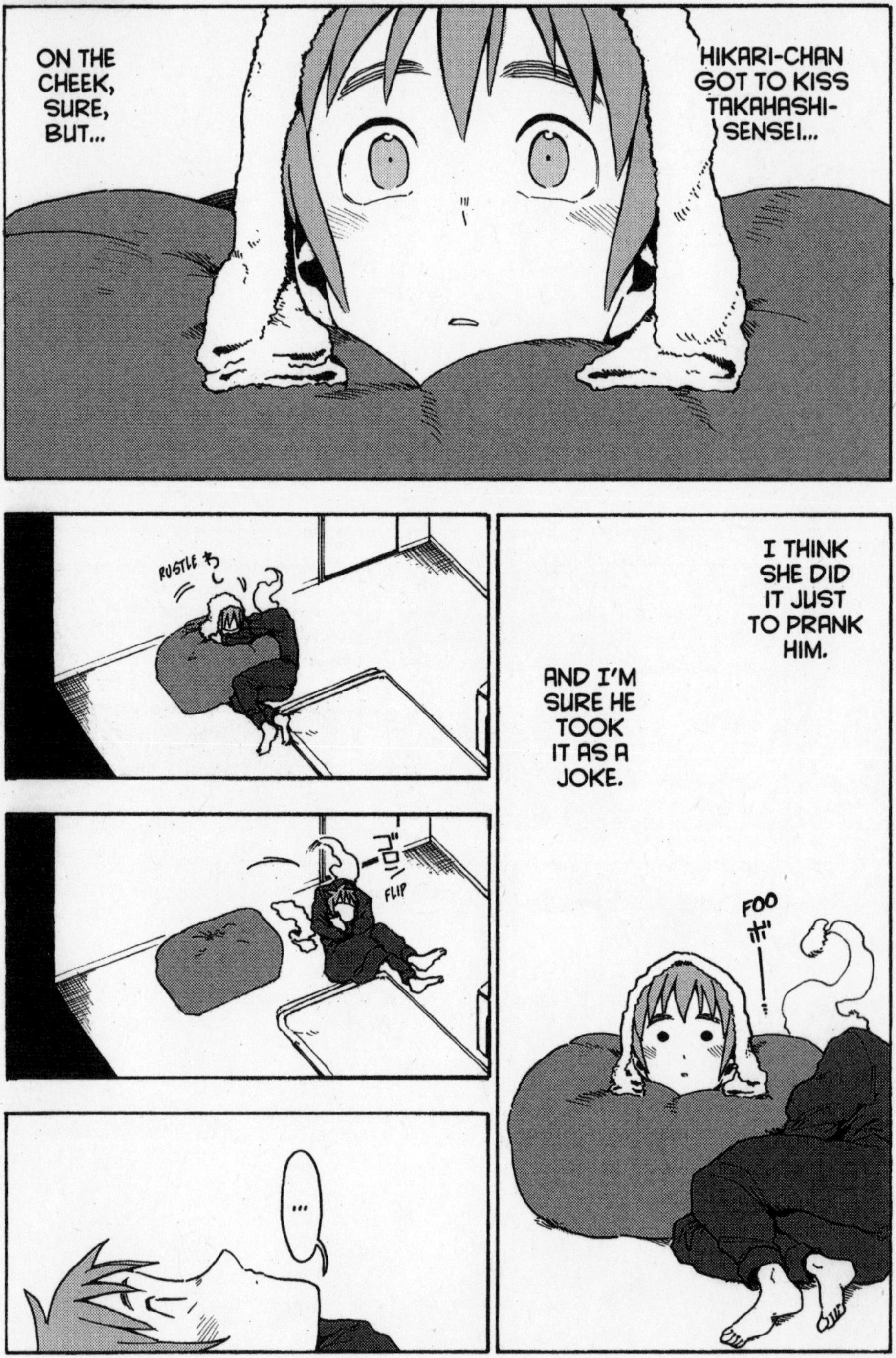
HIKARI-CHAN GOT TO KISS TAKAHASHI-SENSEI...
ON THE CHEEK, SURE, BUT...
I THINK SHE DID IT JUST TO PRANK HIM.
AND I'M SURE HE TOOK IT AS A JOKE.
FOO
ボ—
RUSTLE
ゴロン
FLIP
...

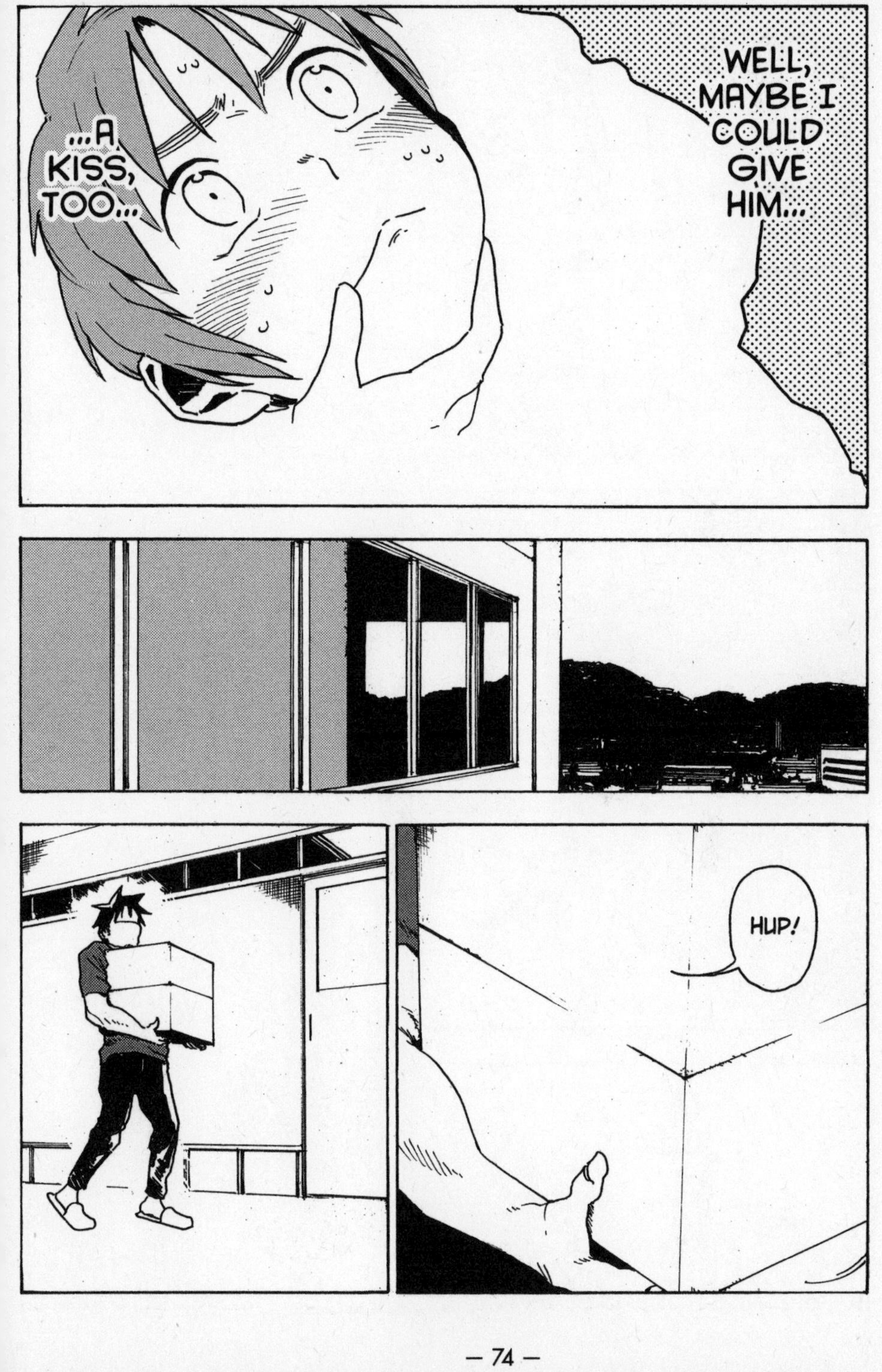
WELL, MAYBE I COULD GIVE HIM...
...A KISS, TOO...
HUP!

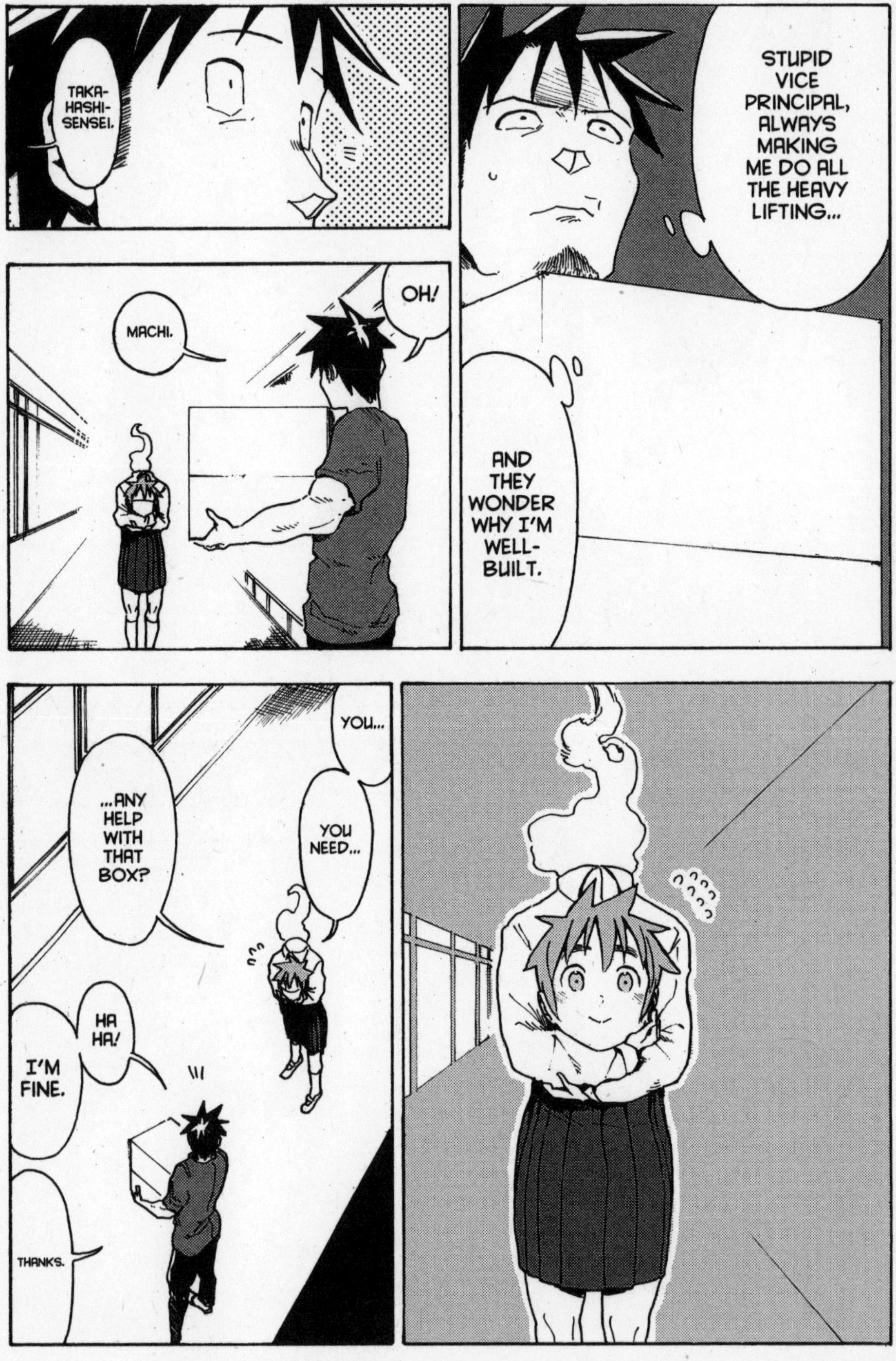

STUPID VICE PRINCIPAL, ALWAYS MAKING ME DO ALL THE HEAVY LIFTING...
AND THEY WONDER WHY I'M WELL-BUILT.
TAKA-HASHI-SENSEI.
OH!
MACHI.
YOU...
YOU NEED...
...ANY HELP WITH THAT BOX?
HA HA!
I'M FINE.
THANKS.

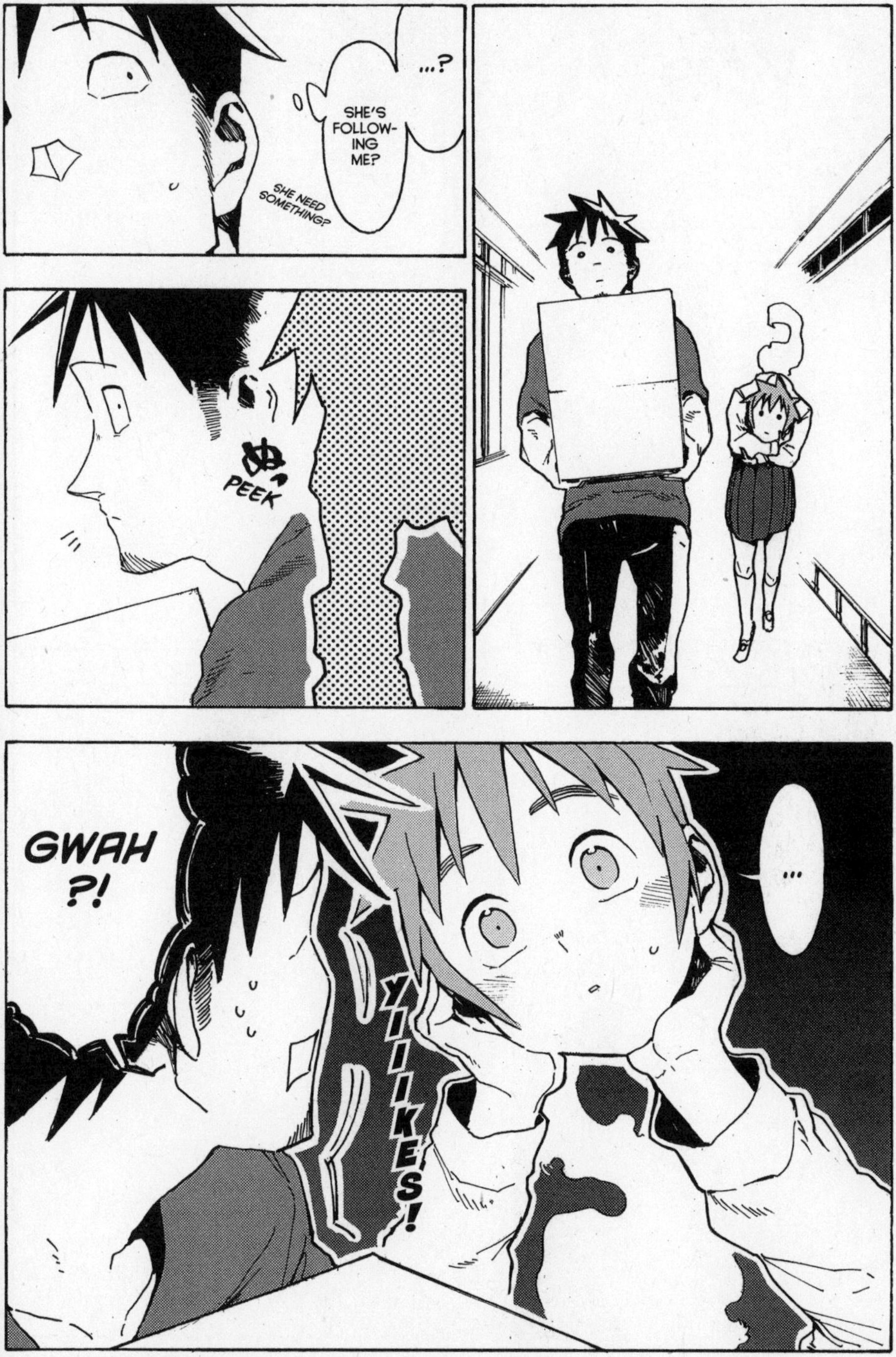
...?
SHE'S FOLLOW-ING ME?
SHE NEED SOMETHING?
PEEK
...
GWAH ?!
YIIIIKES!

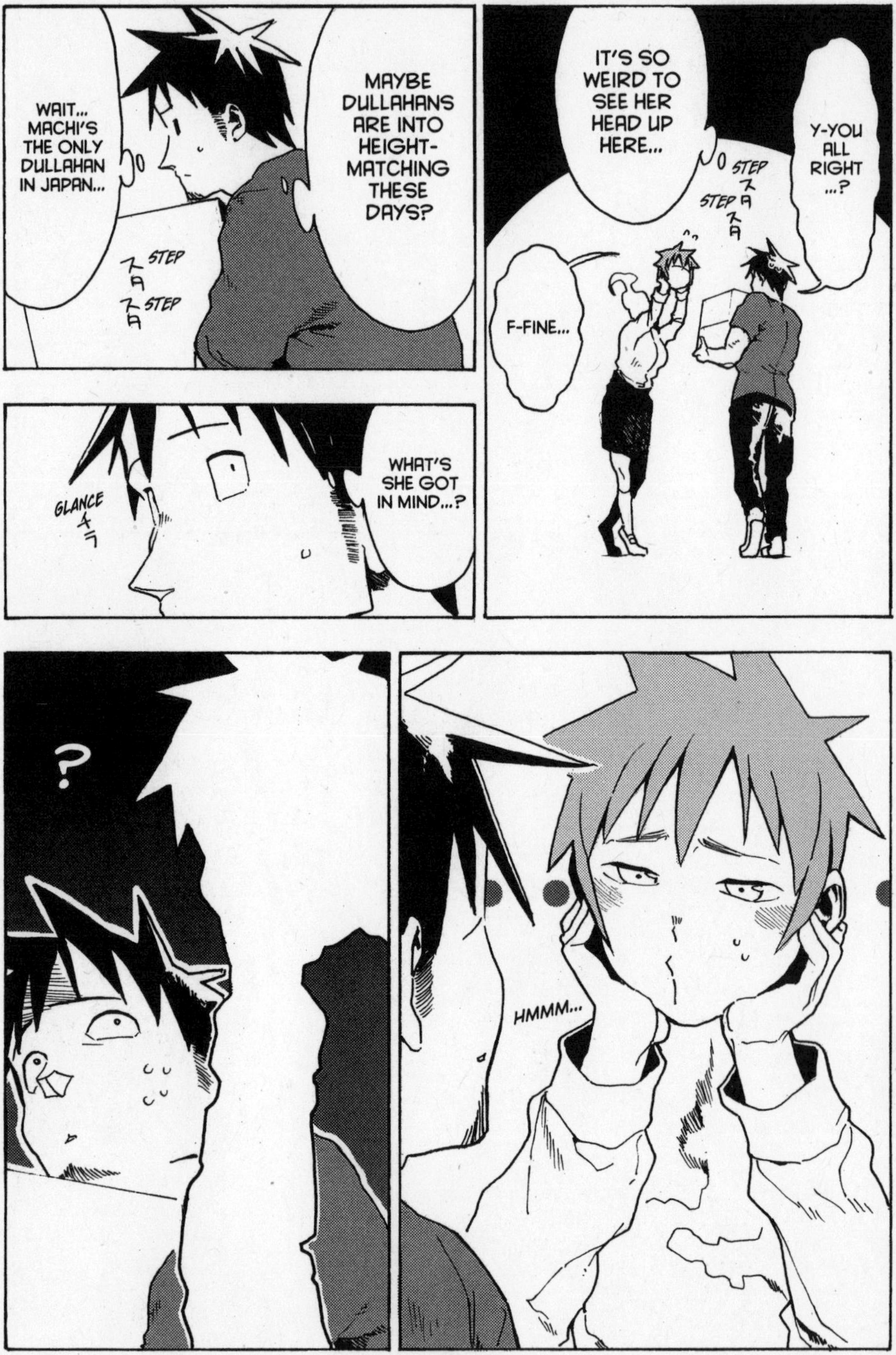
IT'S SO WEIRD TO SEE HER HEAD UP HERE...
Y-YOU ALL RIGHT ...?
STEP スタ
STEP スタ
F-FINE...
MAYBE DULLAHANS ARE INTO HEIGHT-MATCHING THESE DAYS?
WAIT... MACHI'S THE ONLY DULLAHAN IN JAPAN...
STEP スタ
STEP スタ
WHAT'S SHE GOT IN MIND...?
GLANCE チラ
HMMM...
?

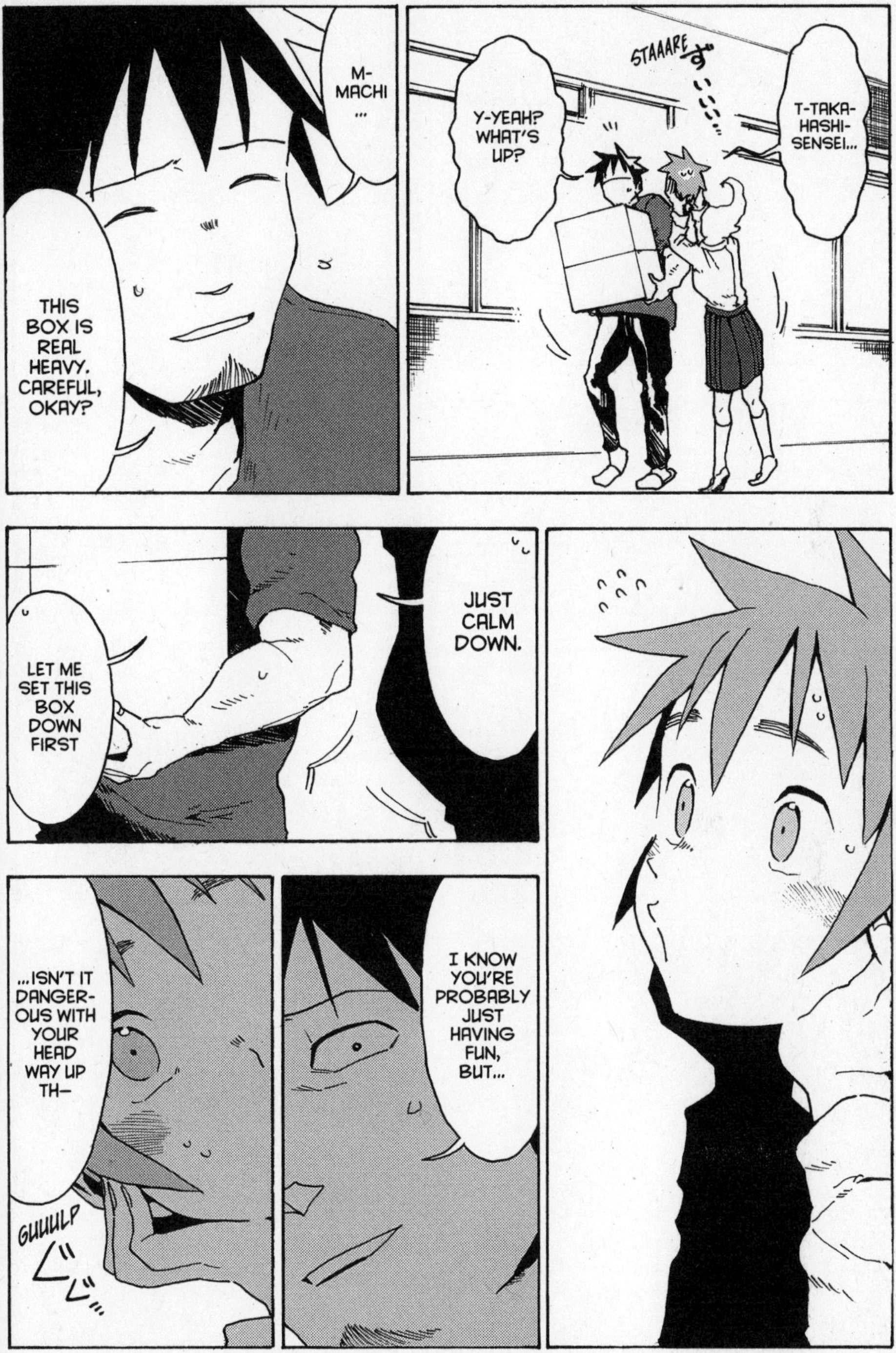
T-TAKA-HASHI-SENSEI...
STAAARE
ずいいいい...
Y-YEAH? WHAT'S UP?
M-MACHI ...
THIS BOX IS REAL HEAVY. CAREFUL, OKAY?
JUST CALM DOWN.
LET ME SET THIS BOX DOWN FIRST
I KNOW YOU'RE PROBABLY JUST HAVING FUN, BUT...
...ISN'T IT DANGEROUS WITH YOUR HEAD WAY UP TH-
GUUULP
ぐぐ...

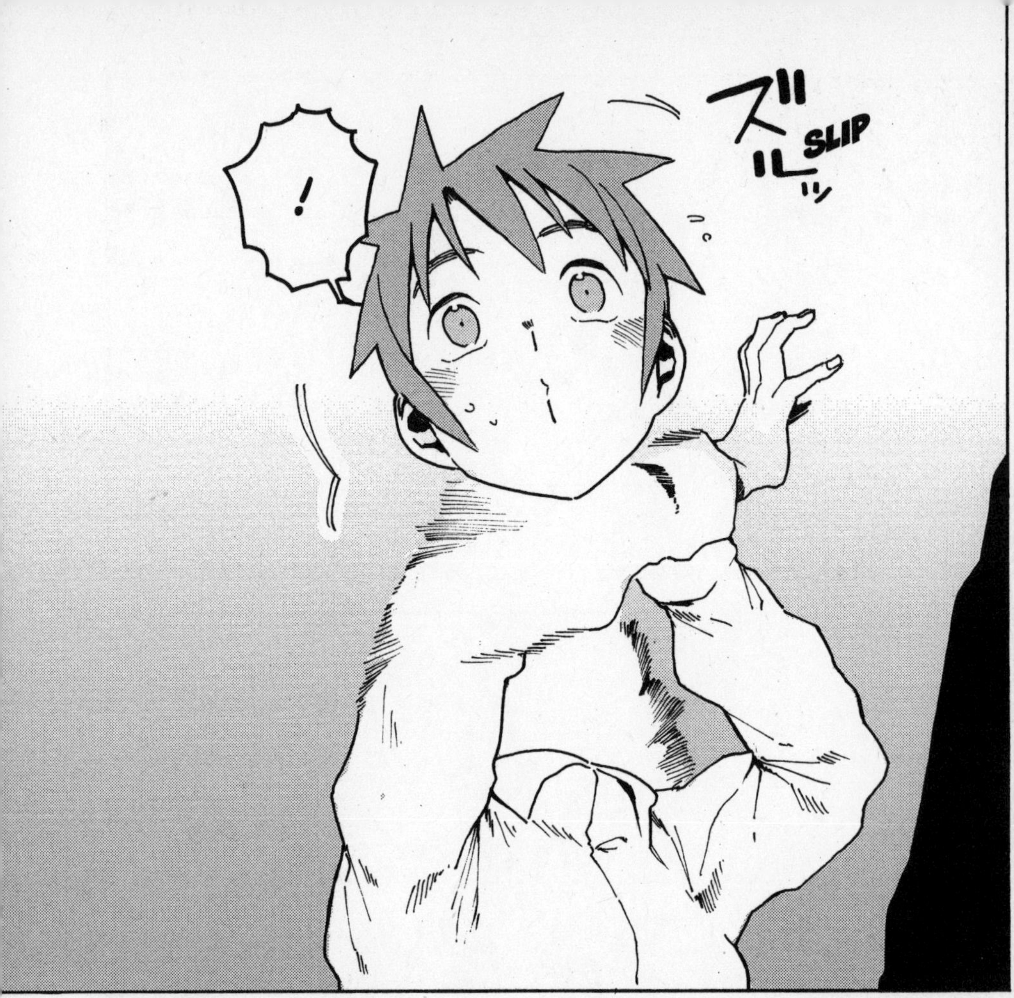
ズルッ
SLIP
!

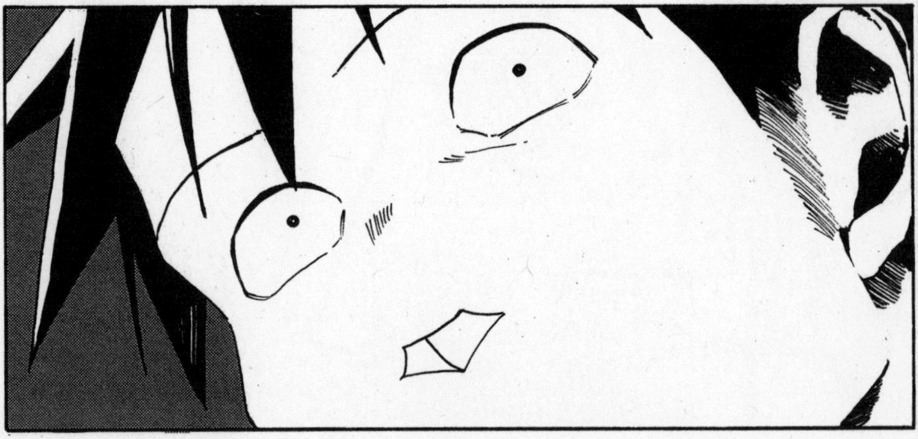

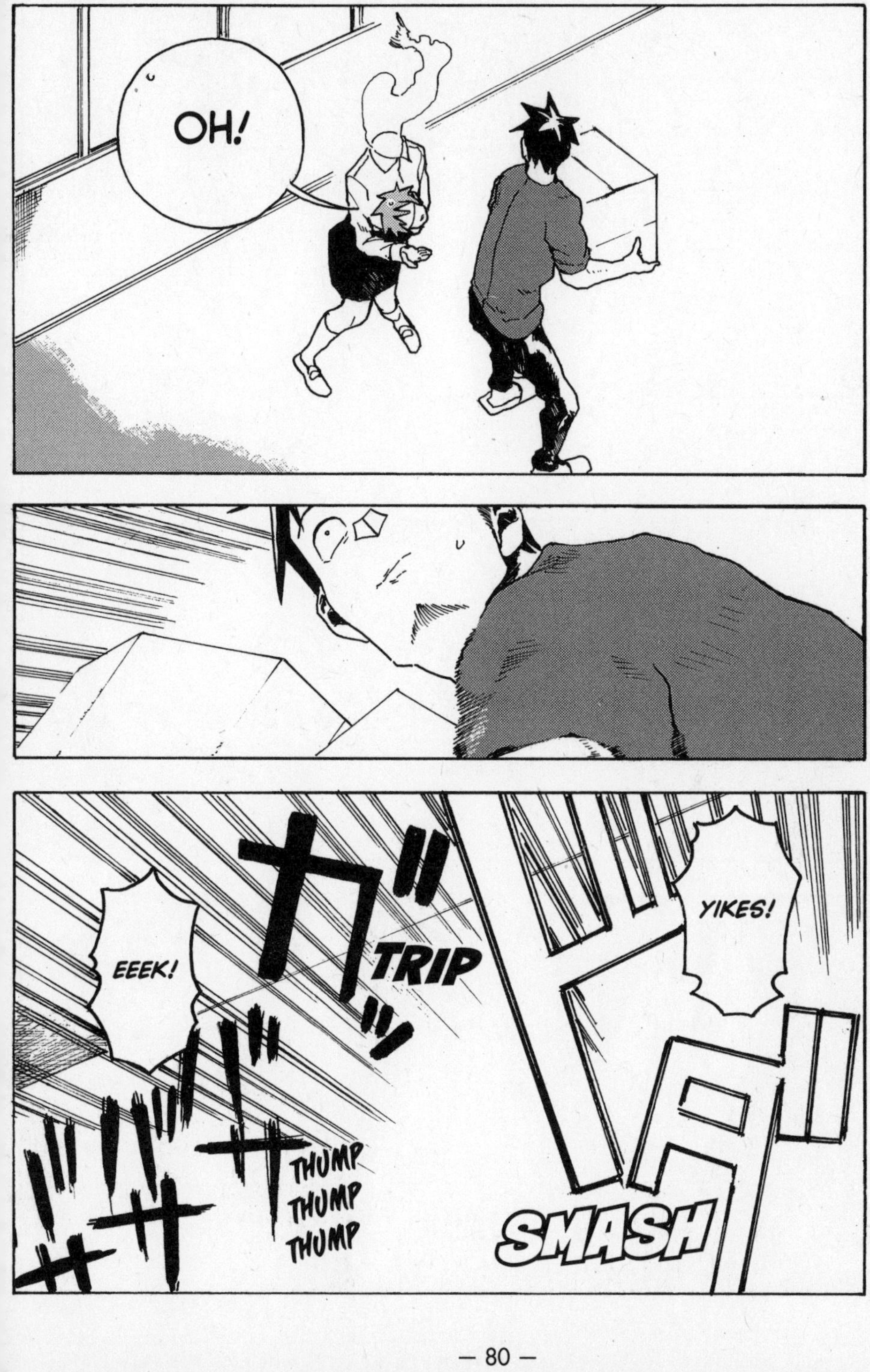
OH!
YIKES!
SMASH
TRIP
EEEK!
THUMP THUMP THUMP

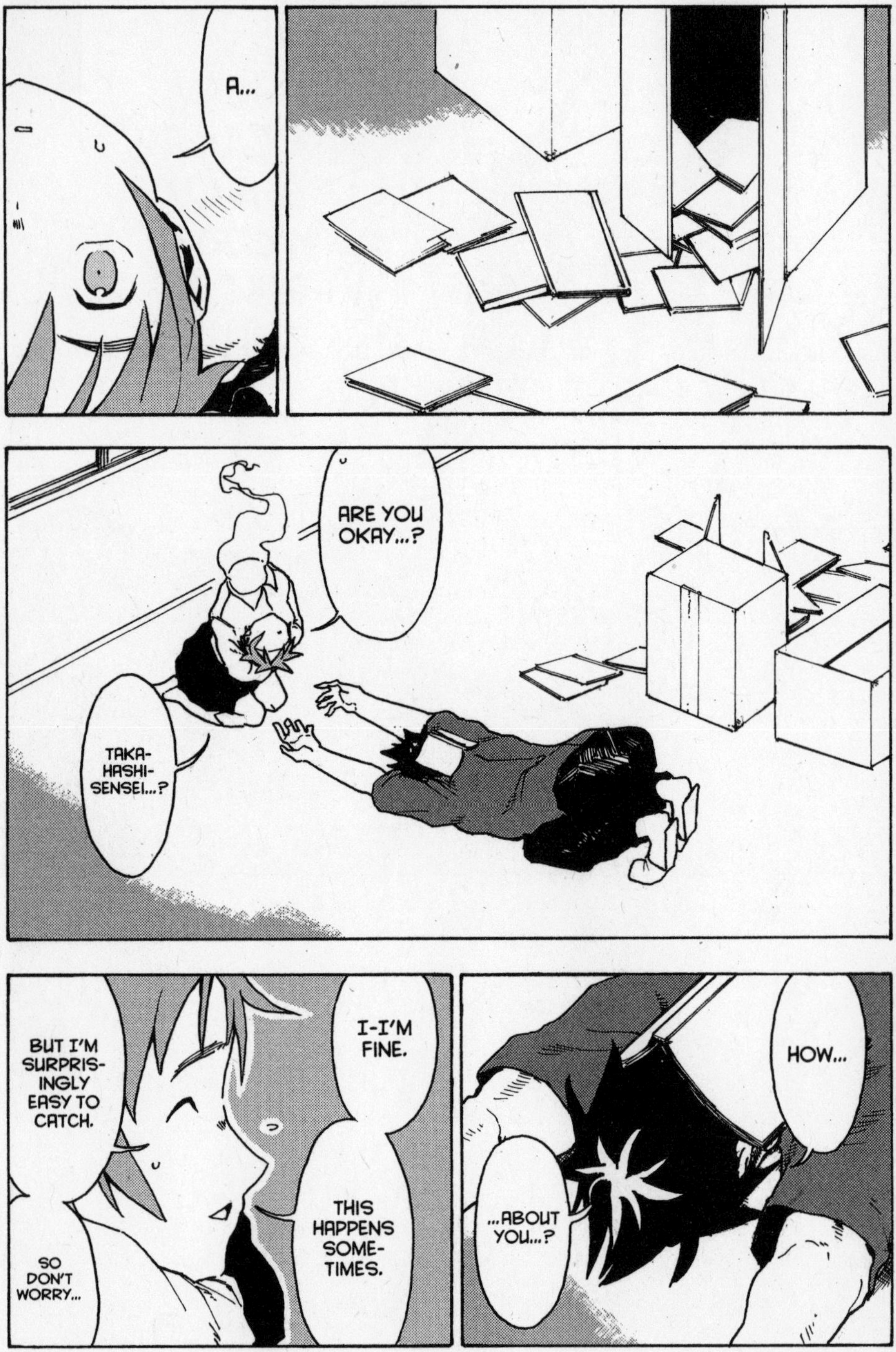
A...
ARE YOU OKAY...?
TAKA-HASHI-SENSEI...?
HOW...
...ABOUT YOU...?
I-I'M FINE.
THIS HAPPENS SOME-TIMES.
BUT I'M SURPRIS-INGLY EASY TO CATCH.
SO DON'T WORRY...

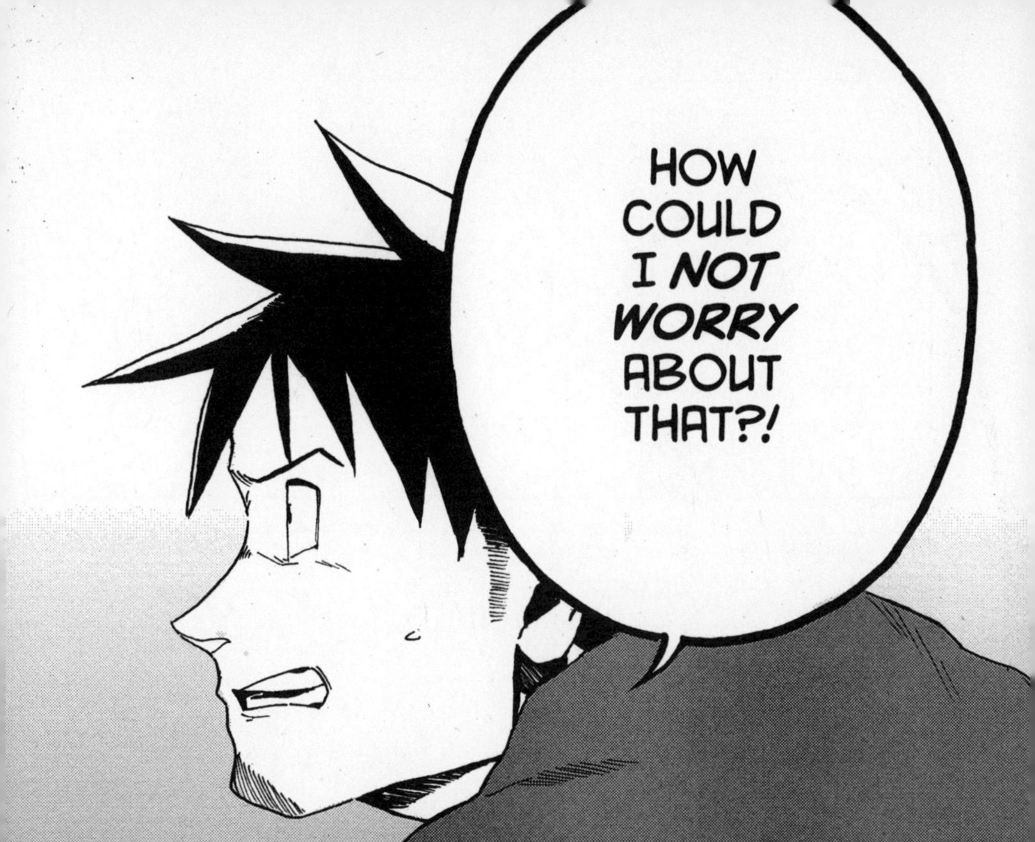
HOW COULD I ***NOT WORRY*** ABOUT THAT?!

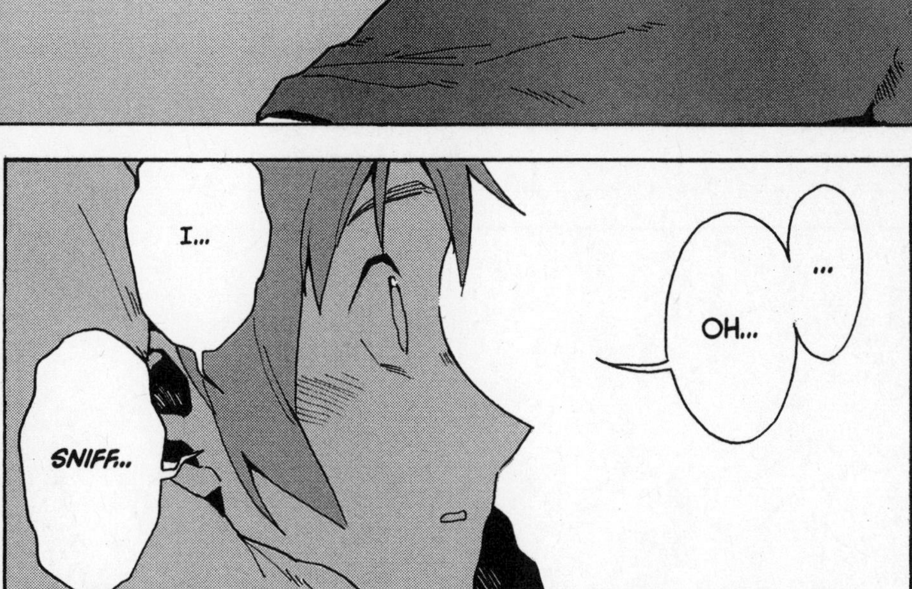
...
OH...
I...
SNIFF...

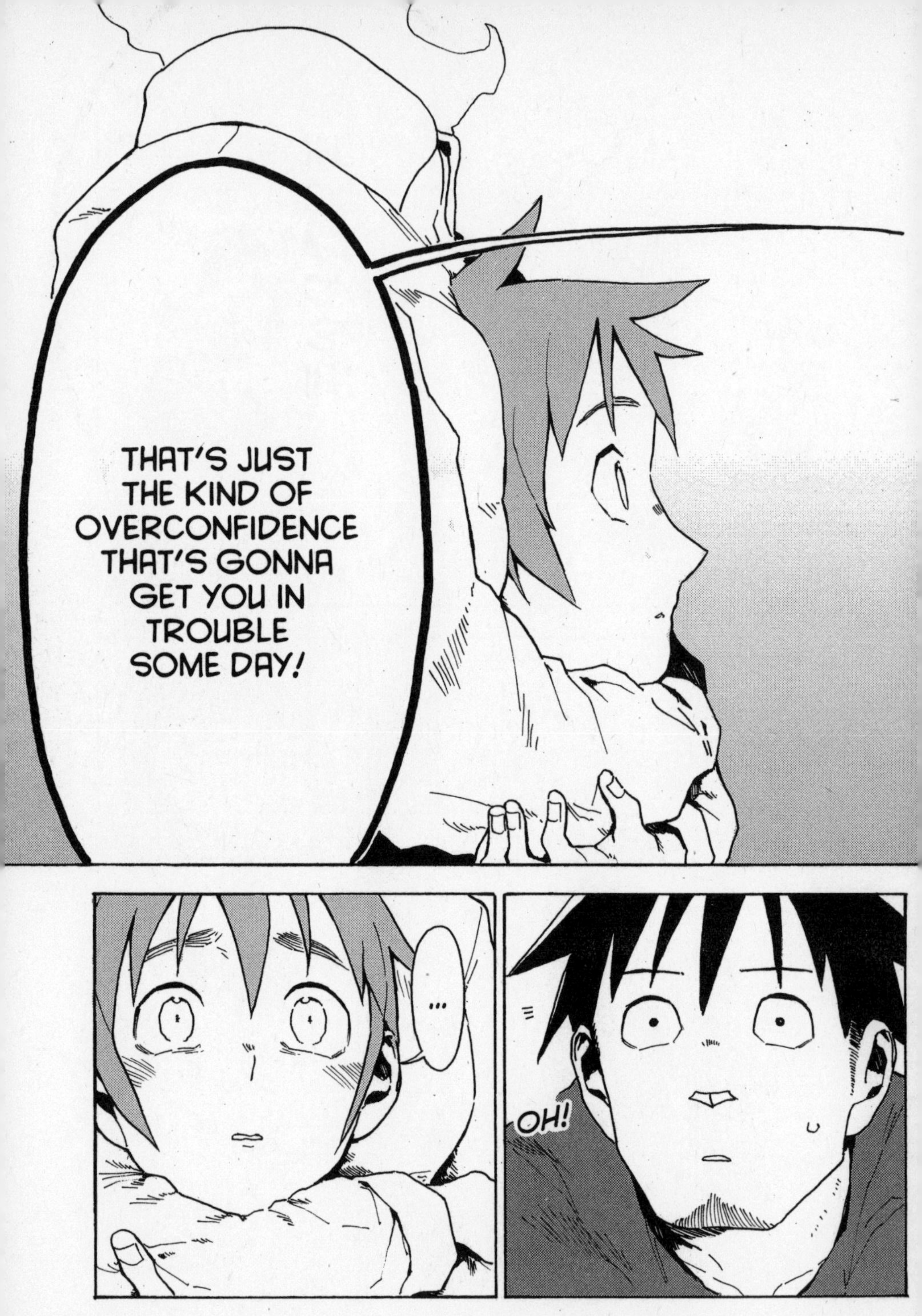
THAT'S JUST THE KIND OF OVERCONFIDENCE THAT'S GONNA GET YOU IN TROUBLE SOME DAY!
OH!
...

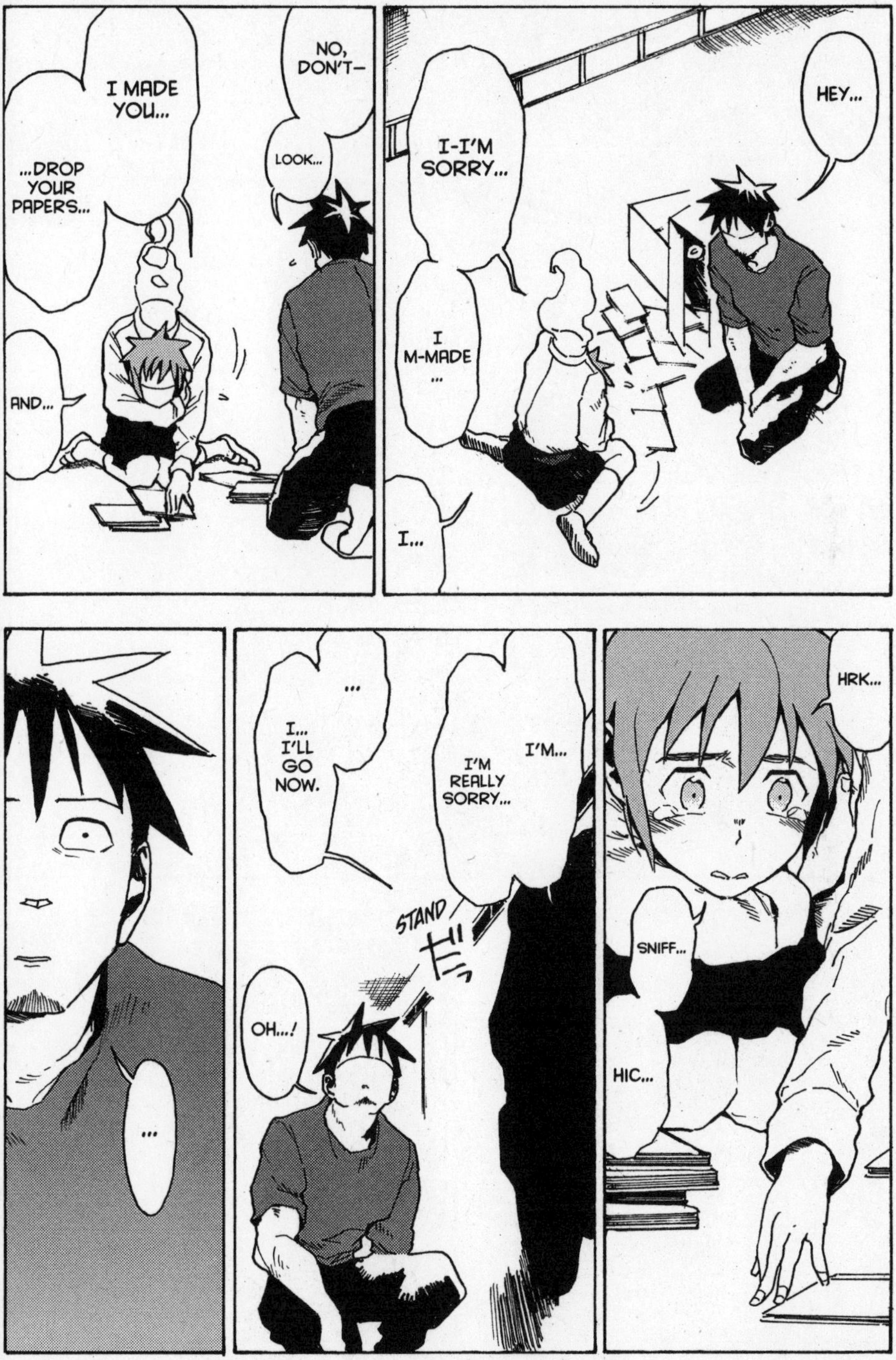
HEY...
I-I'M SORRY...
I M-MADE ...
I...
NO, DON'T—
LOOK...
I MADE YOU...
...DROP YOUR PAPERS...
AND...
HRK...
SNIFF...
HIC...
I'M...
I'M REALLY SORRY...
...
I... I'LL GO NOW.
STAND
OH...!
...

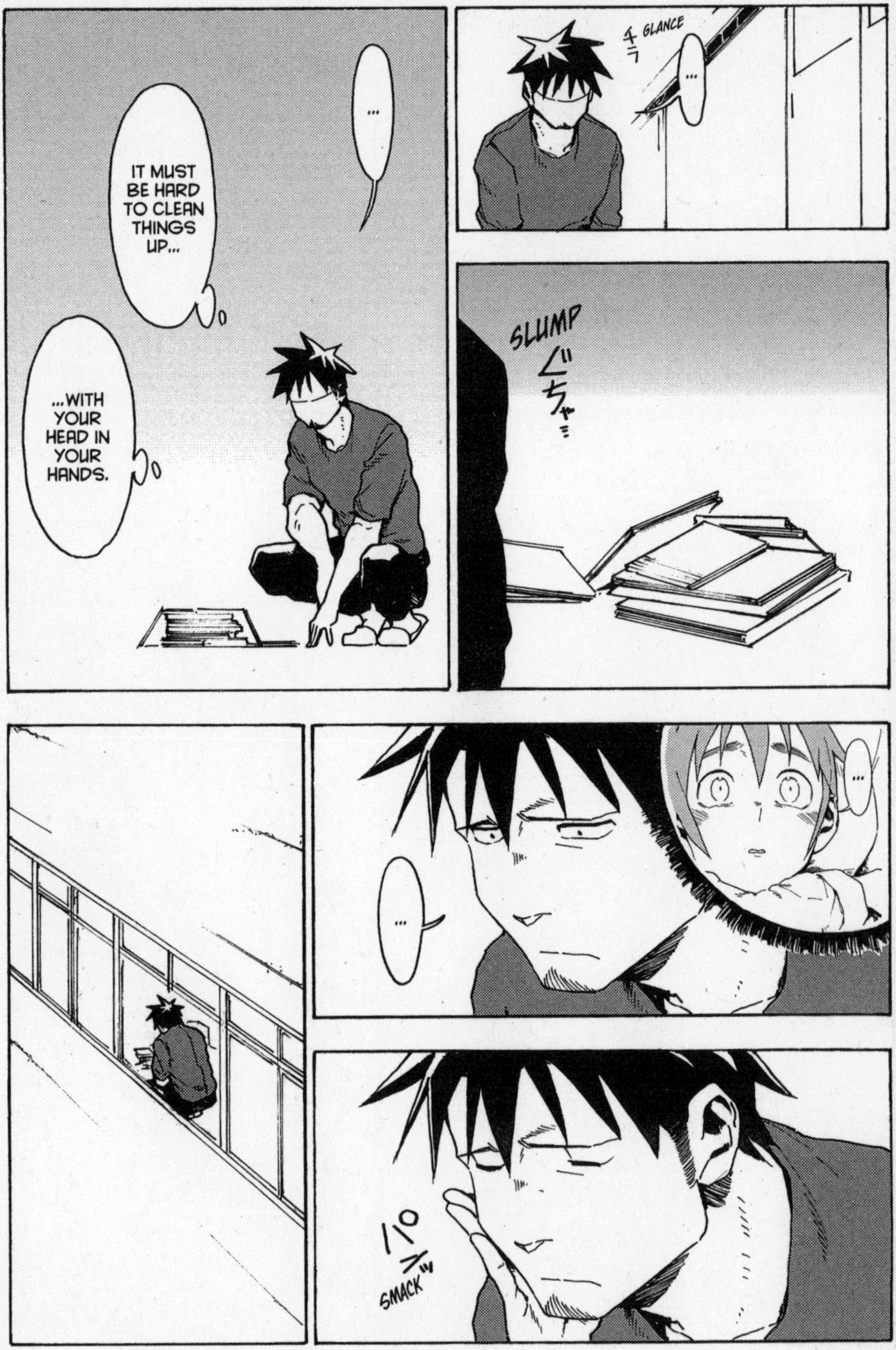
チラ GLANCE
...
SLUMP ぐちゃ
...
IT MUST BE HARD TO CLEAN THINGS UP...
...WITH YOUR HEAD IN YOUR HANDS.
...
...
パン SMACK

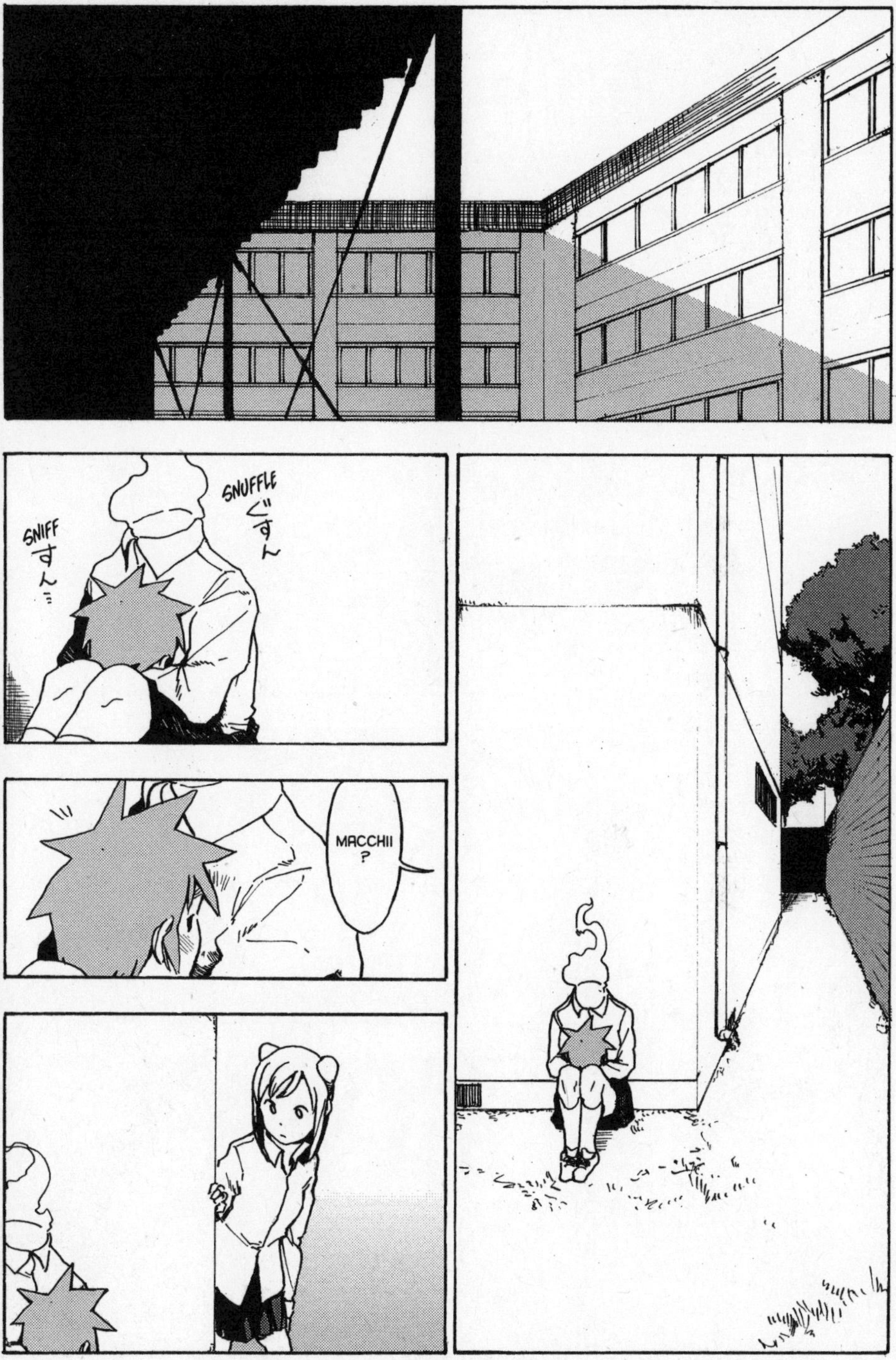
SNUFFLE
ぐすん
SNIFF
すん…
MACCHII ?

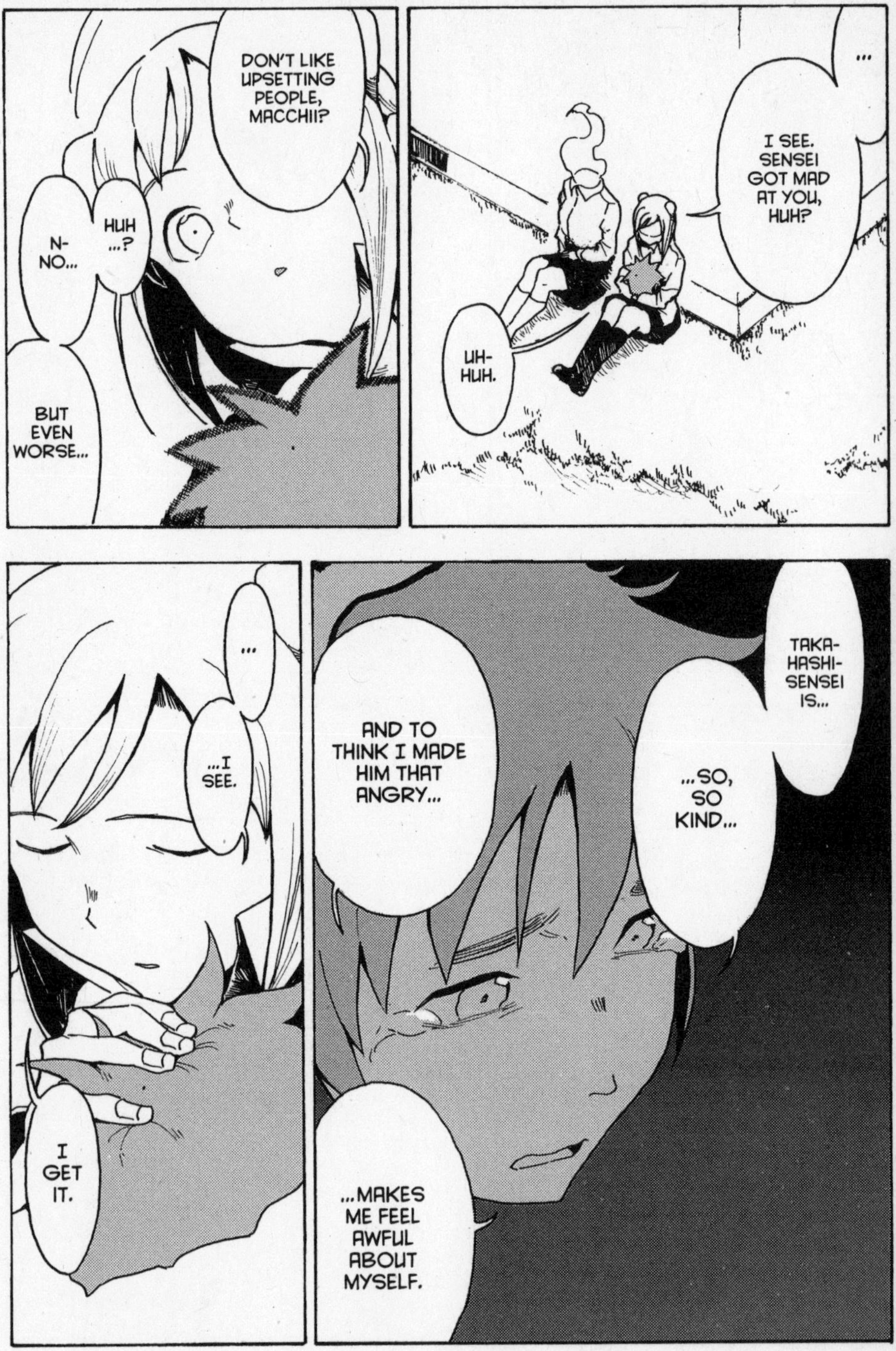
...
I SEE. SENSEI GOT MAD AT YOU, HUH?
UH-HUH.
DON'T LIKE UPSETTING PEOPLE, MACCHII?
HUH ...?
N-NO...
BUT EVEN WORSE...
TAKA-HASHI-SENSEI IS...
...SO, SO KIND...
AND TO THINK I MADE HIM THAT ANGRY...
...MAKES ME FEEL AWFUL ABOUT MYSELF.
...
...I SEE.
I GET IT.

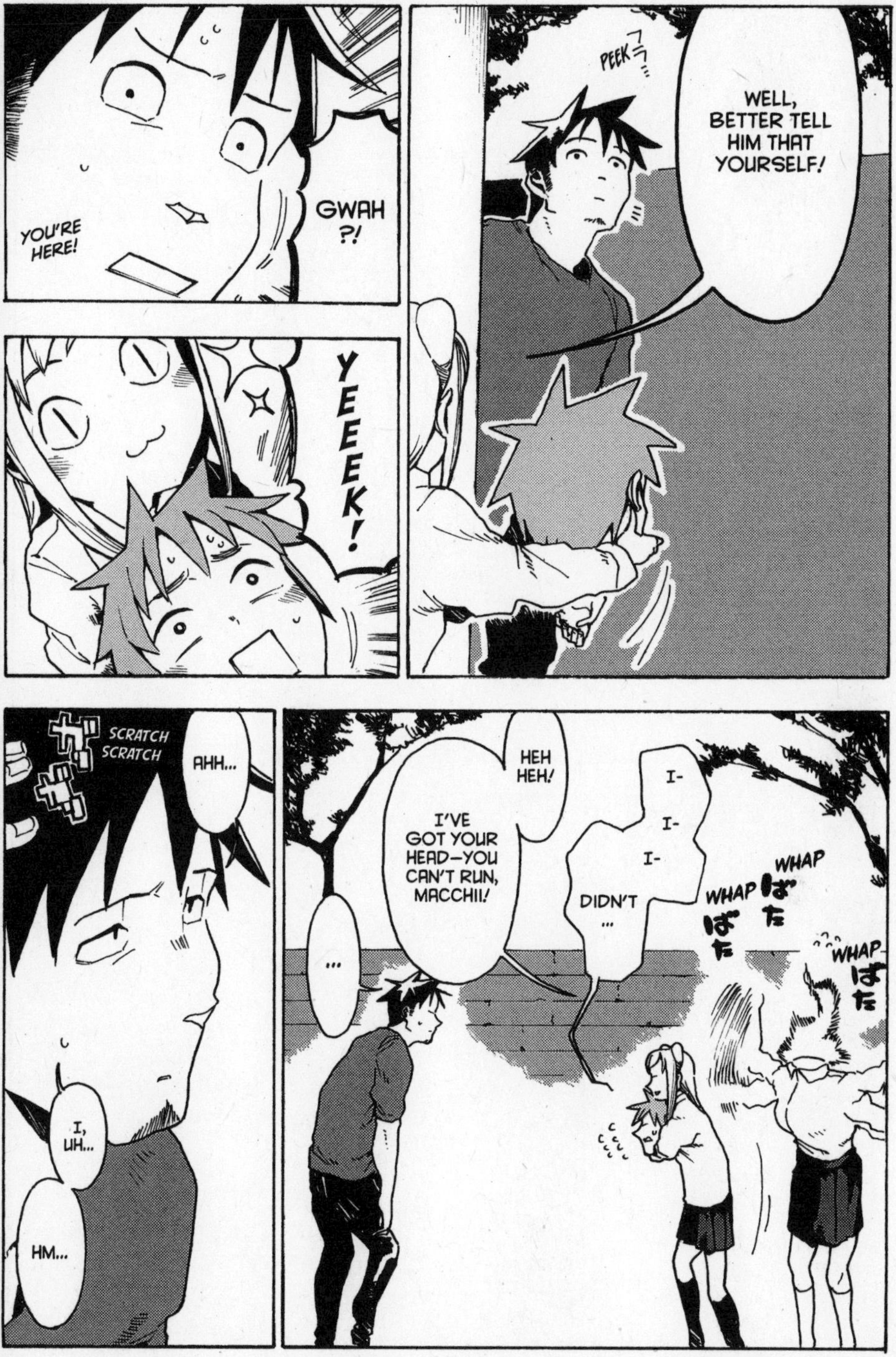
PEEK
WELL, BETTER TELL HIM THAT YOURSELF!
GWAH ?!
YOU'RE HERE!
YEEEEK!
WHAP ばた
WHAP ばた
WHAP ばた
I-
I-
I-
DIDN'T ...
HEH HEH!
I'VE GOT YOUR HEAD—YOU CAN'T RUN, MACCHII!
...
AHH...
SCRATCH SCRATCH
I, UH...
HM...

MACHI.
I'M SORRY ABOUT EARLIER.
VERY SORRY!
?!
A TEACHER HAS TO SCOLD HIS STUDENTS...
...WHEN THEY DON'T KNOW THEY'VE DONE SOMETHING WRONG...
...OR DON'T SEEM TO CARE.
HE MAY HAVE TO SPEAK HARSHLY TO THEM.
BUT THERE WAS NO NEED TO SCOLD YOU.
I REACTED EMOTIONALLY.
I COULD HAVE JUST TOLD YOU IN A NORMAL TONE.
...
I WAS IN THE WRONG.
I SHOULD HAVE SET DOWN...
...MY LORD...
...AND THEN TALKED TO YOU. CALMLY.

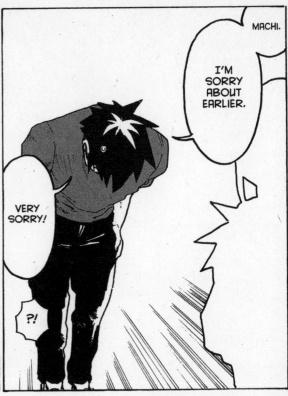

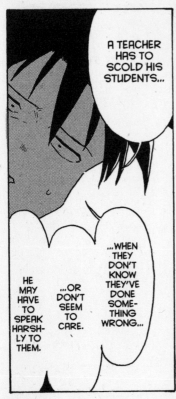

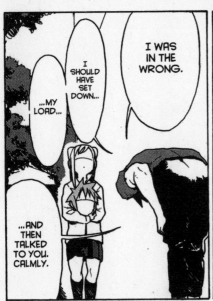

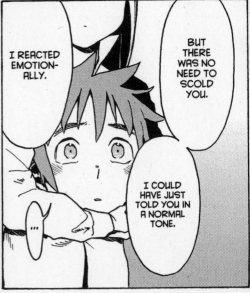

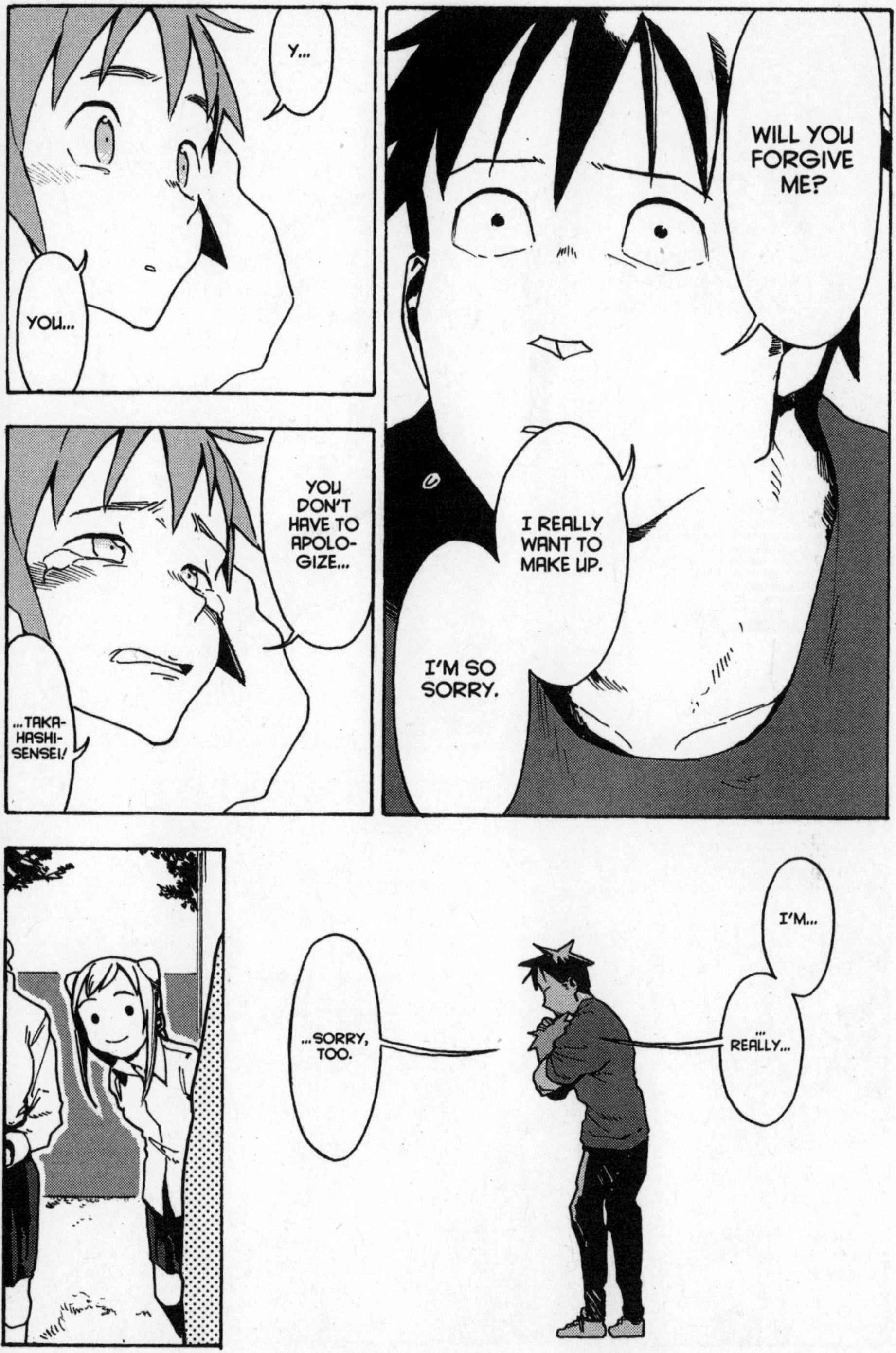
WILL YOU FORGIVE ME?
I REALLY WANT TO MAKE UP.
I'M SO SORRY.
Y...
YOU...
YOU DON'T HAVE TO APOLO-GIZE...
...TAKA-HASHI-SENSEI!
I'M...
...REALLY...
...SORRY, TOO.

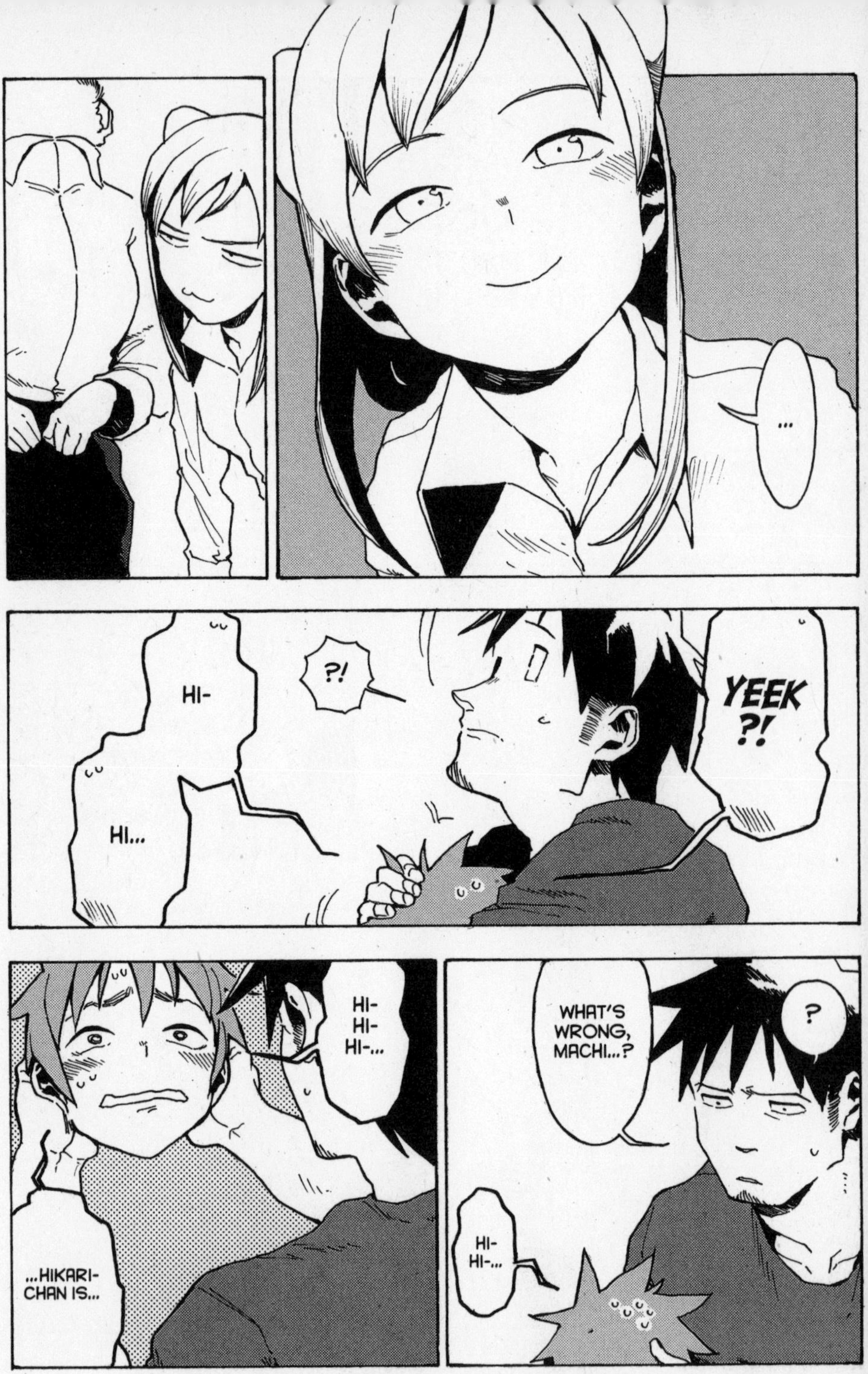
...
YEEK ?!
?!
HI-
HI...
?
WHAT'S WRONG, MACHI...?
HI- HI-...
HI- HI- HI-...
...HIKARI- CHAN IS...

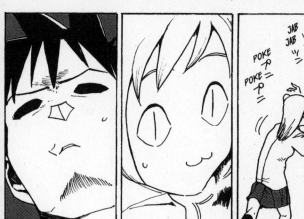

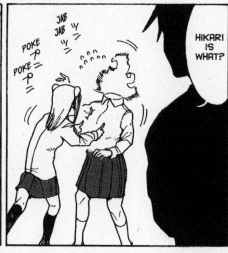

POKE ♪

POKE ♪

JAB JAB ♪

HIKARI IS WHAT?

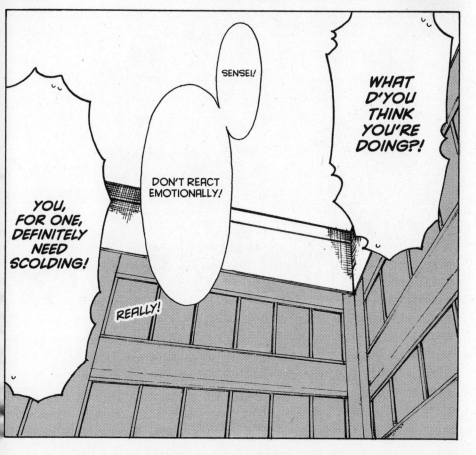

SENSEI!

WHAT D'YOU THINK YOU'RE DOING?!

DON'T REACT EMOTIONALLY!

YOU, FOR ONE, DEFINITELY NEED SCOLDING!

REALLY!

WHOOPS!

ANYWAY, DID YOU WANT SOMETHING?
!
OH, UH...
OH!
IF I SAY I WAS IMITATING HIKARI-CHAN...
...SHE MIGHT FEEL RESPONSIBLE.
...
...
EH HEH HEH!
?
EH HEH HEH!
*JUST 'CAUSE
AH HAH HAH...?
?
GOING WITH THE FLOW.

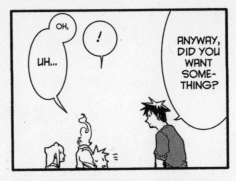

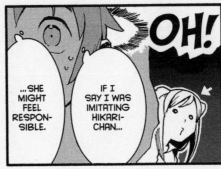

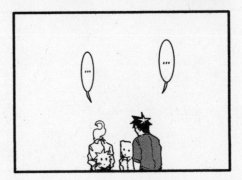

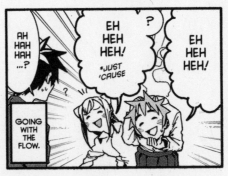

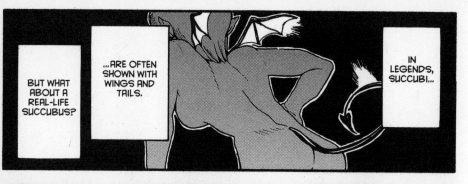

IN LEGENDS, SUCCUBI...

...ARE OFTEN SHOWN WITH WINGS AND TAILS.

BUT WHAT ABOUT A REAL-LIFE SUCCUBUS?

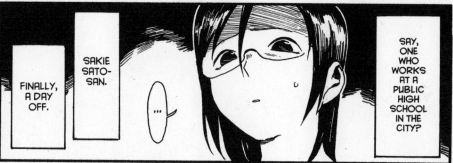

SAY, ONE WHO WORKS AT A PUBLIC HIGH SCHOOL IN THE CITY?

...

SAKIE SATO-SAN.

FINALLY, A DAY OFF.

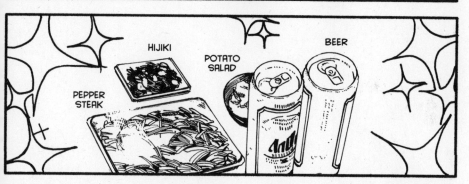

HIJIKI

POTATO SALAD

BEER

PEPPER STEAK

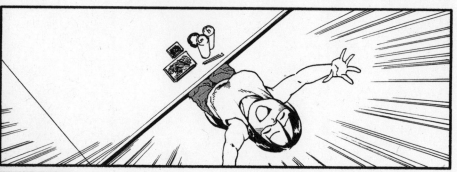

EXTRA STORY: SUCCUBUS'S DAY OFF

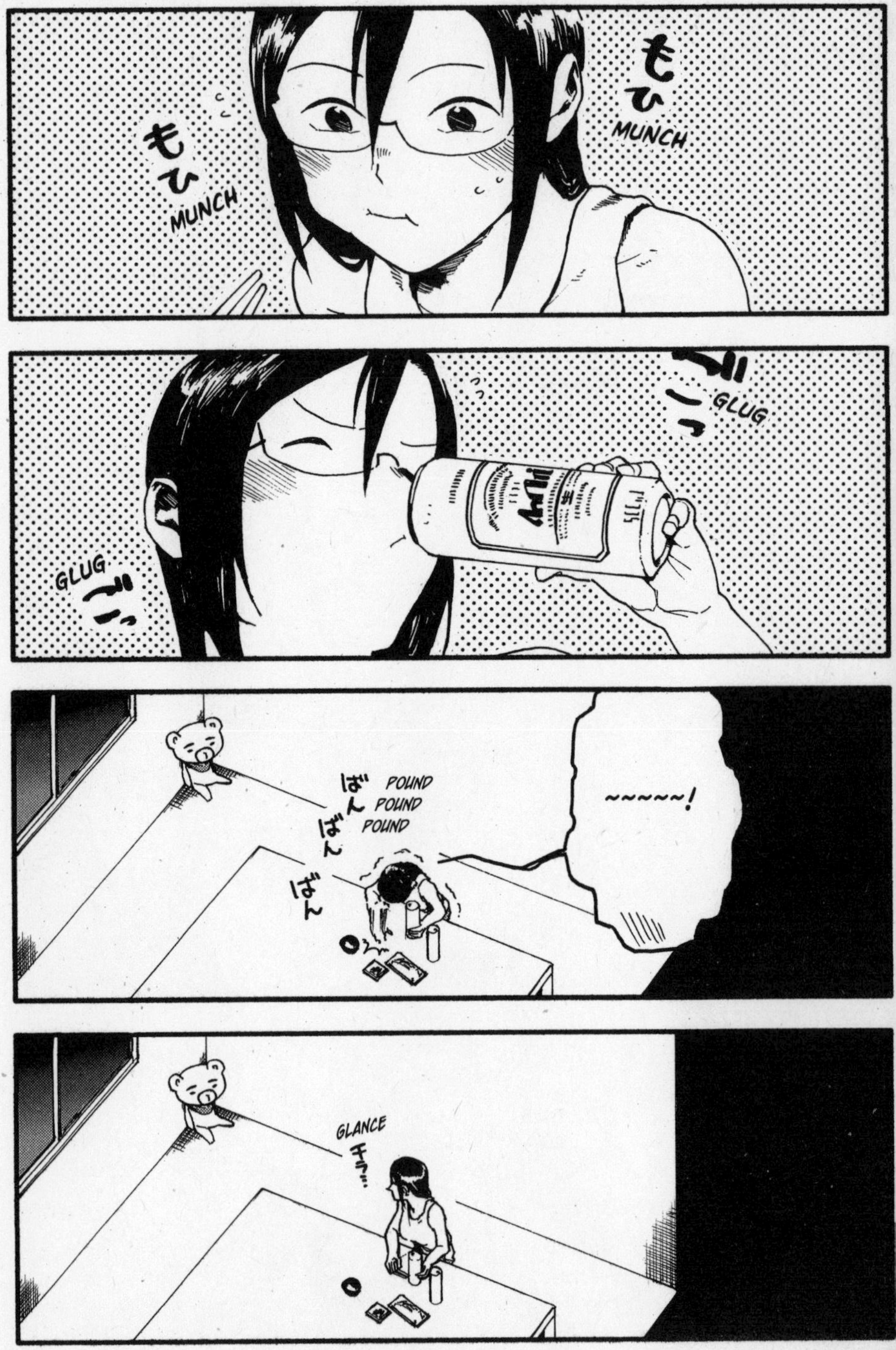
もひ
MUNCH
もひ
MUNCH
ごっ
GLUG
ごっ
GLUG
~~~~~!
ばん ばん ばん
POUND POUND POUND
GLANCE
チラ…
~~~~~

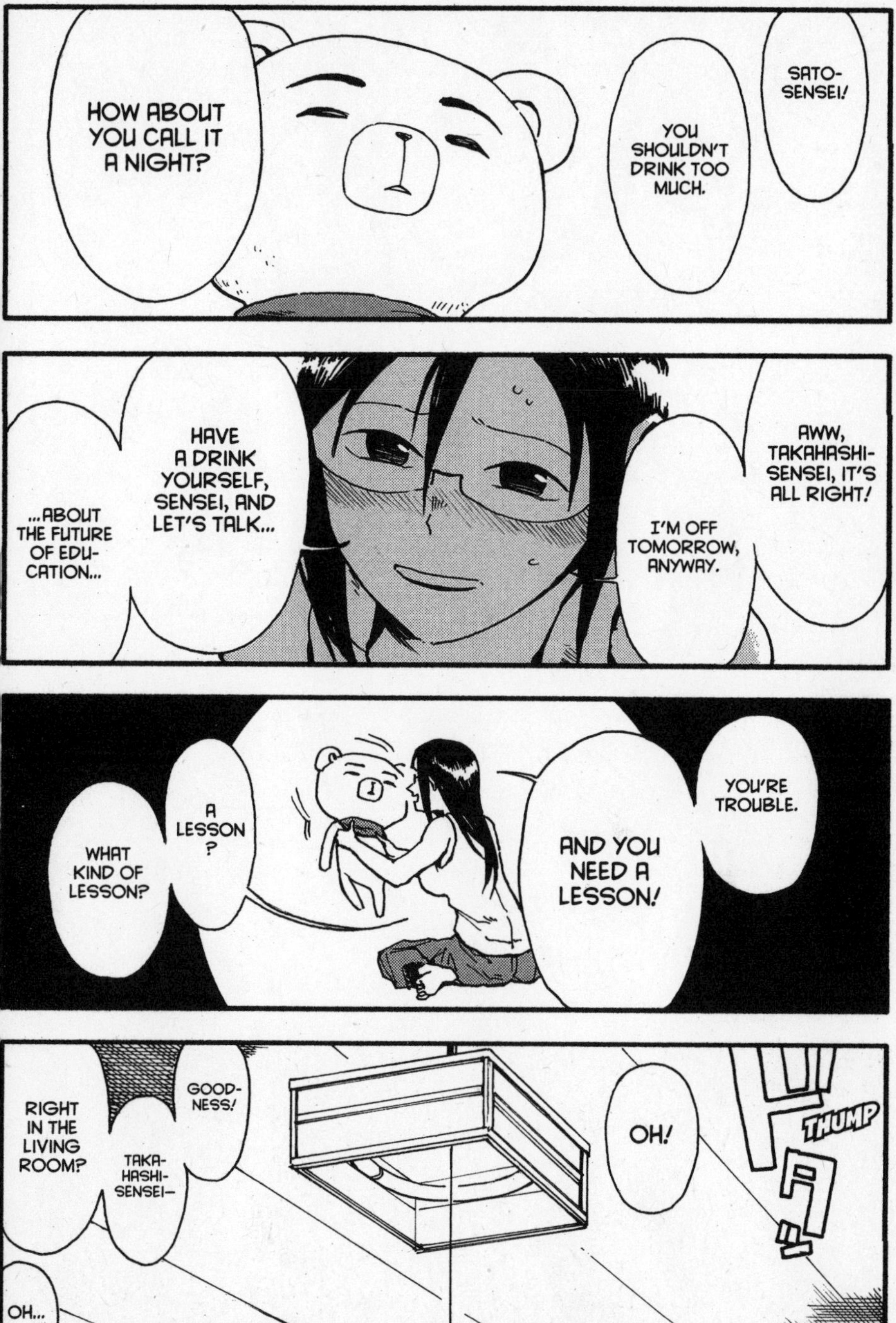
SATO-SENSEI!
YOU SHOULDN'T DRINK TOO MUCH.
HOW ABOUT YOU CALL IT A NIGHT?
AWW, TAKAHASHI-SENSEI, IT'S ALL RIGHT!
I'M OFF TOMORROW, ANYWAY.
HAVE A DRINK YOURSELF, SENSEI, AND LET'S TALK...
...ABOUT THE FUTURE OF EDU-CATION...
YOU'RE TROUBLE.
AND YOU NEED A LESSON!
A LESSON?
WHAT KIND OF LESSON?
THUMP
OH!
GOOD-NESS!
TAKA-HASHI-SENSEI—
RIGHT IN THE LIVING ROOM?
OH...

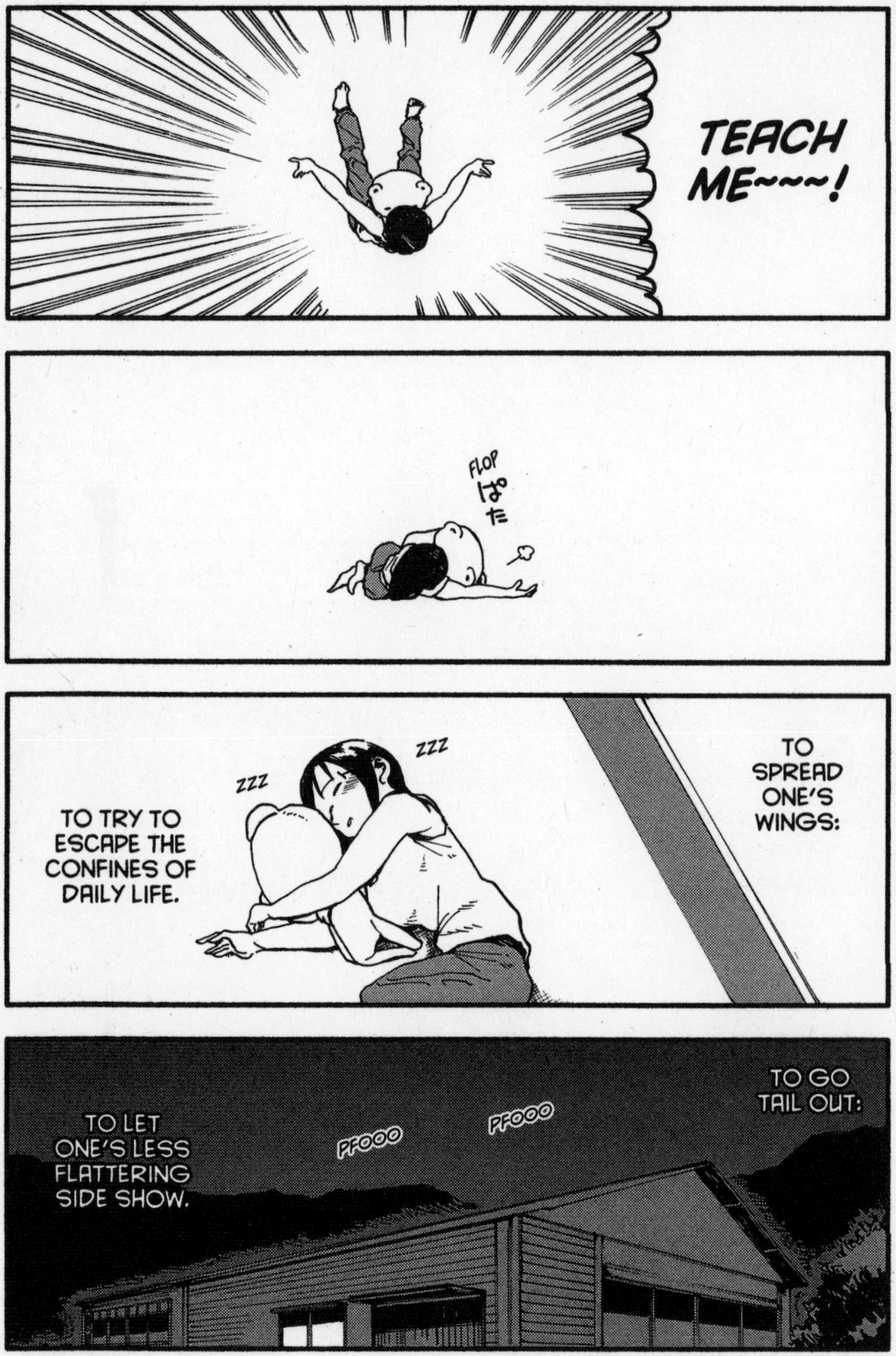
TEACH ME~~~!
FLOP
ぱた
TO SPREAD ONE'S WINGS:
ZZZ
ZZZ
TO TRY TO ESCAPE THE CONFINES OF DAILY LIFE.
TO GO TAIL OUT:
PFOOO
PFOOO
TO LET ONE'S LESS FLATTERING SIDE SHOW.

INTERVIEWS WITH MONSTER GIRLS

Chapter 22: Step Up, Succubus!

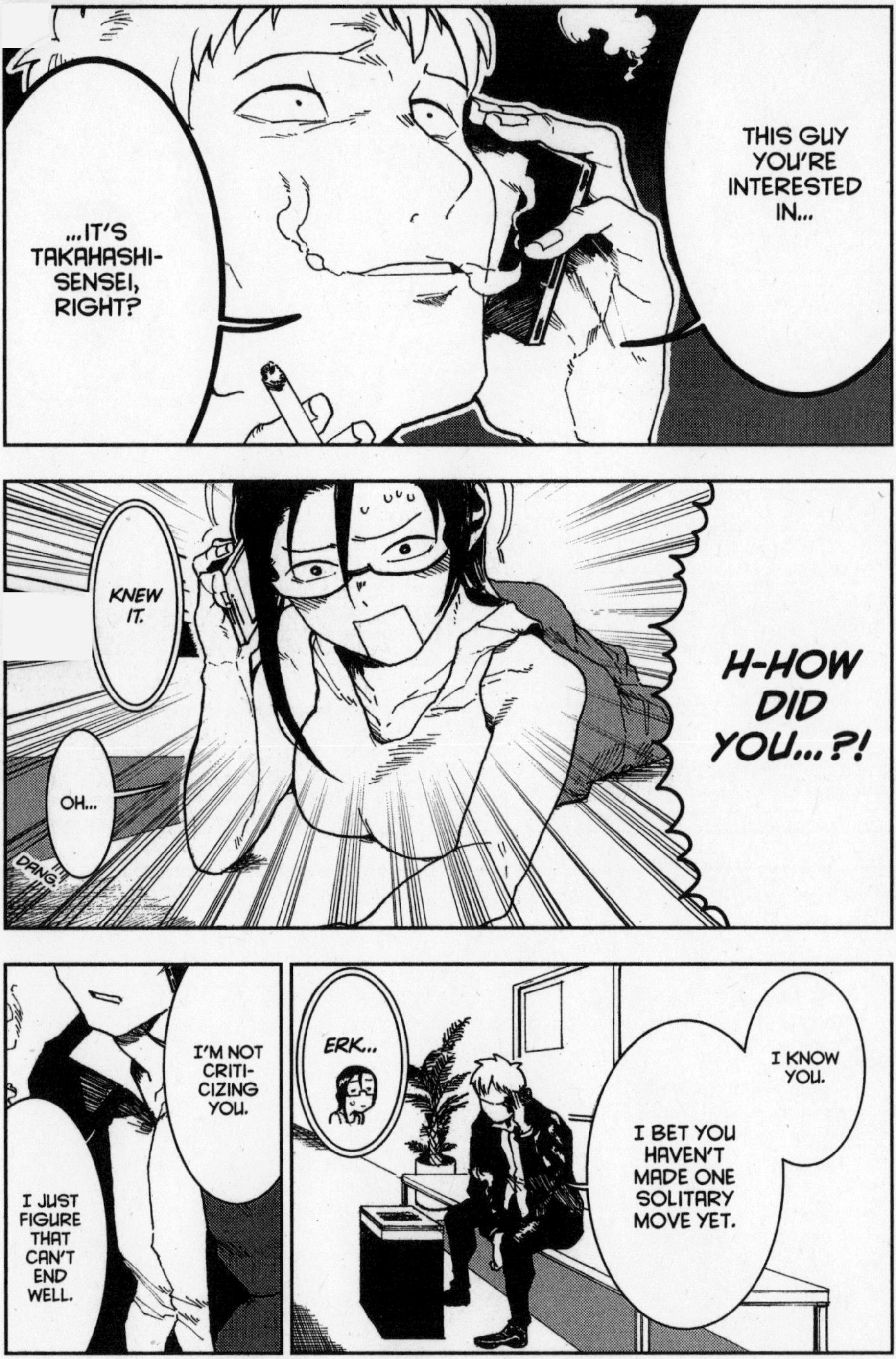
THIS GUY YOU'RE INTERESTED IN...
...IT'S TAKAHASHI-SENSEI, RIGHT?
H-HOW DID YOU...?!
KNEW IT.
OH...
DANG.
I KNOW YOU.
I BET YOU HAVEN'T MADE ONE SOLITARY MOVE YET.
ERK...
I'M NOT CRITI-CIZING YOU.
I JUST FIGURE THAT CAN'T END WELL.

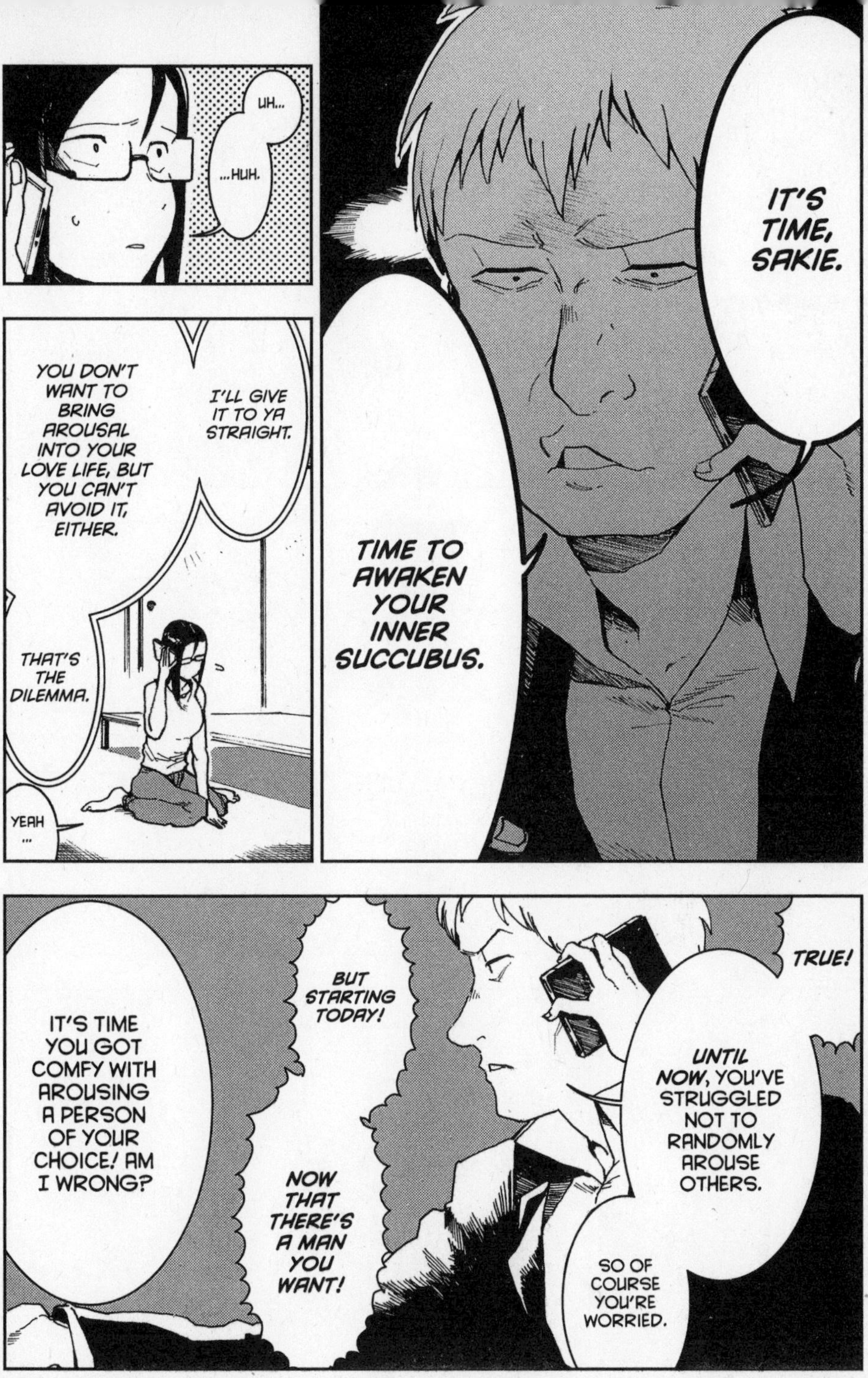
IT'S TIME, SAKIE.
TIME TO AWAKEN YOUR INNER SUCCUBUS.
UH...
...HUH.
I'LL GIVE IT TO YA STRAIGHT.
YOU DON'T WANT TO BRING AROUSAL INTO YOUR LOVE LIFE, BUT YOU CAN'T AVOID IT, EITHER.
THAT'S THE DILEMMA.
YEAH ...
TRUE!
UNTIL NOW, YOU'VE STRUGGLED NOT TO RANDOMLY AROUSE OTHERS.
SO OF COURSE YOU'RE WORRIED.
BUT STARTING TODAY!
NOW THAT THERE'S A MAN YOU WANT!
IT'S TIME YOU GOT COMFY WITH AROUSING A PERSON OF YOUR CHOICE! AM I WRONG?

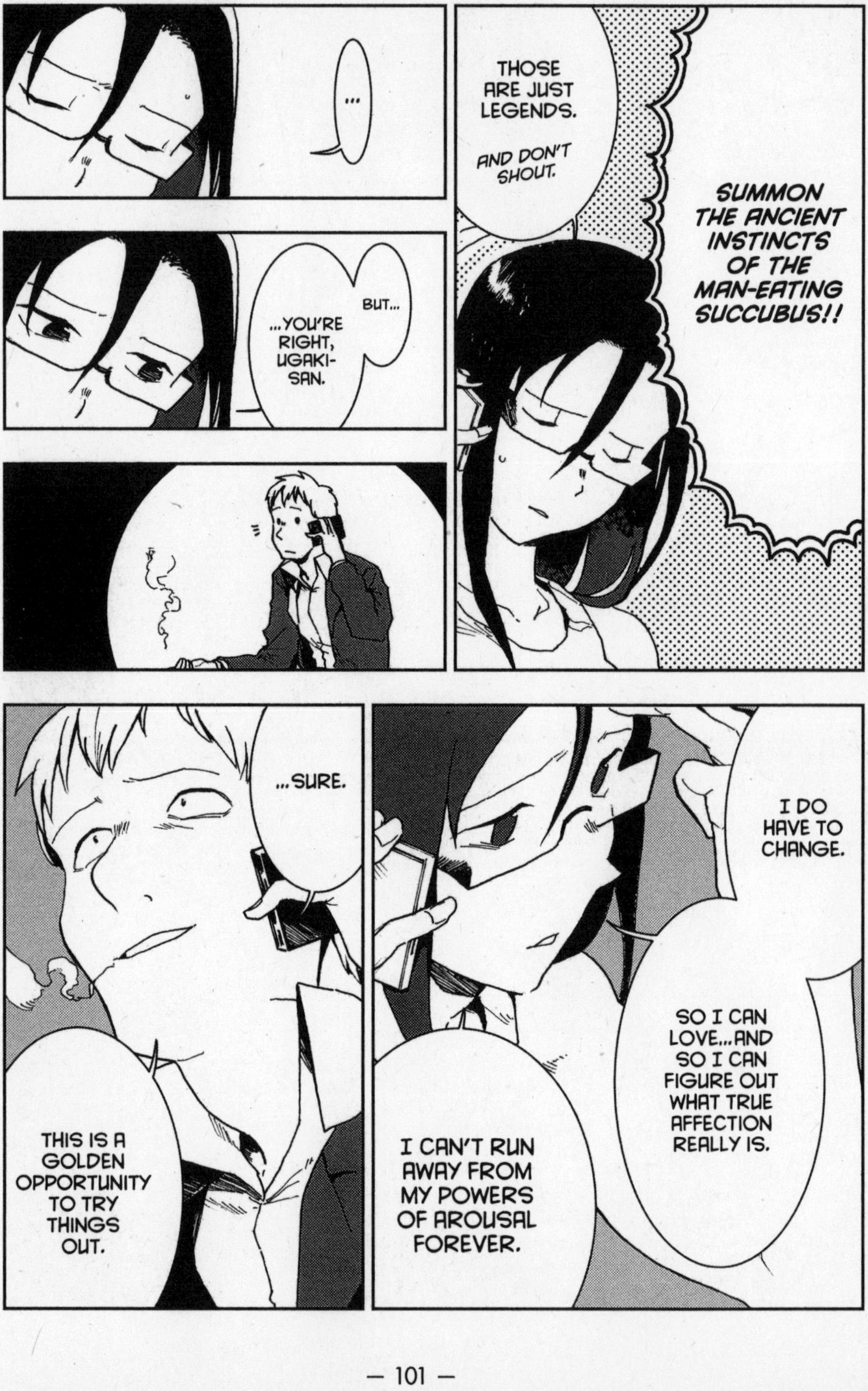

SUMMON THE ANCIENT INSTINCTS OF THE MAN-EATING SUCCUBUS!!
THOSE ARE JUST LEGENDS.
AND DON'T SHOUT.
...
BUT...
...YOU'RE RIGHT, UGAKI-SAN.
I DO HAVE TO CHANGE.
SO I CAN LOVE...AND SO I CAN FIGURE OUT WHAT TRUE AFFECTION REALLY IS.
I CAN'T RUN AWAY FROM MY POWERS OF AROUSAL FOREVER.
...SURE.
THIS IS A GOLDEN OPPORTUNITY TO TRY THINGS OUT.

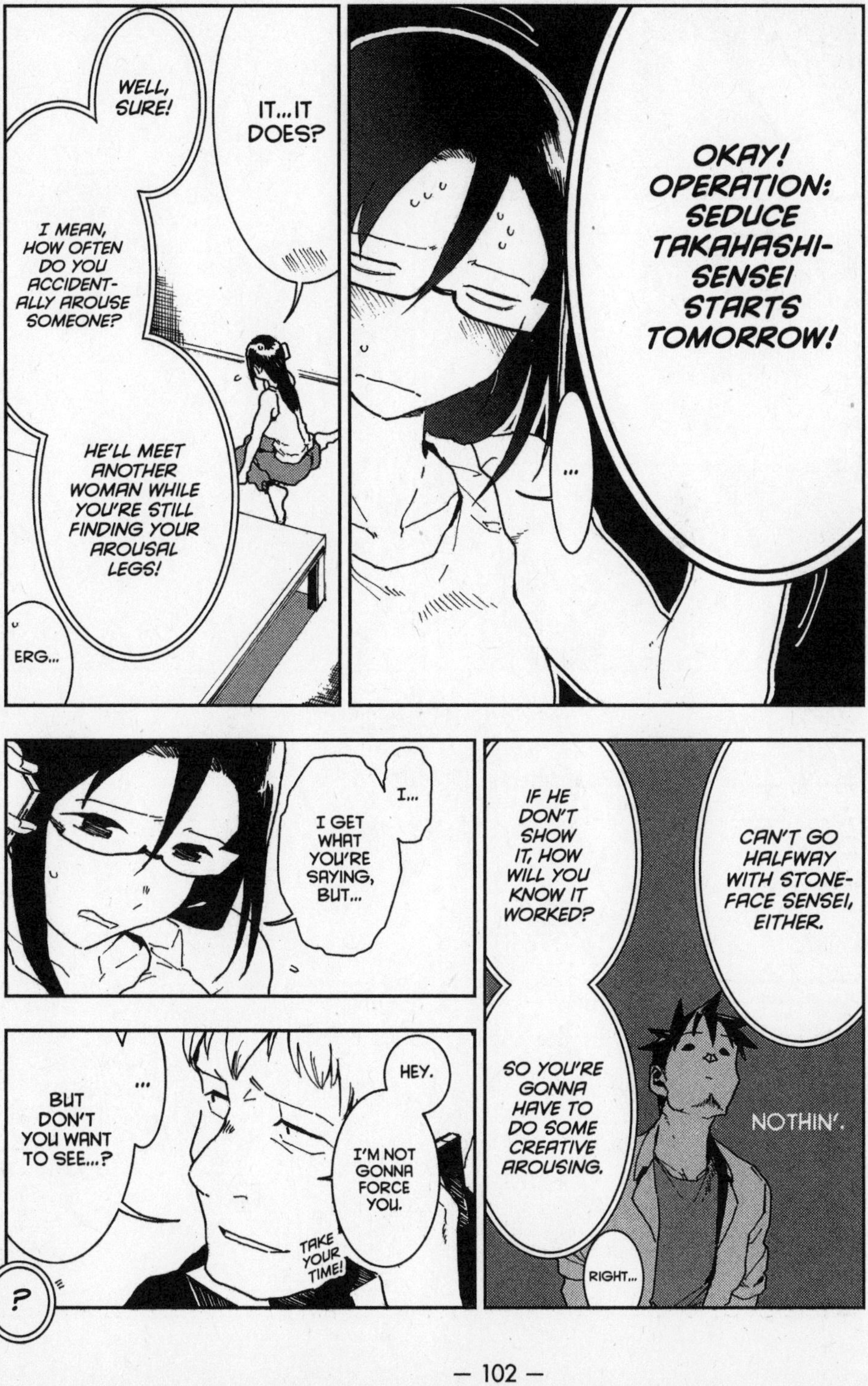
OKAY! OPERATION: SEDUCE TAKAHASHI-SENSEI STARTS TOMORROW!
...
IT...IT DOES?
WELL, SURE!
I MEAN, HOW OFTEN DO YOU ACCIDENT-ALLY AROUSE SOMEONE?
HE'LL MEET ANOTHER WOMAN WHILE YOU'RE STILL FINDING YOUR AROUSAL LEGS!
ERG...
CAN'T GO HALFWAY WITH STONE-FACE SENSEI, EITHER.
IF HE DON'T SHOW IT, HOW WILL YOU KNOW IT WORKED?
NOTHIN'.
SO YOU'RE GONNA HAVE TO DO SOME CREATIVE AROUSING.
RIGHT...
I...
I GET WHAT YOU'RE SAYING, BUT...
HEY.
I'M NOT GONNA FORCE YOU.
TAKE YOUR TIME!
...
BUT DON'T YOU WANT TO SEE...?
?

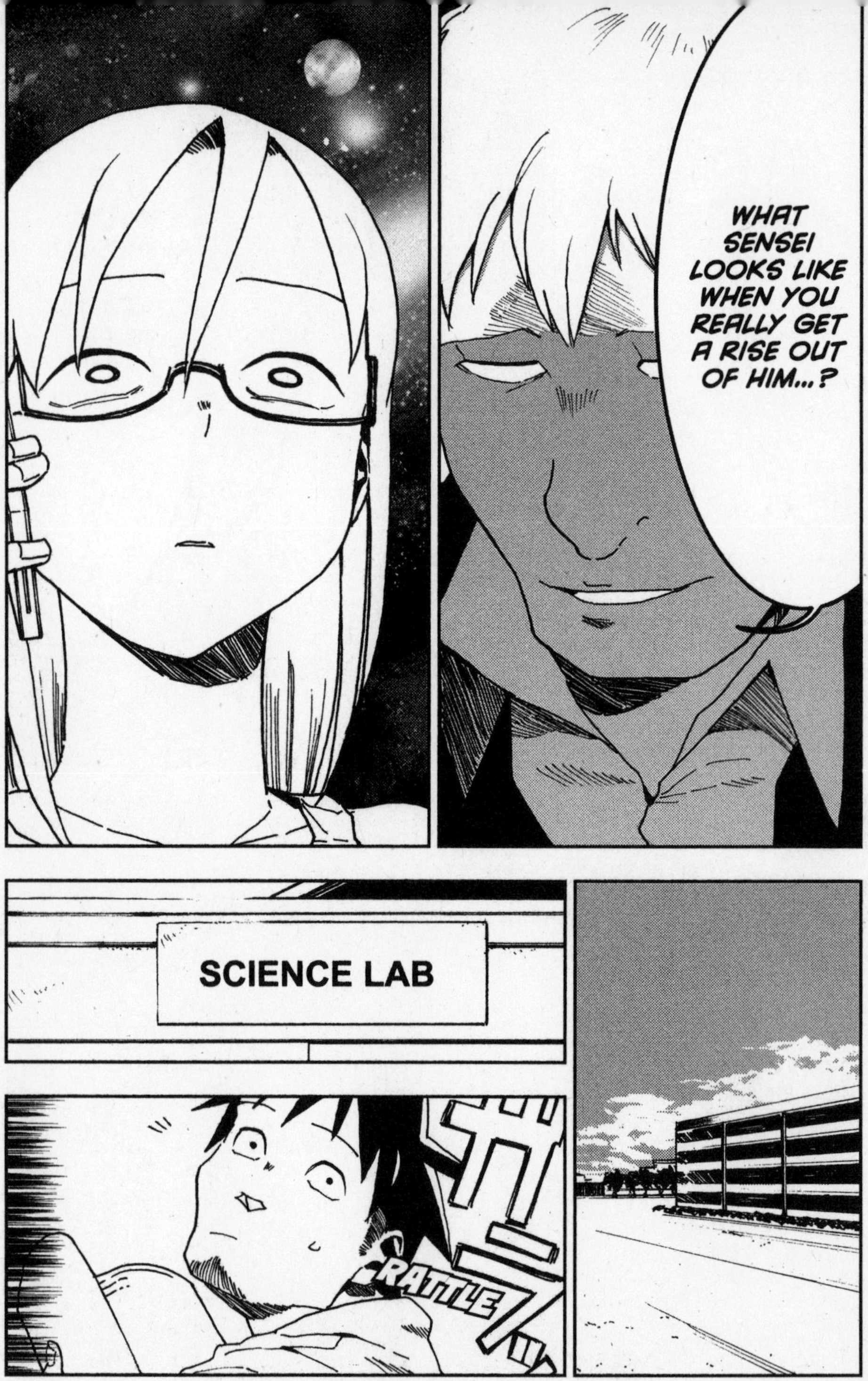
WHAT SENSEI LOOKS LIKE WHEN YOU REALLY GET A RISE OUT OF HIM...?
SCIENCE LAB
RATTLE

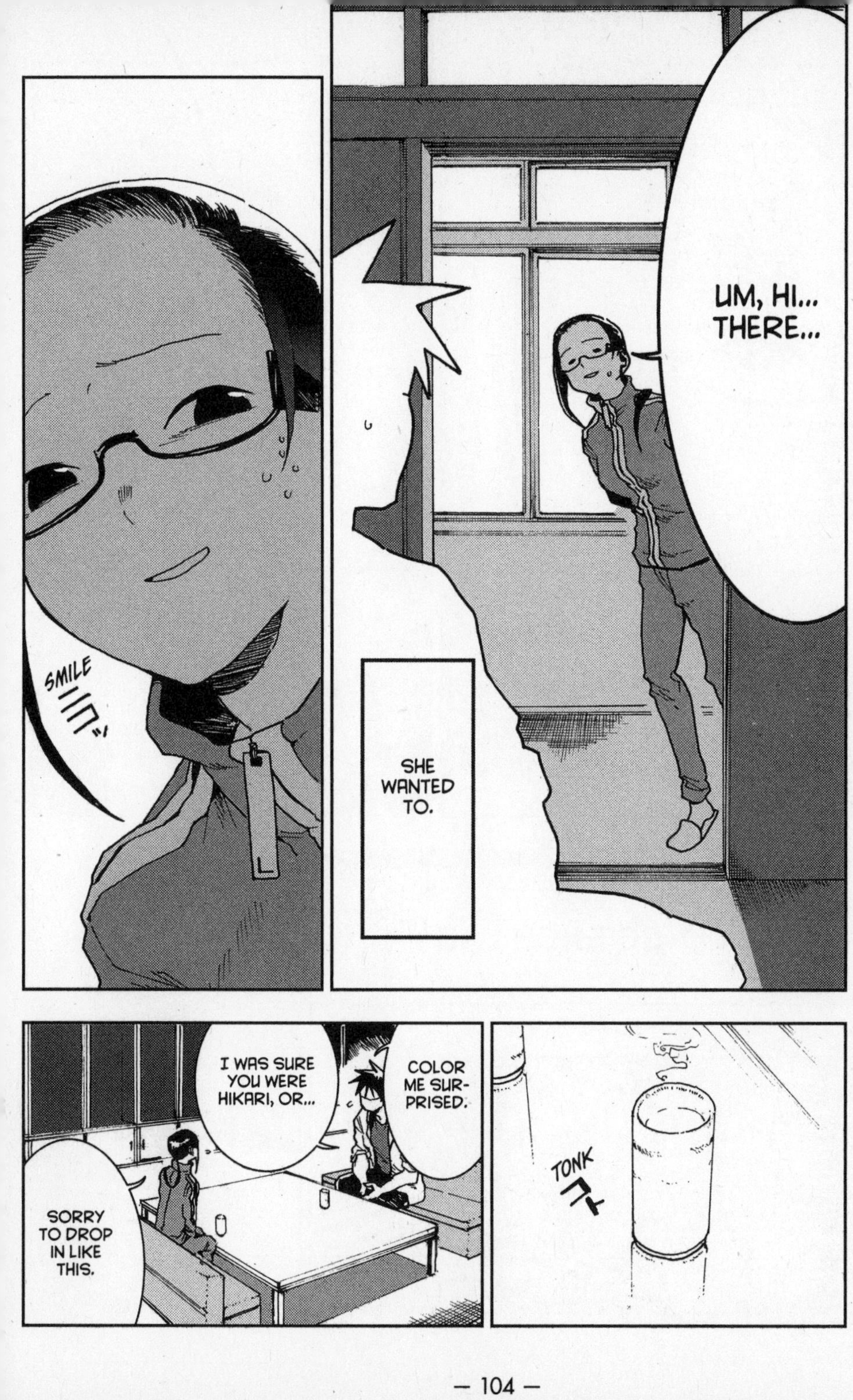
UM, HI... THERE...
SHE WANTED TO.
SMILE
TONK
COLOR ME SUR-PRISED.
I WAS SURE YOU WERE HIKARI, OR...
SORRY TO DROP IN LIKE THIS.

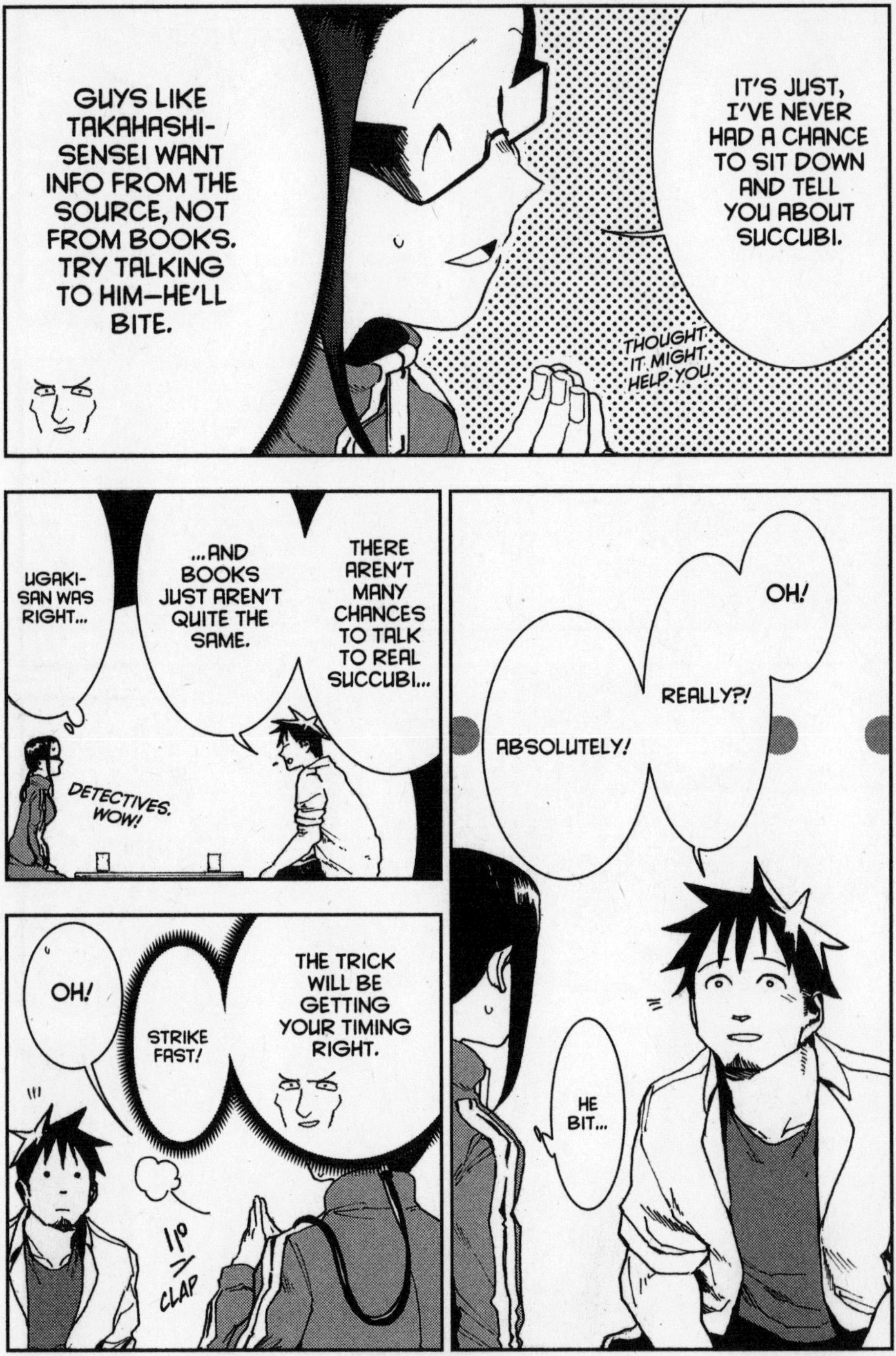
IT'S JUST, I'VE NEVER HAD A CHANCE TO SIT DOWN AND TELL YOU ABOUT SUCCUBI.
THOUGHT IT MIGHT HELP YOU.
GUYS LIKE TAKAHASHI-SENSEI WANT INFO FROM THE SOURCE, NOT FROM BOOKS. TRY TALKING TO HIM—HE'LL BITE.
OH!
REALLY?!
ABSOLUTELY!
HE BIT...
THERE AREN'T MANY CHANCES TO TALK TO REAL SUCCUBI...
...AND BOOKS JUST AREN'T QUITE THE SAME.
UGAKI-SAN WAS RIGHT...
DETECTIVES. WOW!
THE TRICK WILL BE GETTING YOUR TIMING RIGHT.
STRIKE FAST!
OH!
CLAP

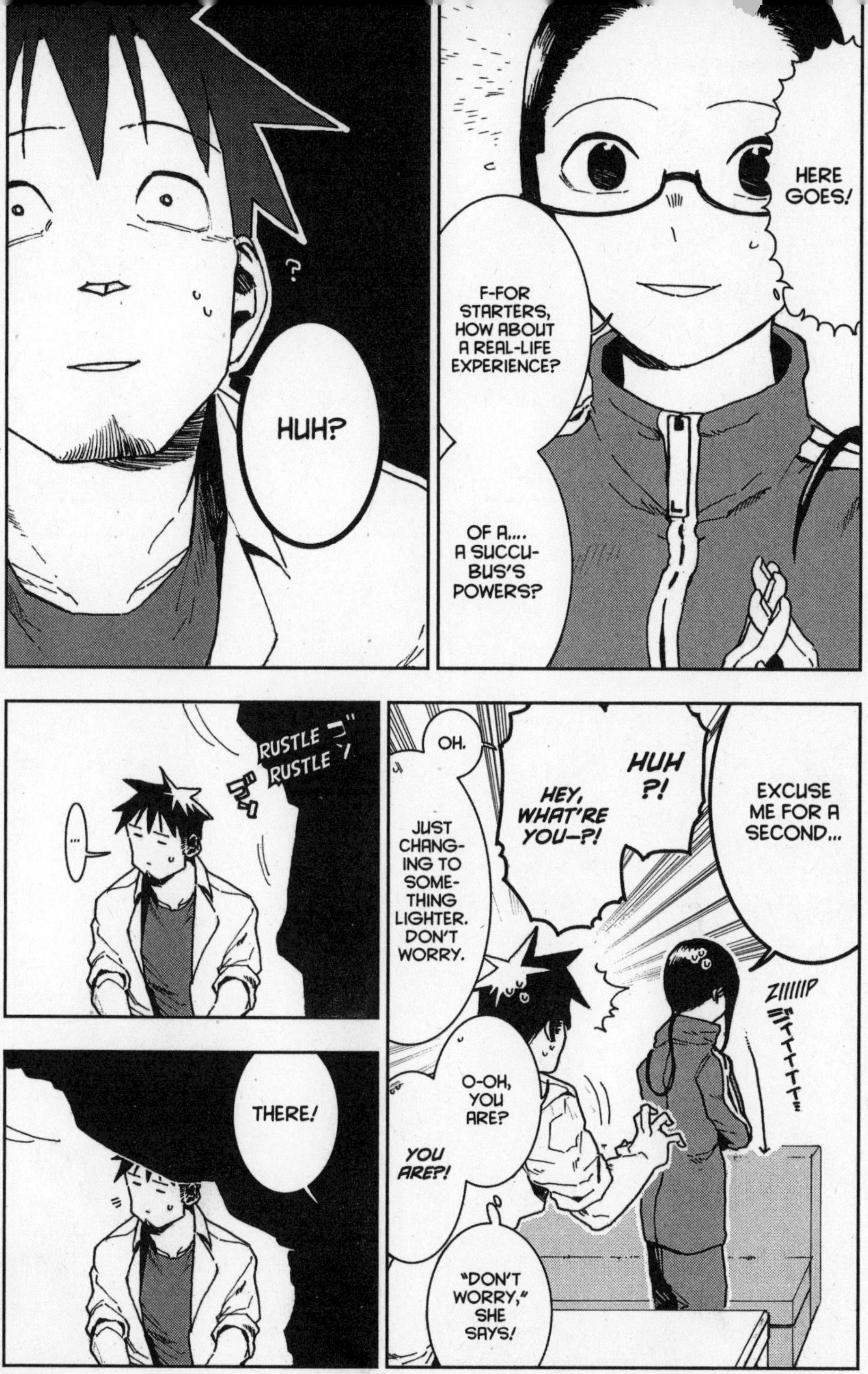
HERE GOES!
F-FOR STARTERS, HOW ABOUT A REAL-LIFE EXPERIENCE?
OF A.... A SUCCU-BUS'S POWERS?
?
HUH?
EXCUSE ME FOR A SECOND...
HUH ?!
HEY, WHAT'RE YOU—?!
OH.
JUST CHANG-ING TO SOME-THING LIGHTER. DON'T WORRY.
ZIIIIP
O-OH, YOU ARE?
YOU ARE?!
"DON'T WORRY," SHE SAYS!
RUSTLE RUSTLE
...
THERE!

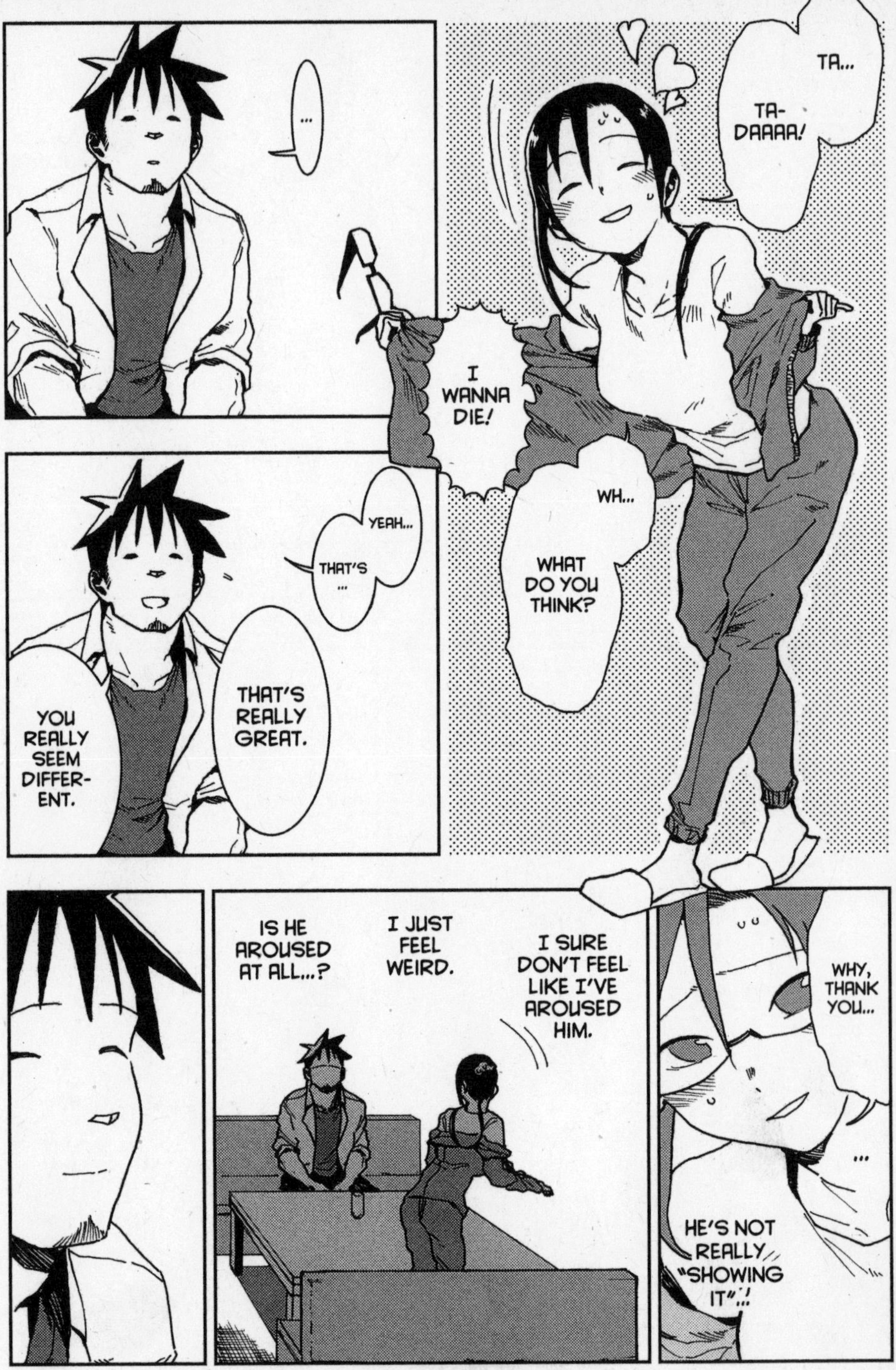

TA...
TA-DAAAA!
I WANNA DIE!
WH...
WHAT DO YOU THINK?
...
YEAH...
THAT'S...
THAT'S REALLY GREAT.
YOU REALLY SEEM DIFFER-ENT.
WHY, THANK YOU...
...
HE'S NOT REALLY "SHOWING IT"...!
I SURE DON'T FEEL LIKE I'VE AROUSED HIM.
I JUST FEEL WEIRD.
IS HE AROUSED AT ALL...?

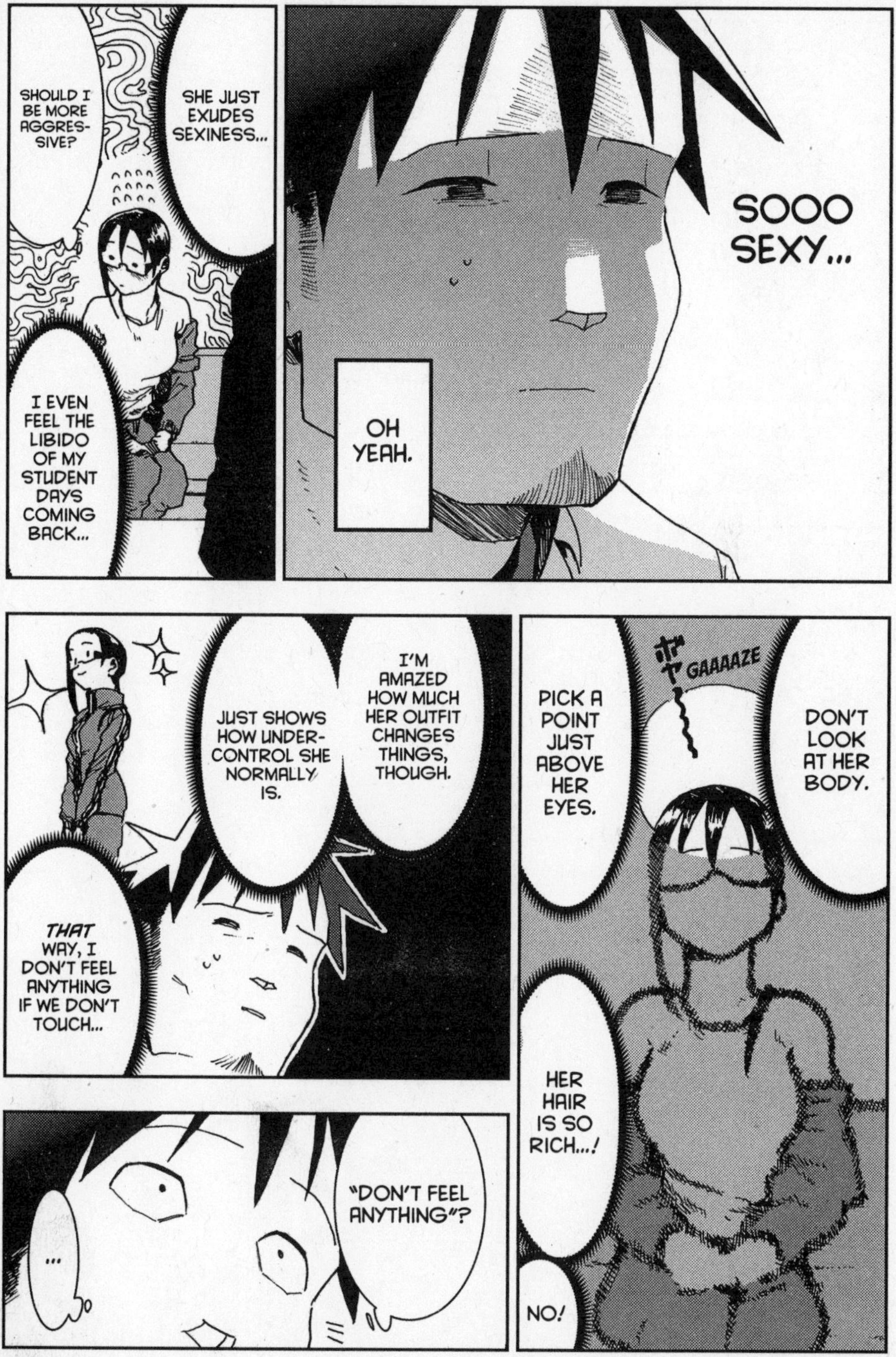
SOOO SEXY...
OH YEAH.
SHE JUST EXUDES SEXINESS...
SHOULD I BE MORE AGGRES-SIVE?
I EVEN FEEL THE LIBIDO OF MY STUDENT DAYS COMING BACK...
DON'T LOOK AT HER BODY.
GAAAAZE
PICK A POINT JUST ABOVE HER EYES.
HER HAIR IS SO RICH...!
NO!
I'M AMAZED HOW MUCH HER OUTFIT CHANGES THINGS, THOUGH.
JUST SHOWS HOW UNDER-CONTROL SHE NORMALLY IS.
THAT WAY, I DON'T FEEL ANYTHING IF WE DON'T TOUCH...
"DON'T FEEL ANYTHING"?
...

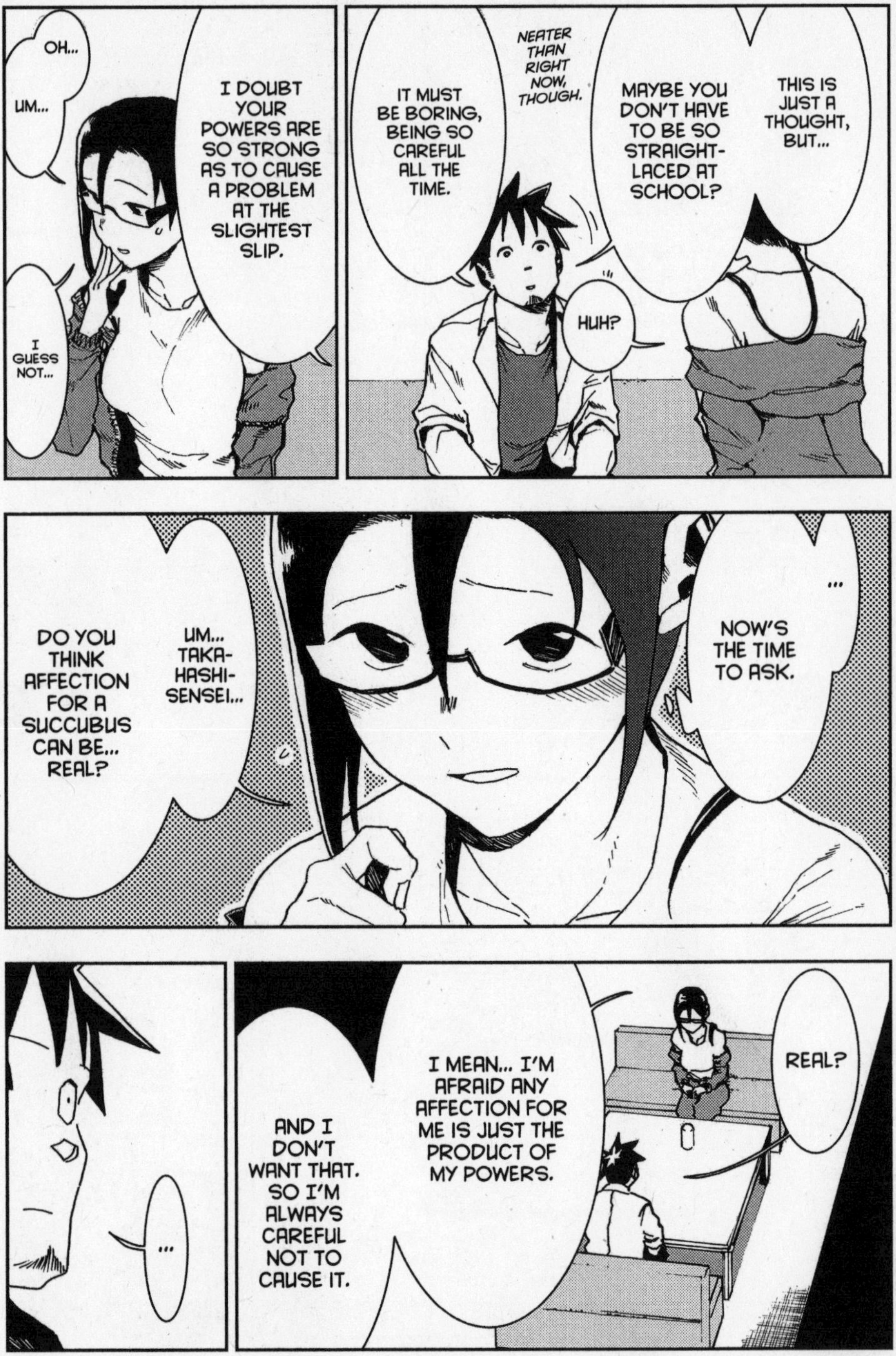
THIS IS JUST A THOUGHT, BUT...
MAYBE YOU DON'T HAVE TO BE SO STRAIGHT-LACED AT SCHOOL?
HUH?
NEATER THAN RIGHT NOW, THOUGH.
IT MUST BE BORING, BEING SO CAREFUL ALL THE TIME.
I DOUBT YOUR POWERS ARE SO STRONG AS TO CAUSE A PROBLEM AT THE SLIGHTEST SLIP.
OH...
UM...
I GUESS NOT...
...
NOW'S THE TIME TO ASK.
UM... TAKA-HASHI-SENSEI...
DO YOU THINK AFFECTION FOR A SUCCUBUS CAN BE... REAL?
REAL?
I MEAN... I'M AFRAID ANY AFFECTION FOR ME IS JUST THE PRODUCT OF MY POWERS.
AND I DON'T WANT THAT. SO I'M ALWAYS CAREFUL NOT TO CAUSE IT.
...

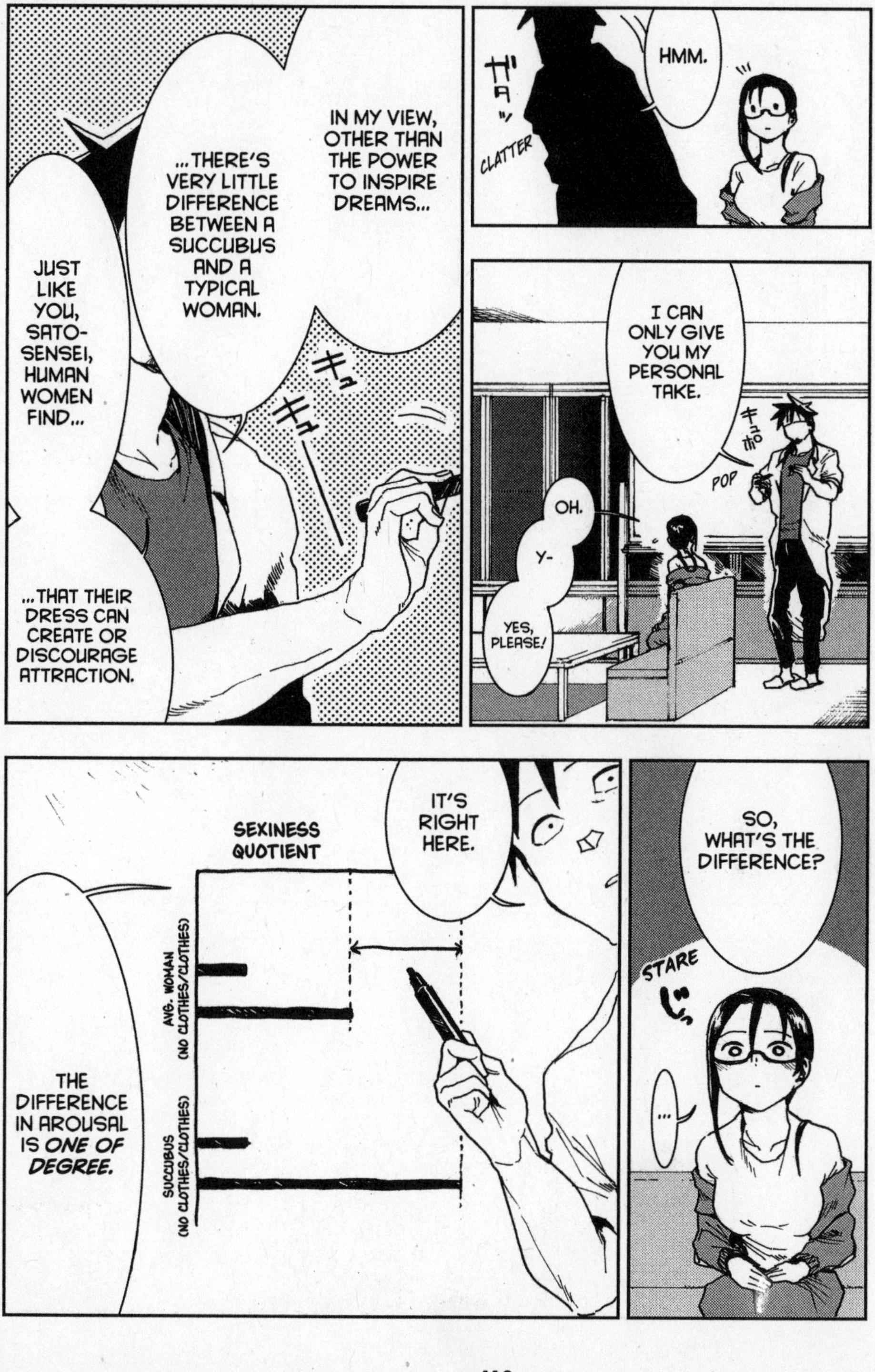
ガタッ
CLATTER
HMM.
I CAN ONLY GIVE YOU MY PERSONAL TAKE.
キュポ
POP
OH.
Y-
YES, PLEASE!
IN MY VIEW, OTHER THAN THE POWER TO INSPIRE DREAMS...
...THERE'S VERY LITTLE DIFFERENCE BETWEEN A SUCCUBUS AND A TYPICAL WOMAN.
キュ
キュ
JUST LIKE YOU, SATO-SENSEI, HUMAN WOMEN FIND...
...THAT THEIR DRESS CAN CREATE OR DISCOURAGE ATTRACTION.
SO, WHAT'S THE DIFFERENCE?
STARE
じっ
...
IT'S RIGHT HERE.
SEXINESS QUOTIENT
AVG. WOMAN (NO CLOTHES/CLOTHES)
SUCCUBUS (NO CLOTHES/CLOTHES)
THE DIFFERENCE IN AROUSAL IS *ONE OF DEGREE.*

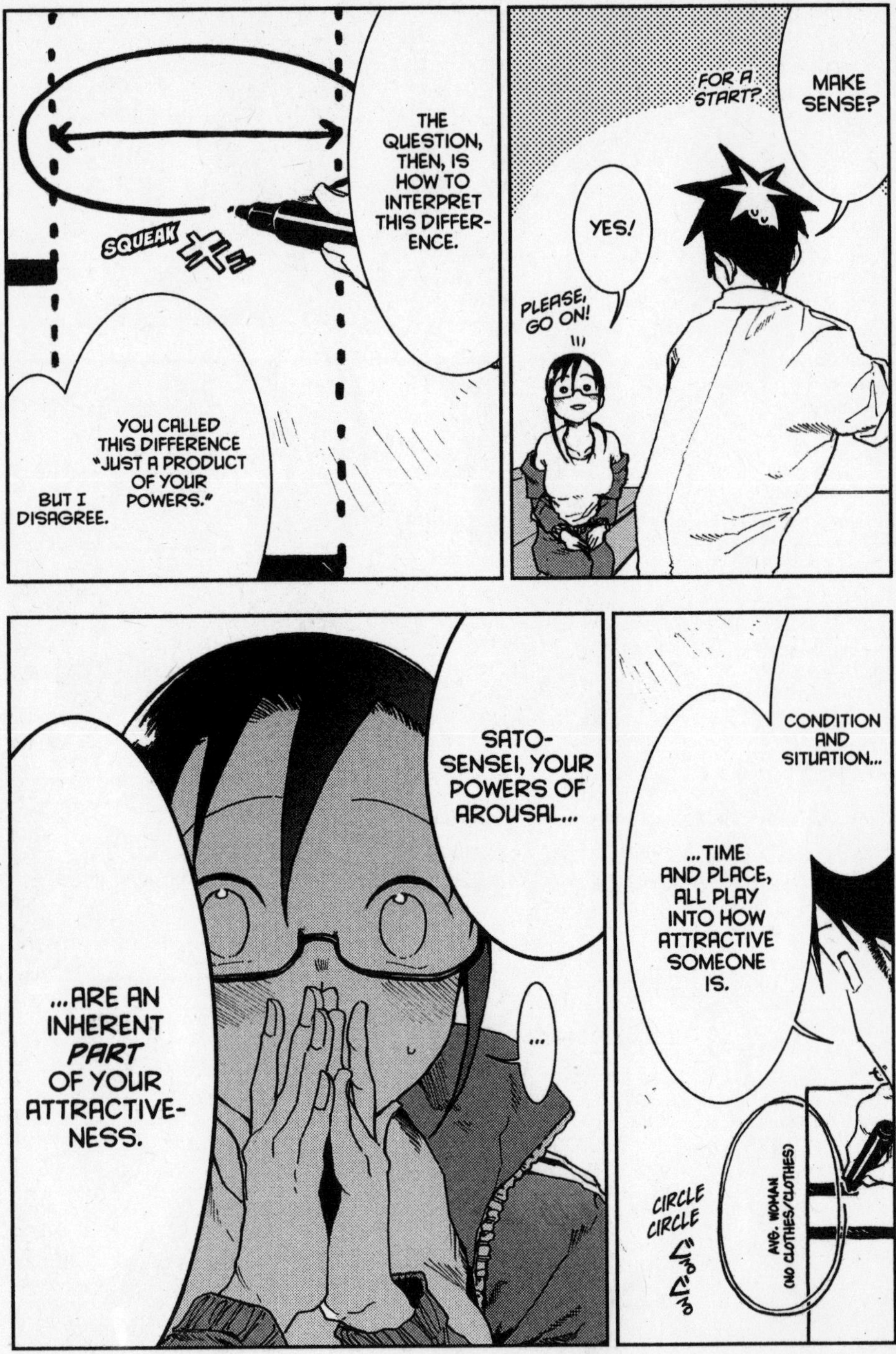
MAKE SENSE?
FOR A START?
YES!
PLEASE, GO ON!
THE QUESTION, THEN, IS HOW TO INTERPRET THIS DIFFERENCE.
SQUEAK
YOU CALLED THIS DIFFERENCE "JUST A PRODUCT OF YOUR POWERS."
BUT I DISAGREE.
CONDITION AND SITUATION...
...TIME AND PLACE, ALL PLAY INTO HOW ATTRACTIVE SOMEONE IS.
CIRCLE CIRCLE
AVG. WOMAN (NO CLOTHES/CLOTHES)
SATO-SENSEI, YOUR POWERS OF AROUSAL...
...
...ARE AN INHERENT *PART* OF YOUR ATTRACTIVENESS.

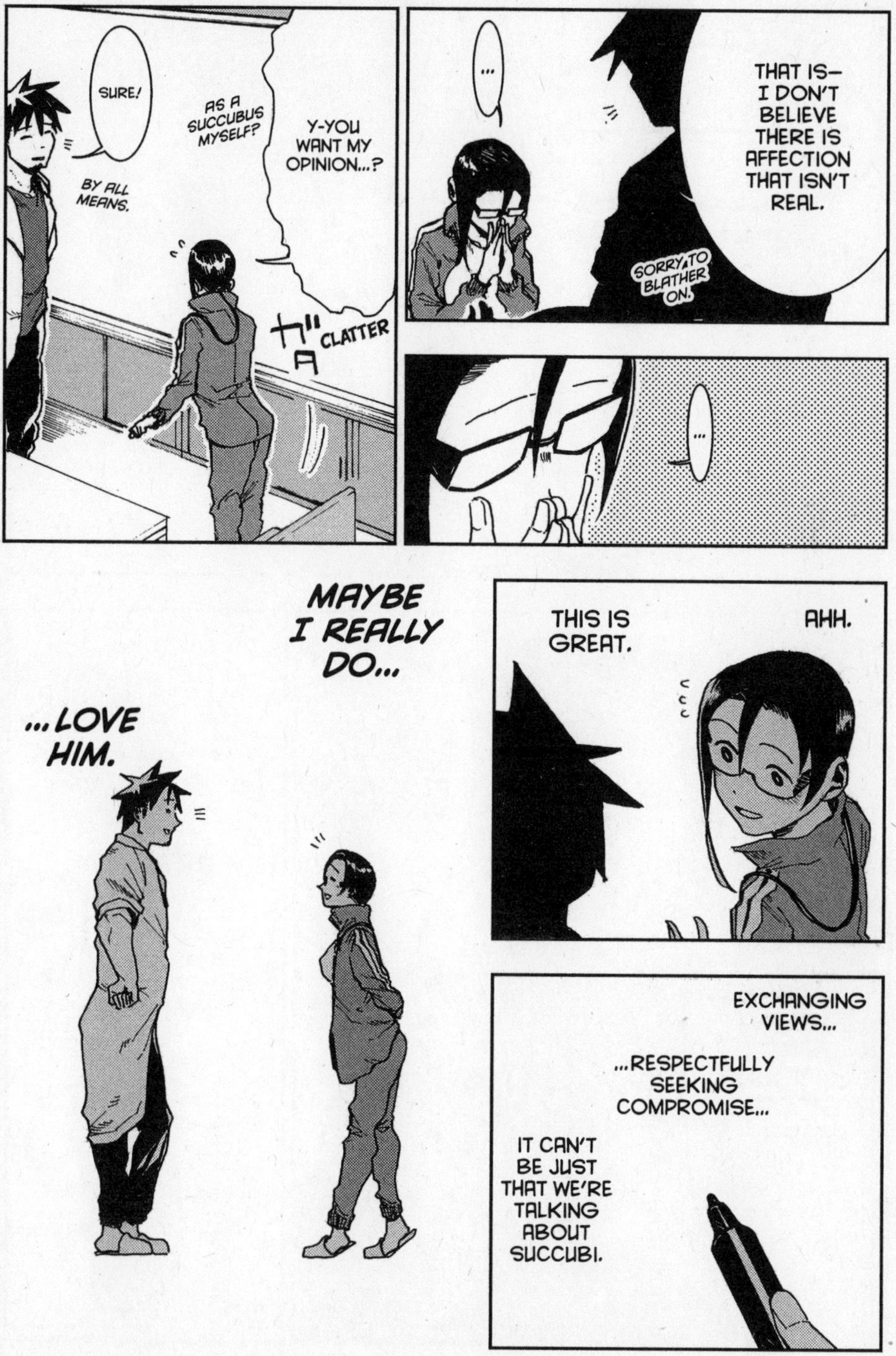
...
THAT IS— I DON'T BELIEVE THERE IS AFFECTION THAT ISN'T REAL.
SORRY TO BLATHER ON.
...
Y-YOU WANT MY OPINION...?
AS A SUCCUBUS MYSELF?
SURE!
BY ALL MEANS.
CLATTER
AHH.
THIS IS GREAT.
EXCHANGING VIEWS...
...RESPECTFULLY SEEKING COMPROMISE...
IT CAN'T BE JUST THAT WE'RE TALKING ABOUT SUCCUBI.
MAYBE I REALLY DO...
...LOVE HIM.

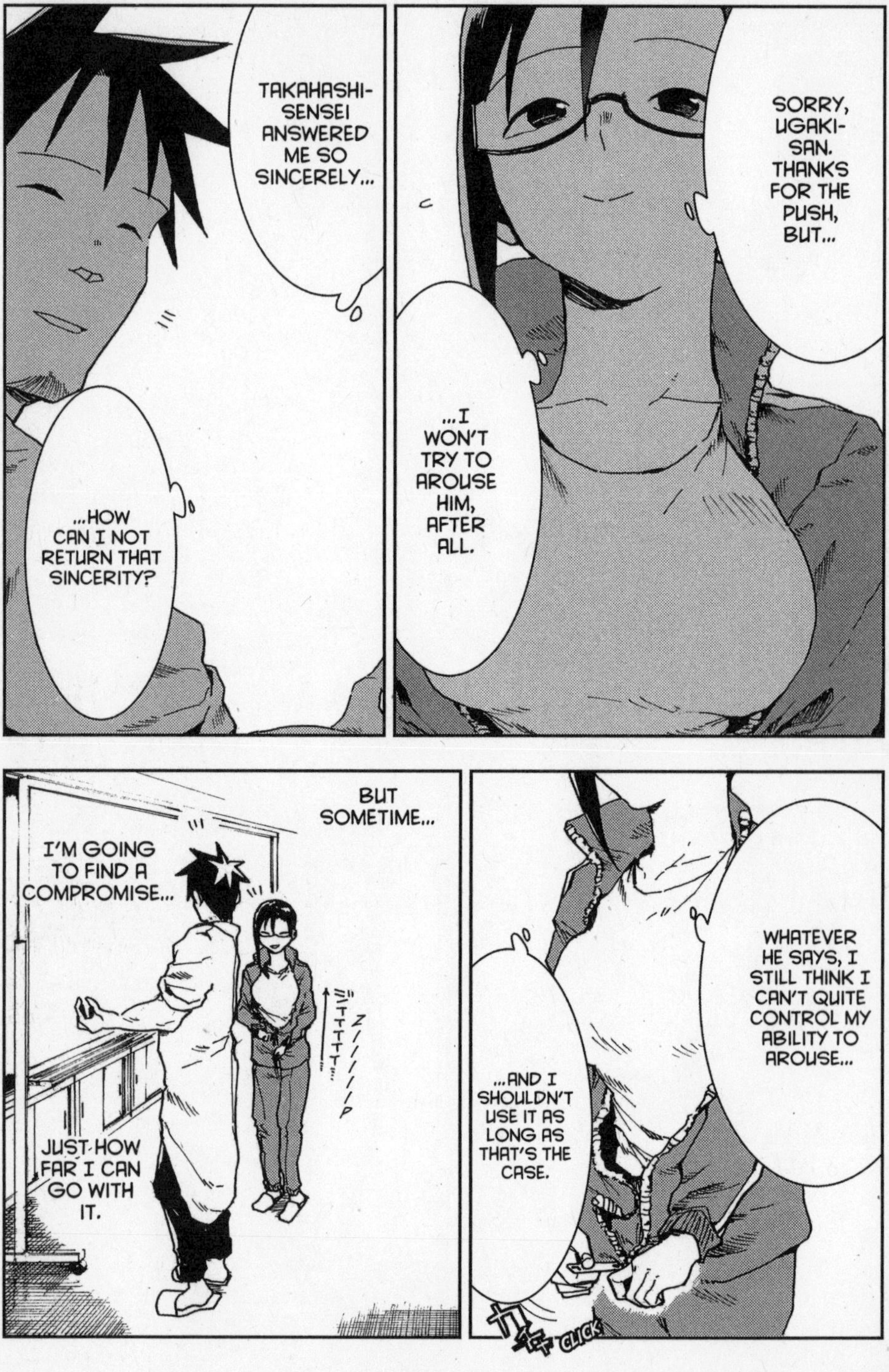
SORRY, UGAKI-SAN. THANKS FOR THE PUSH, BUT...
...I WON'T TRY TO AROUSE HIM, AFTER ALL.
TAKAHASHI-SENSEI ANSWERED ME SO SINCERELY...
...HOW CAN I NOT RETURN THAT SINCERITY?
WHATEVER HE SAYS, I STILL THINK I CAN'T QUITE CONTROL MY ABILITY TO AROUSE...
...AND I SHOULDN'T USE IT AS LONG AS THAT'S THE CASE.
CLICK
BUT SOMETIME...
I'M GOING TO FIND A COMPROMISE...
JUST HOW FAR I CAN GO WITH IT.

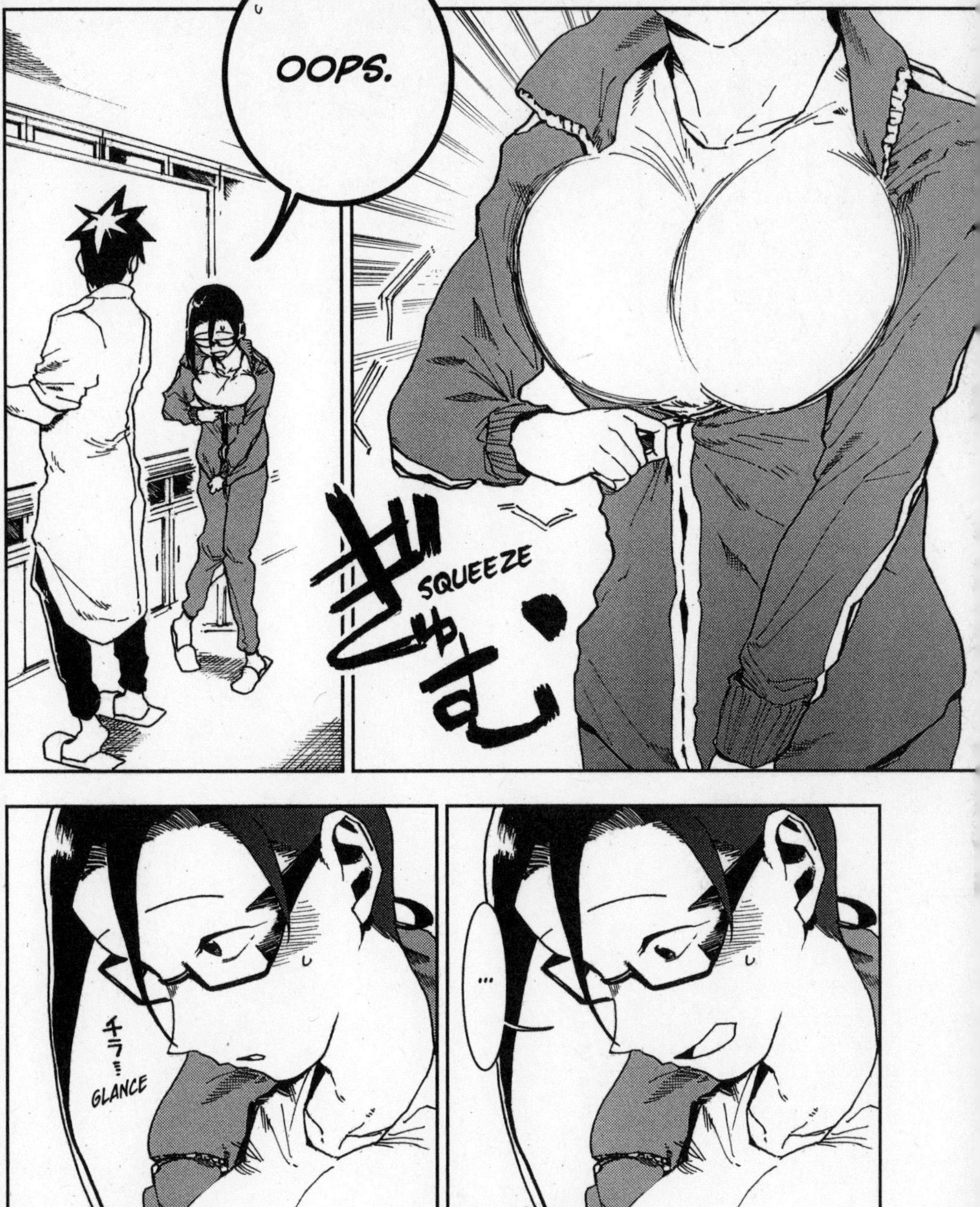
ぎゅむ
SQUEEZE
OOPS.
...
チラ
GLANCE

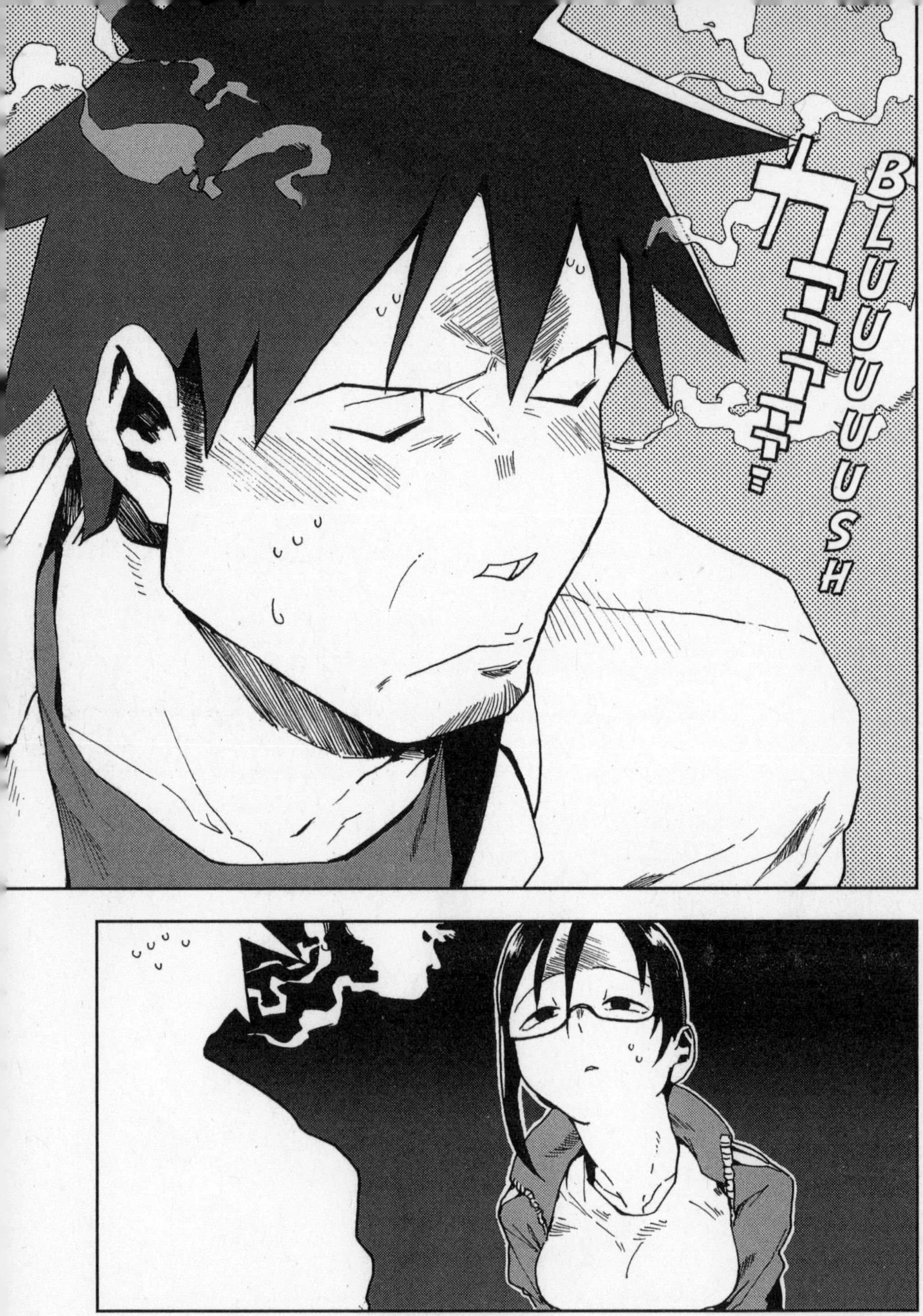
BLUUUUUSH

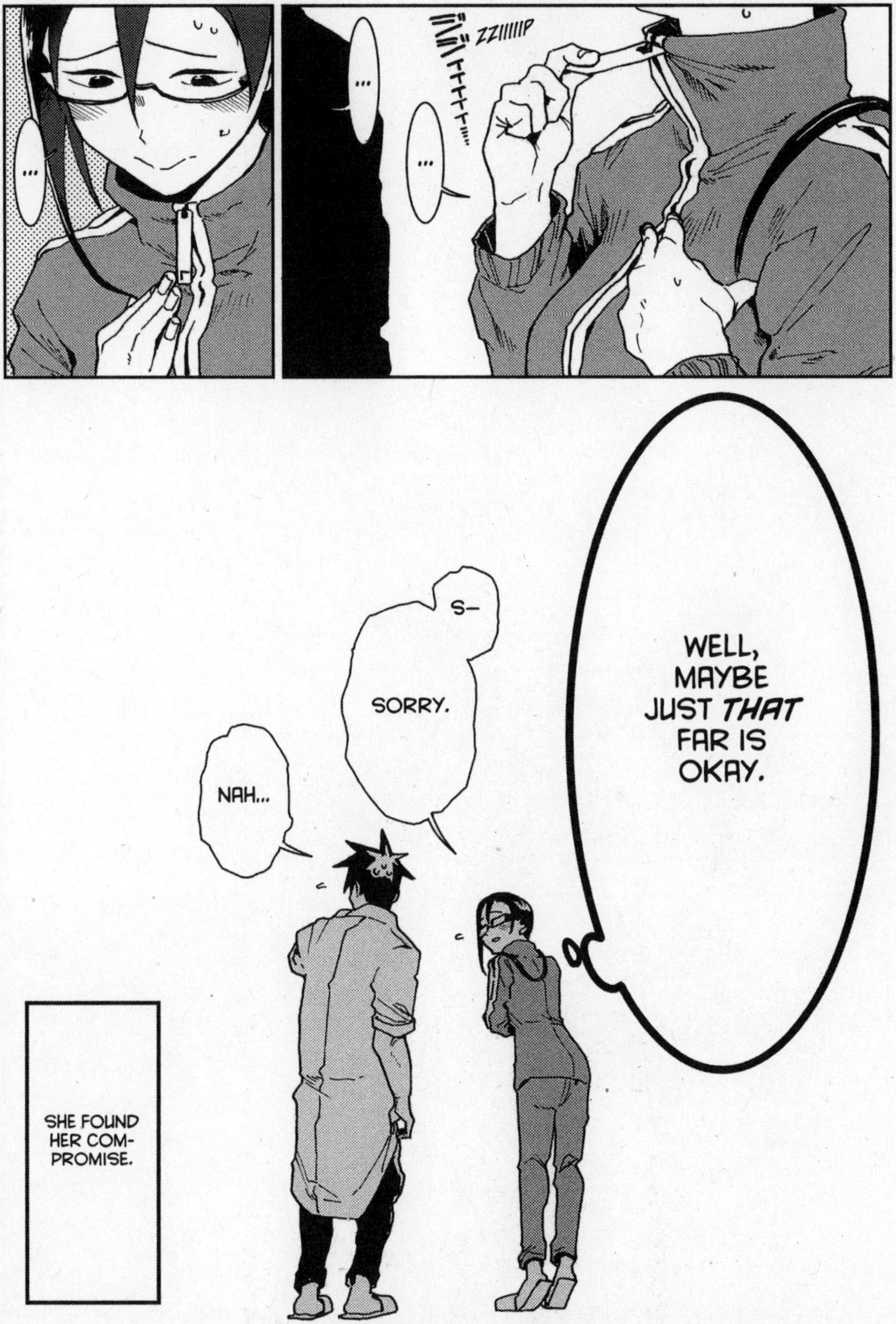

...
...
ZZIIIIIP
...
WELL, MAYBE JUST *THAT* FAR IS OKAY.
S—
SORRY.
NAH...
SHE FOUND HER COMPROMISE.

...AND HE WAS TOTALLY EMBARRASSED!
NICE GOING!
AND WE SHARED OUR THOUGHTS ON THE NATURE OF SUCCUBI...
OOH, A LI'L ARGUMENT? GONNA BE OKAY?
BETTER! I LOVE A GOOD DIFFERENCE OF OPINION!
POSITIONS!
POINTS!
COMPROMISES!
YOU DON'T GET IT AT ALL, DO YOU, UGAKI-SAN?!
GUESS NOT...
YAAAY!
WOO!
GOOD FOR YOU.
SAD THAT HIS "DAUGHTER" IS LEAVING THE NEST...

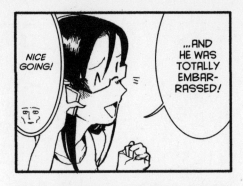

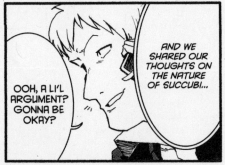

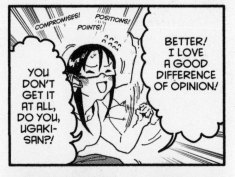

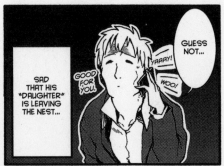

INTERVIEWS WITH MONSTER GIRLS

Chapter 23: When Demis Don't Interview

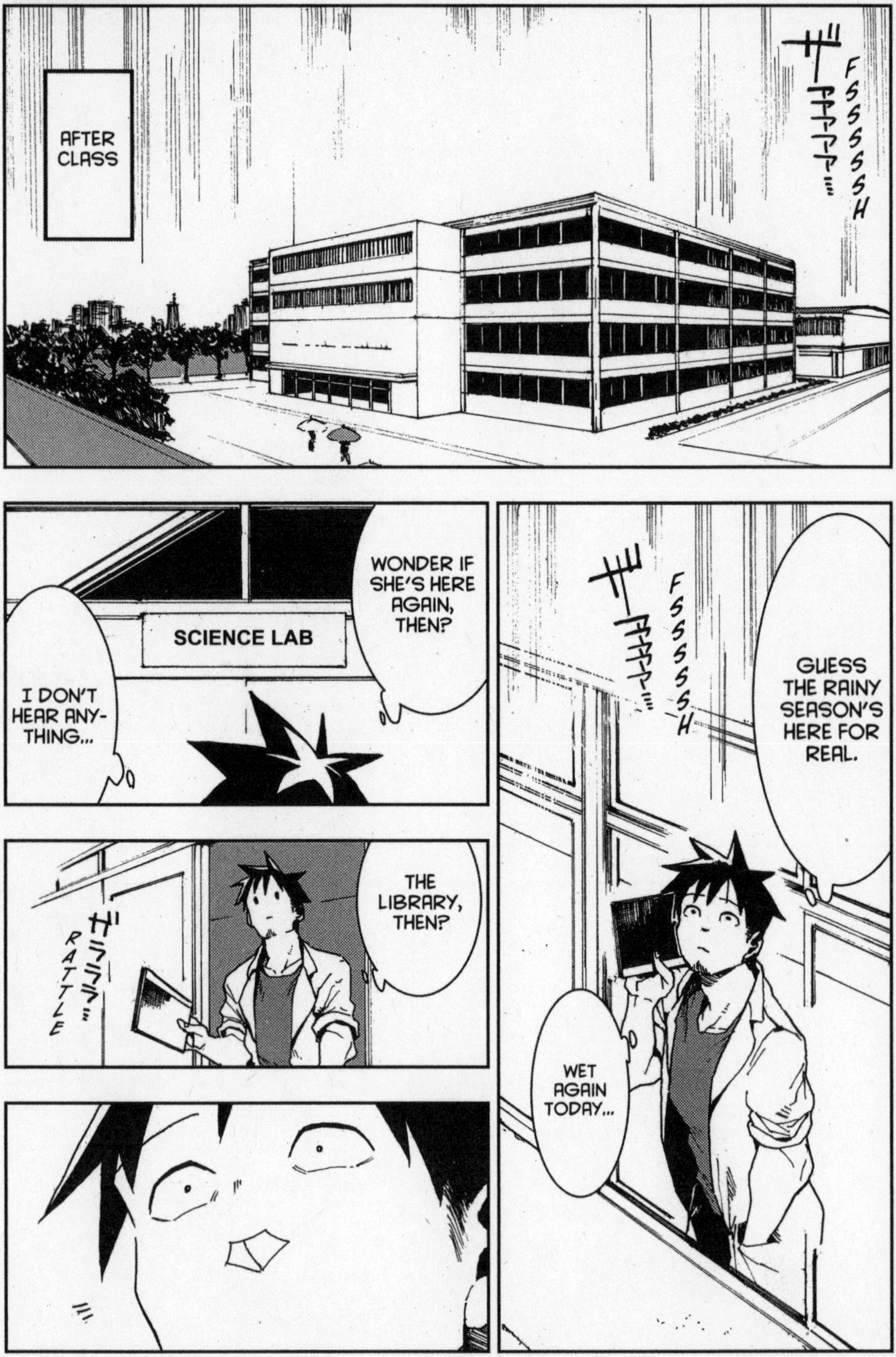
AFTER CLASS
FSSSSSH
GUESS THE RAINY SEASON'S HERE FOR REAL.
FSSSSSH
WET AGAIN TODAY...
WONDER IF SHE'S HERE AGAIN, THEN?
SCIENCE LAB
I DON'T HEAR ANY-THING...
THE LIBRARY, THEN?
RATTLE

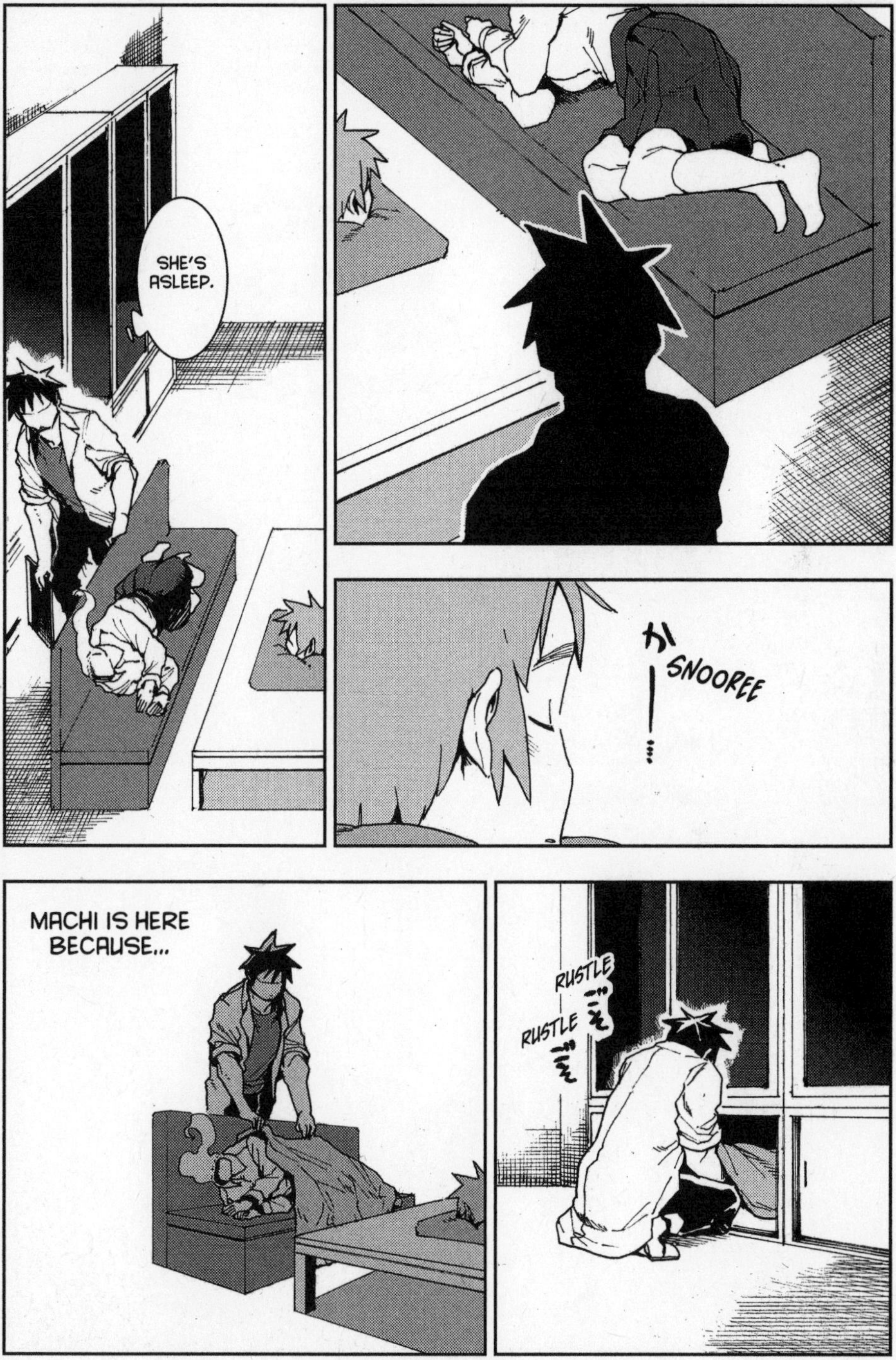
かー…
SNOOREE
SHE'S ASLEEP.
RUSTLE
RUSTLE
MACHI IS HERE BECAUSE...

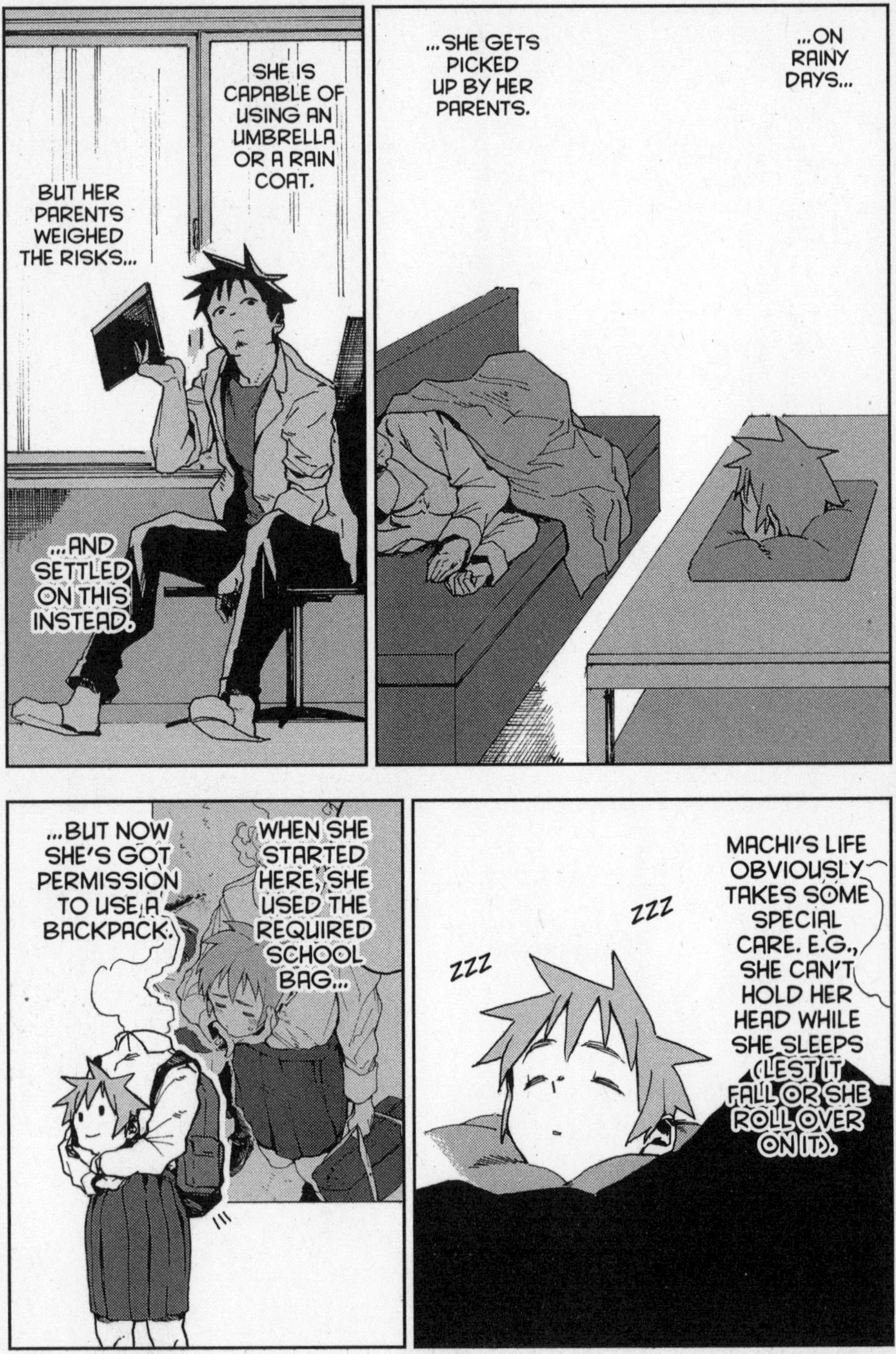
...ON RAINY DAYS...
...SHE GETS PICKED UP BY HER PARENTS.
SHE IS CAPABLE OF USING AN UMBRELLA OR A RAIN COAT.
BUT HER PARENTS WEIGHED THE RISKS...
...AND SETTLED ON THIS INSTEAD.
MACHI'S LIFE OBVIOUSLY TAKES SOME SPECIAL CARE. E.G., SHE CAN'T HOLD HER HEAD WHILE SHE SLEEPS (LEST IT FALL OR SHE ROLL OVER ON IT).
ZZZ
ZZZ
WHEN SHE STARTED HERE, SHE USED THE REQUIRED SCHOOL BAG...
...BUT NOW SHE'S GOT PERMISSION TO USE A BACKPACK.

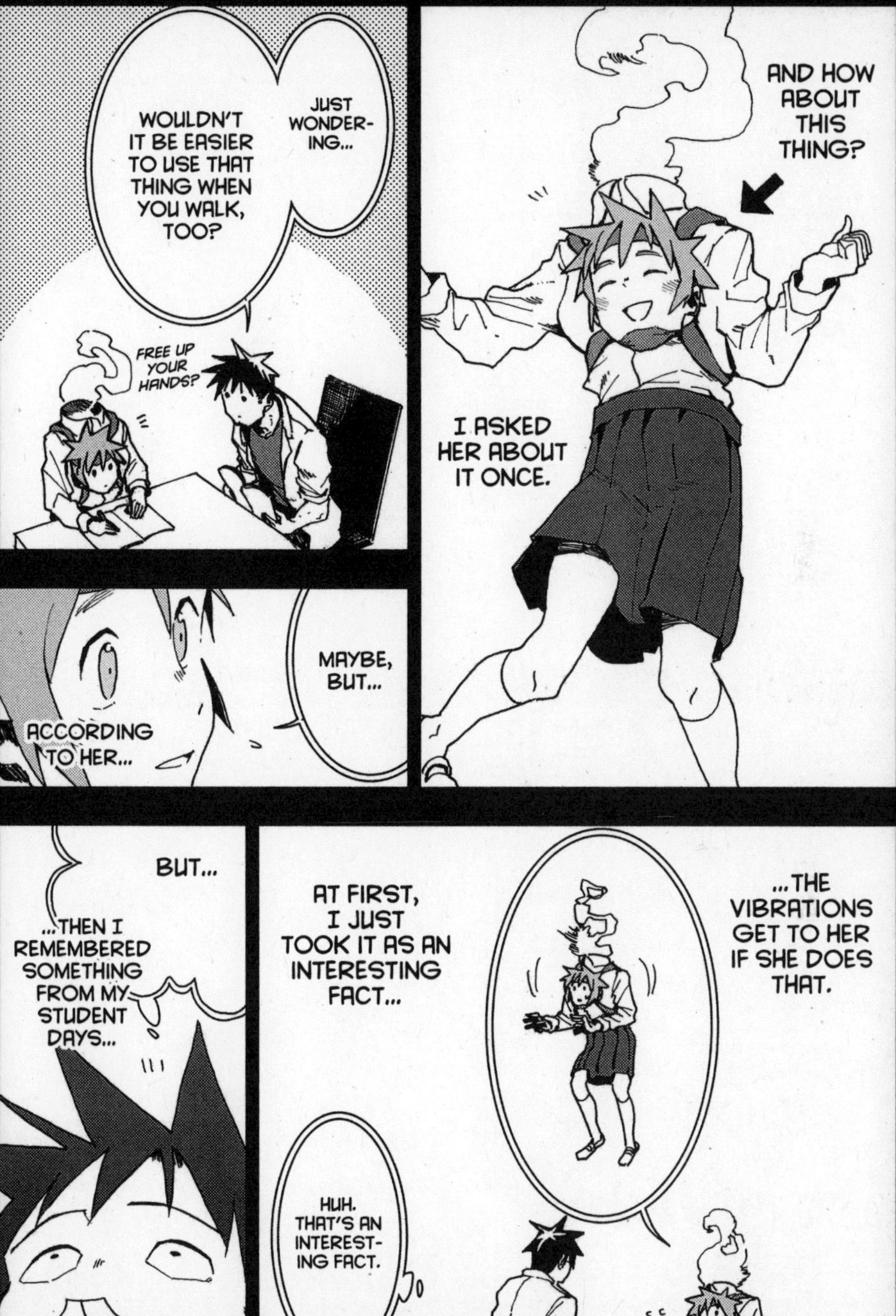
AND HOW ABOUT THIS THING?
I ASKED HER ABOUT IT ONCE.
JUST WONDERING...
WOULDN'T IT BE EASIER TO USE THAT THING WHEN YOU WALK, TOO?
FREE UP YOUR HANDS?
MAYBE, BUT...
ACCORDING TO HER...
...THE VIBRATIONS GET TO HER IF SHE DOES THAT.
AT FIRST, I JUST TOOK IT AS AN INTERESTING FACT...
HUH. THAT'S AN INTEREST-ING FACT.
BUT...
...THEN I REMEMBERED SOMETHING FROM MY STUDENT DAYS...

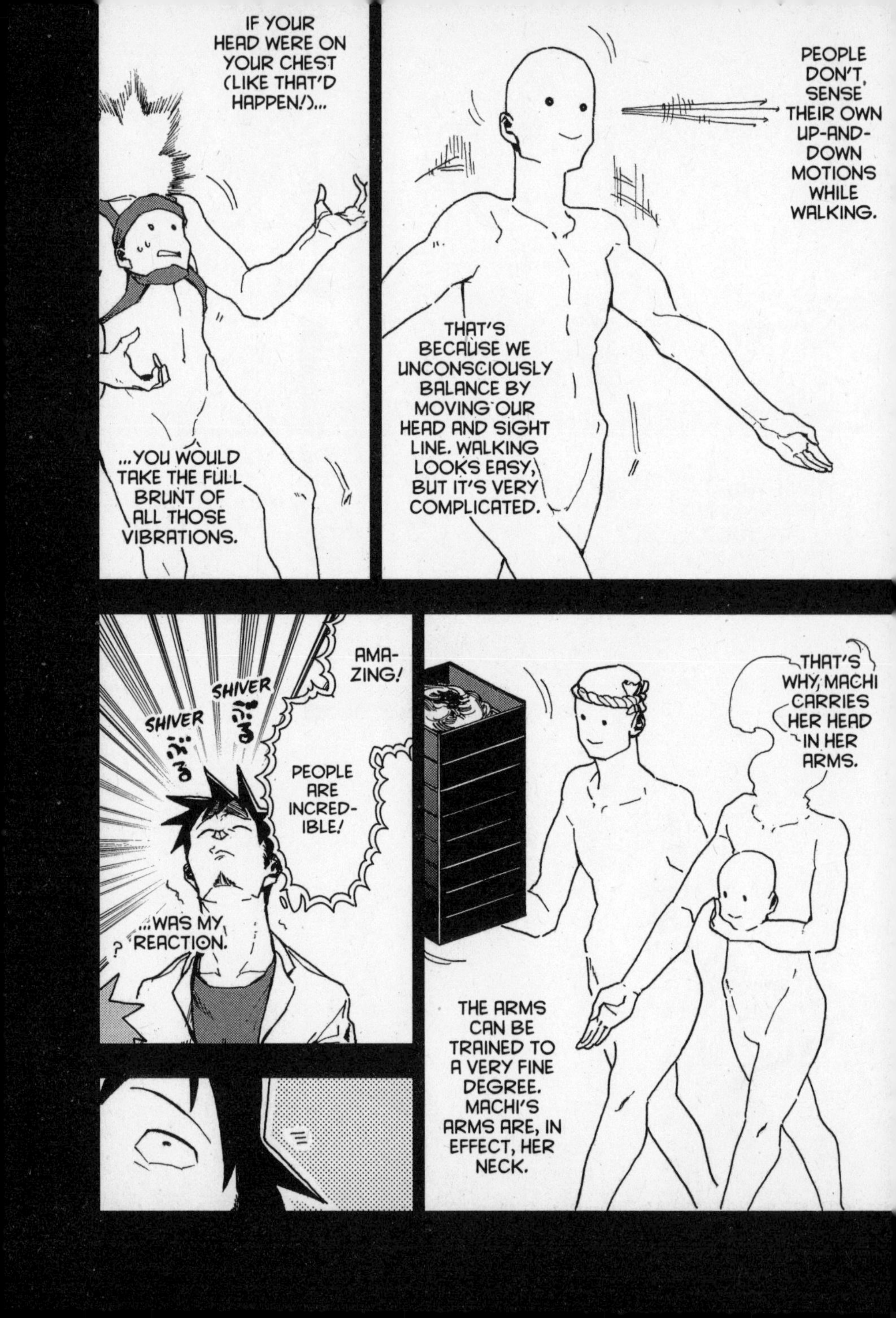
PEOPLE DON'T SENSE THEIR OWN UP-AND-DOWN MOTIONS WHILE WALKING.
THAT'S BECAUSE WE UNCONSCIOUSLY BALANCE BY MOVING OUR HEAD AND SIGHT LINE. WALKING LOOKS EASY, BUT IT'S VERY COMPLICATED.
IF YOUR HEAD WERE ON YOUR CHEST (LIKE THAT'D HAPPEN!)...
...YOU WOULD TAKE THE FULL BRUNT OF ALL THOSE VIBRATIONS.
THAT'S WHY, MACHI CARRIES HER HEAD IN HER ARMS.
THE ARMS CAN BE TRAINED TO A VERY FINE DEGREE. MACHI'S ARMS ARE, IN EFFECT, HER NECK.
AMA-ZING!
PEOPLE ARE INCRED-IBLE!
SHIVER
SHIVER
...WAS MY REACTION.

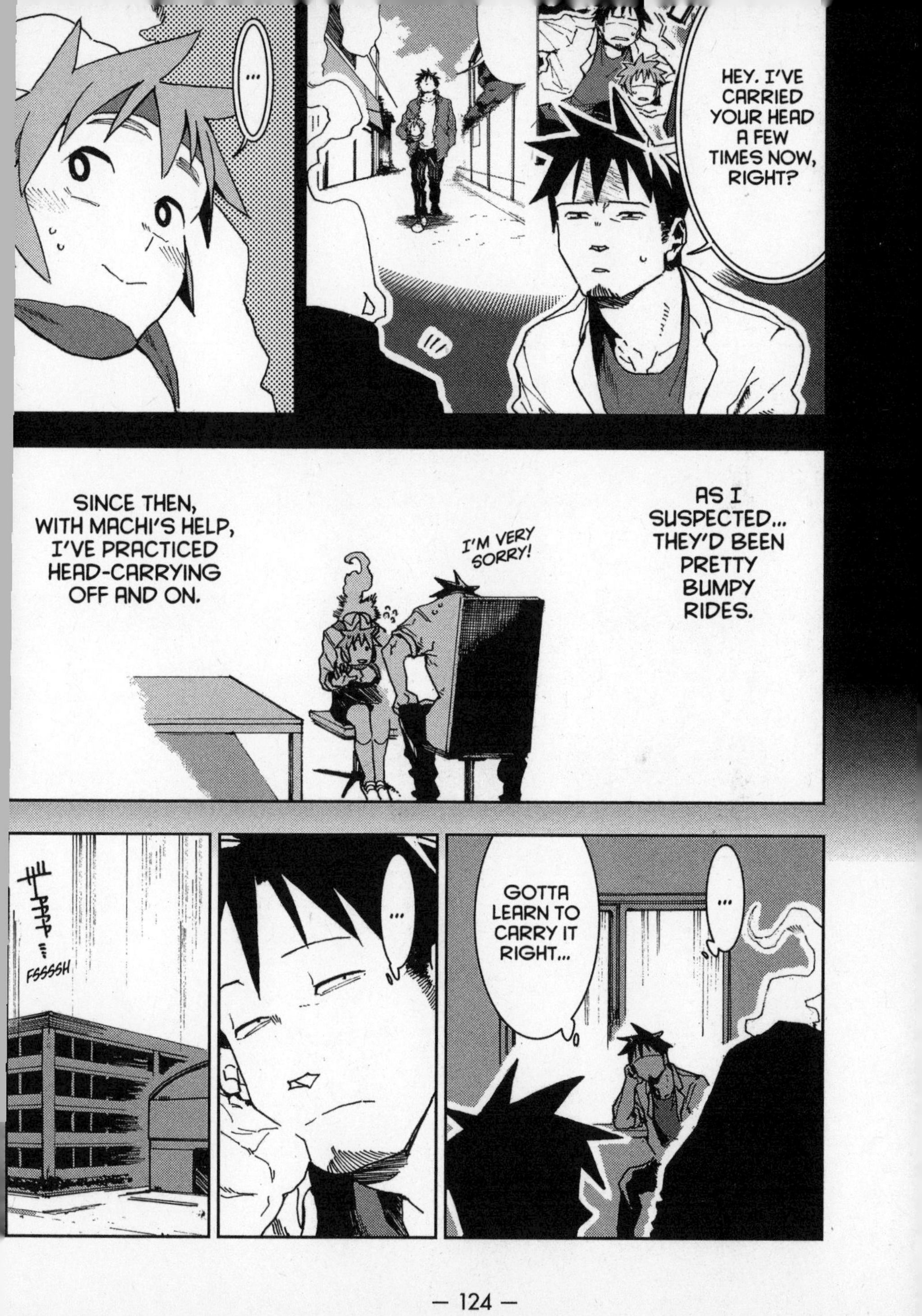
HEY. I'VE CARRIED YOUR HEAD A FEW TIMES NOW, RIGHT?
...
AS I SUSPECTED... THEY'D BEEN PRETTY BUMPY RIDES.
I'M VERY SORRY!
SINCE THEN, WITH MACHI'S HELP, I'VE PRACTICED HEAD-CARRYING OFF AND ON.
...
GOTTA LEARN TO CARRY IT RIGHT...
...
FSSSSH

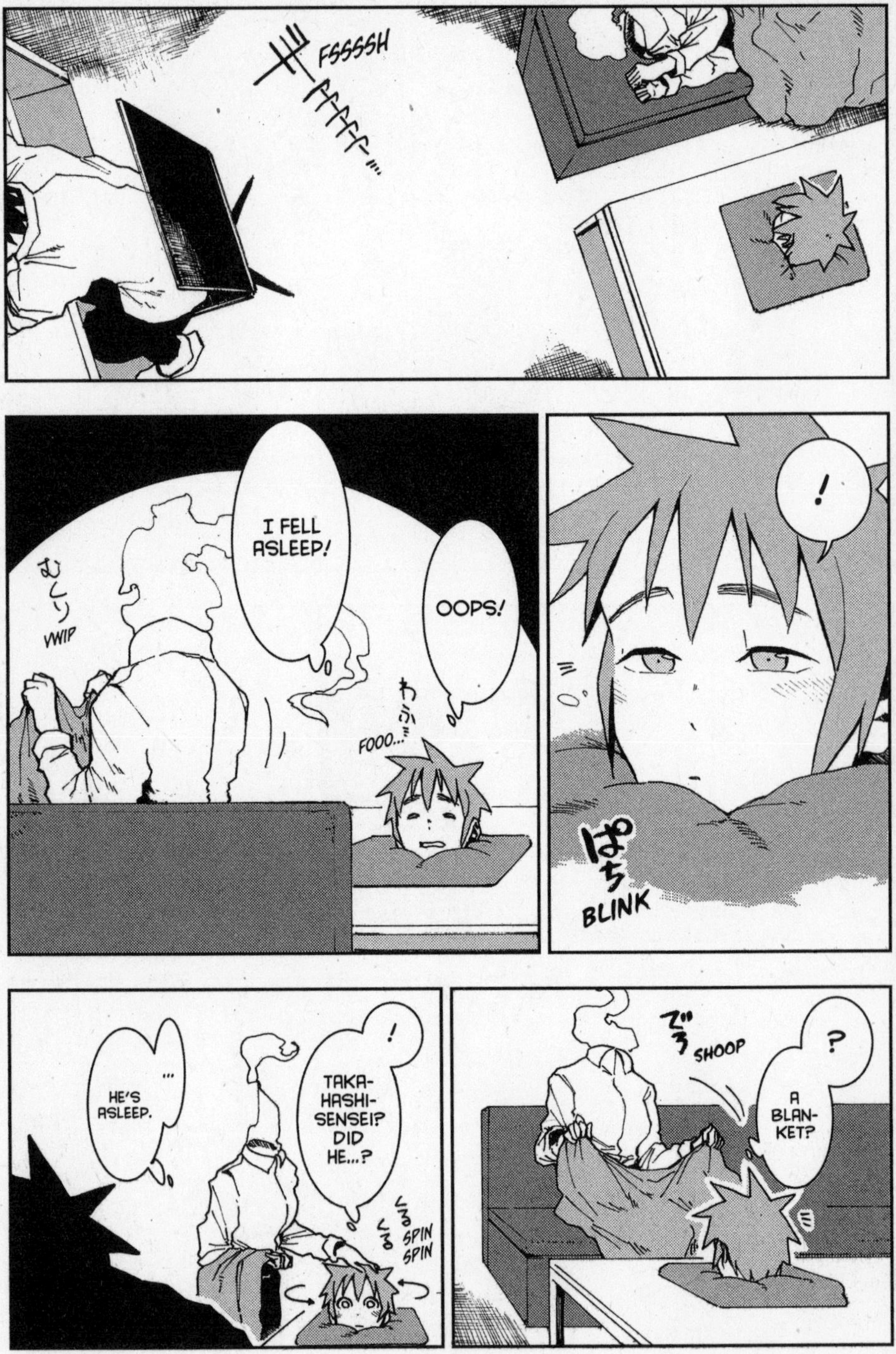
FSSSSH
!
ぱち
BLINK
I FELL ASLEEP!
OOPS!
わふ
FOOO...
むくり
VWIP
ぞろ
SHOOP
?
A BLAN-KET?
!
TAKA-HASHI-SENSEI? DID HE...?
くる くる
SPIN SPIN
...
HE'S ASLEEP.

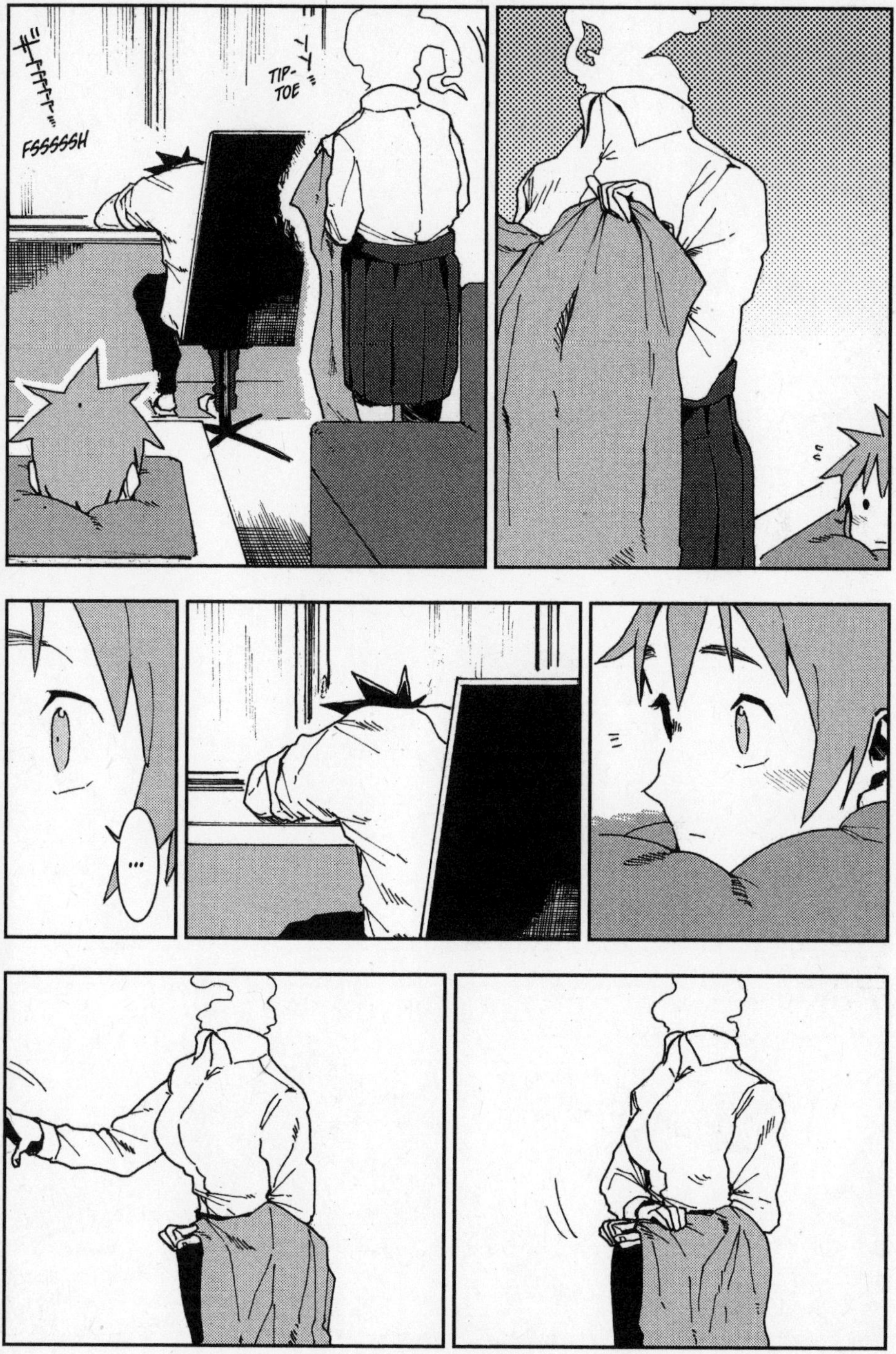
TIP-
TOE
FSSSSSH
...

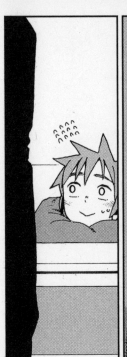
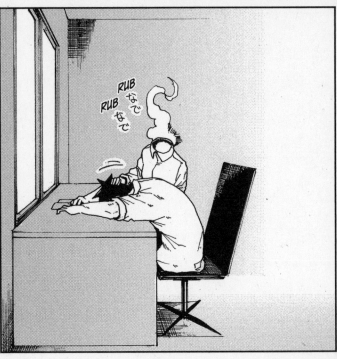

RUB なで
RUB なで

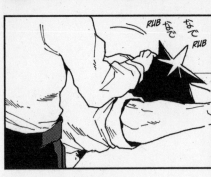

RUB なで
RUB なで
RUB

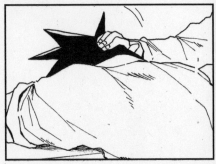

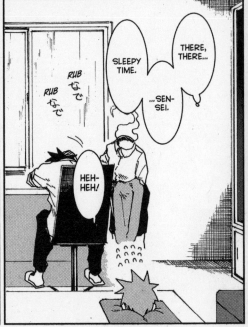

RUB なで
RUB なで

SLEEPY TIME.

...SEN-SEI.

THERE, THERE...

HEH-HEH!

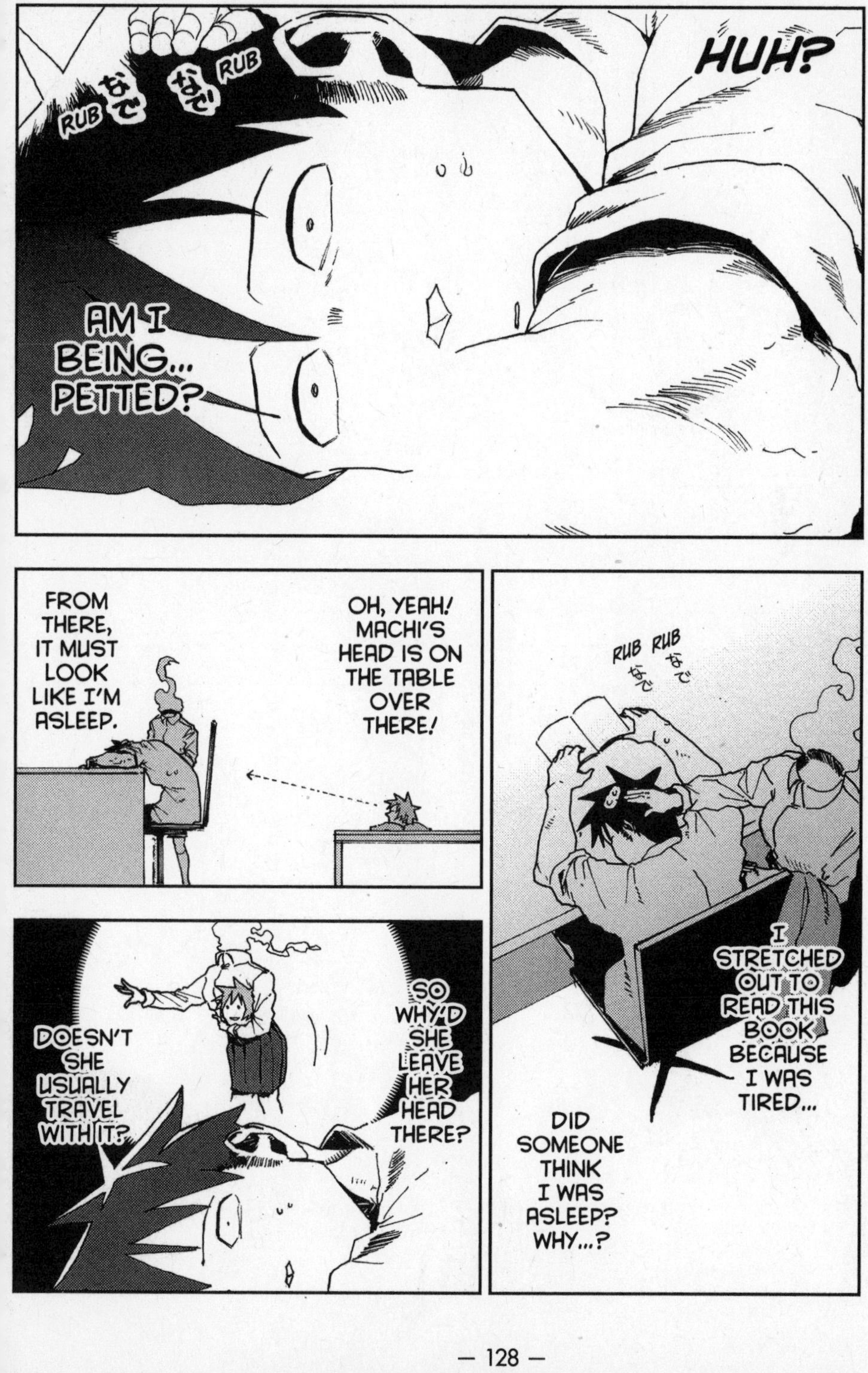
HUH?
RUB なで
なで RUB
AM I BEING... PETTED?
RUB RUB なで なで
I STRETCHED OUT TO READ THIS BOOK BECAUSE I WAS TIRED...
DID SOMEONE THINK I WAS ASLEEP? WHY...?
OH, YEAH! MACHI'S HEAD IS ON THE TABLE OVER THERE!
FROM THERE, IT MUST LOOK LIKE I'M ASLEEP.
SO WHY'D SHE LEAVE HER HEAD THERE?
DOESN'T SHE USUALLY TRAVEL WITH IT?

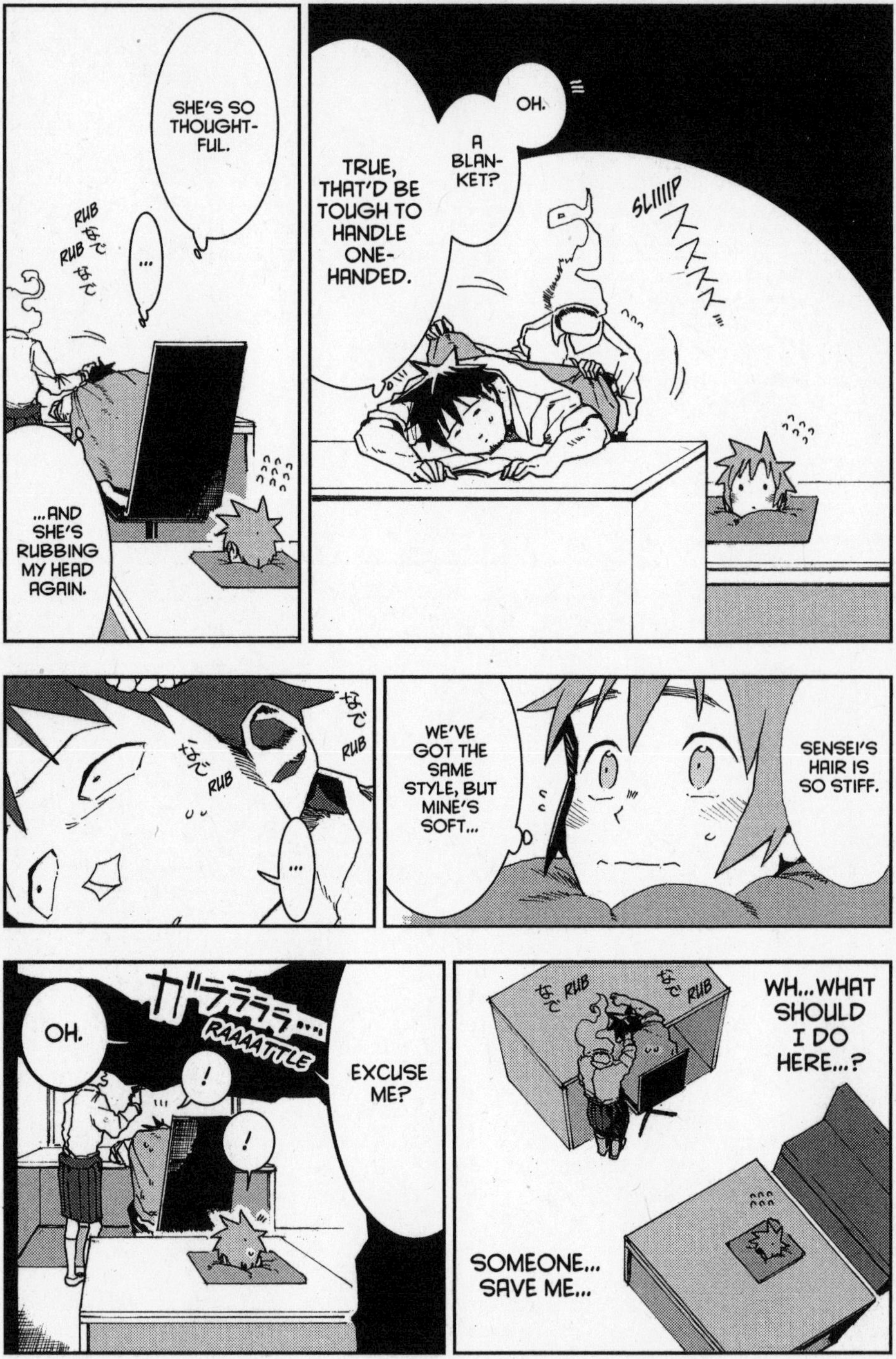
SLIIIIP
スススス
OH.
A BLANKET?
TRUE, THAT'D BE TOUGH TO HANDLE ONE-HANDED.
SHE'S SO THOUGHTFUL.
RUB なで
RUB なで
...
...AND SHE'S RUBBING MY HEAD AGAIN.
SENSEI'S HAIR IS SO STIFF.
WE'VE GOT THE SAME STYLE, BUT MINE'S SOFT...
なで RUB
なで RUB
...
WH...WHAT SHOULD I DO HERE...?
なで RUB
なで RUB
SOMEONE... SAVE ME...
EXCUSE ME?
ガラララララ...
RAAAATTLE
!
!
OH.

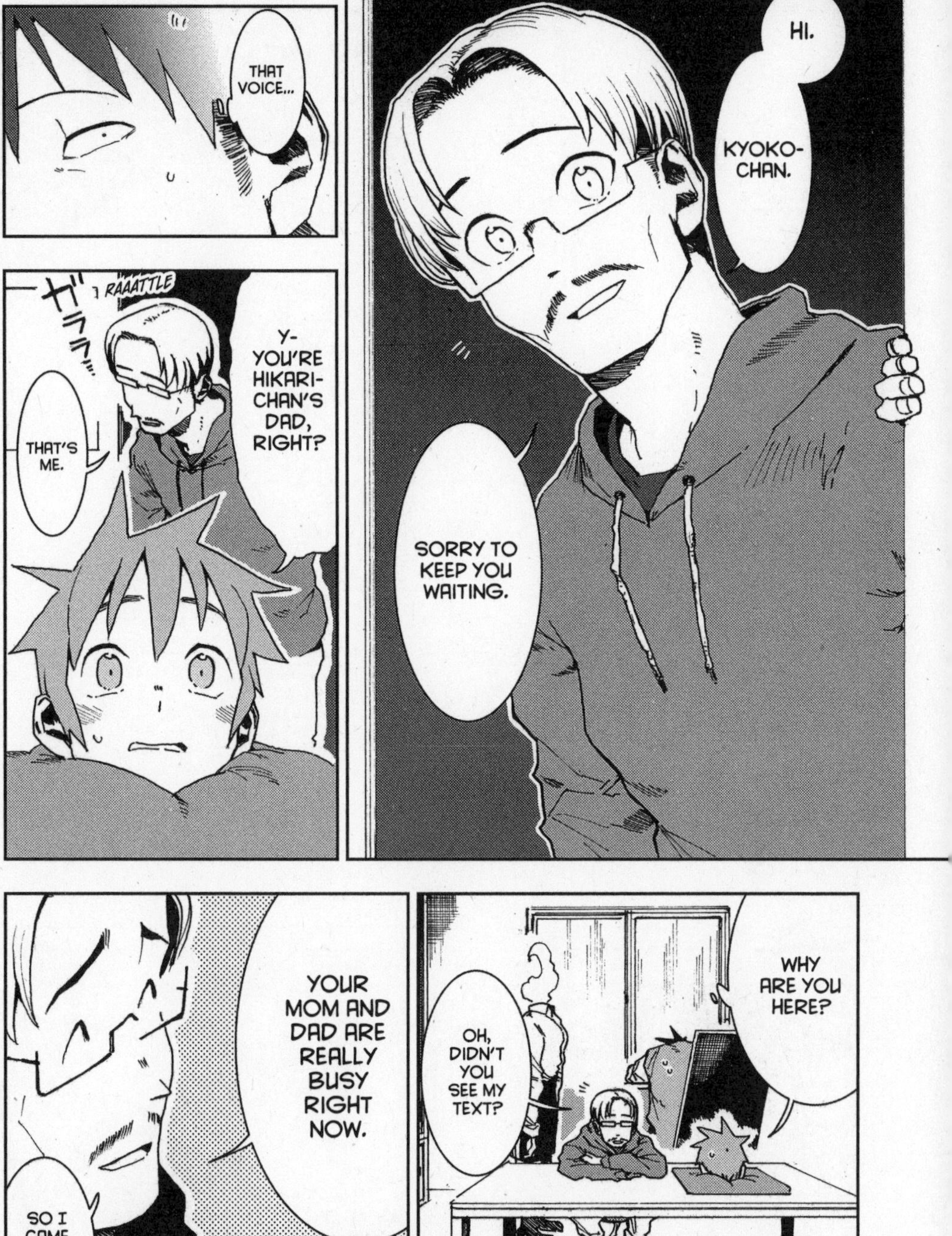
HI.
KYOKO-CHAN.
SORRY TO KEEP YOU WAITING.
THAT VOICE...
ガララ
RAAATTLE
Y-YOU'RE HIKARI-CHAN'S DAD, RIGHT?
THAT'S ME.
WHY ARE YOU HERE?
OH, DIDN'T YOU SEE MY TEXT?
YOUR MOM AND DAD ARE REALLY BUSY RIGHT NOW.
SO I CAME TO GET YOU.

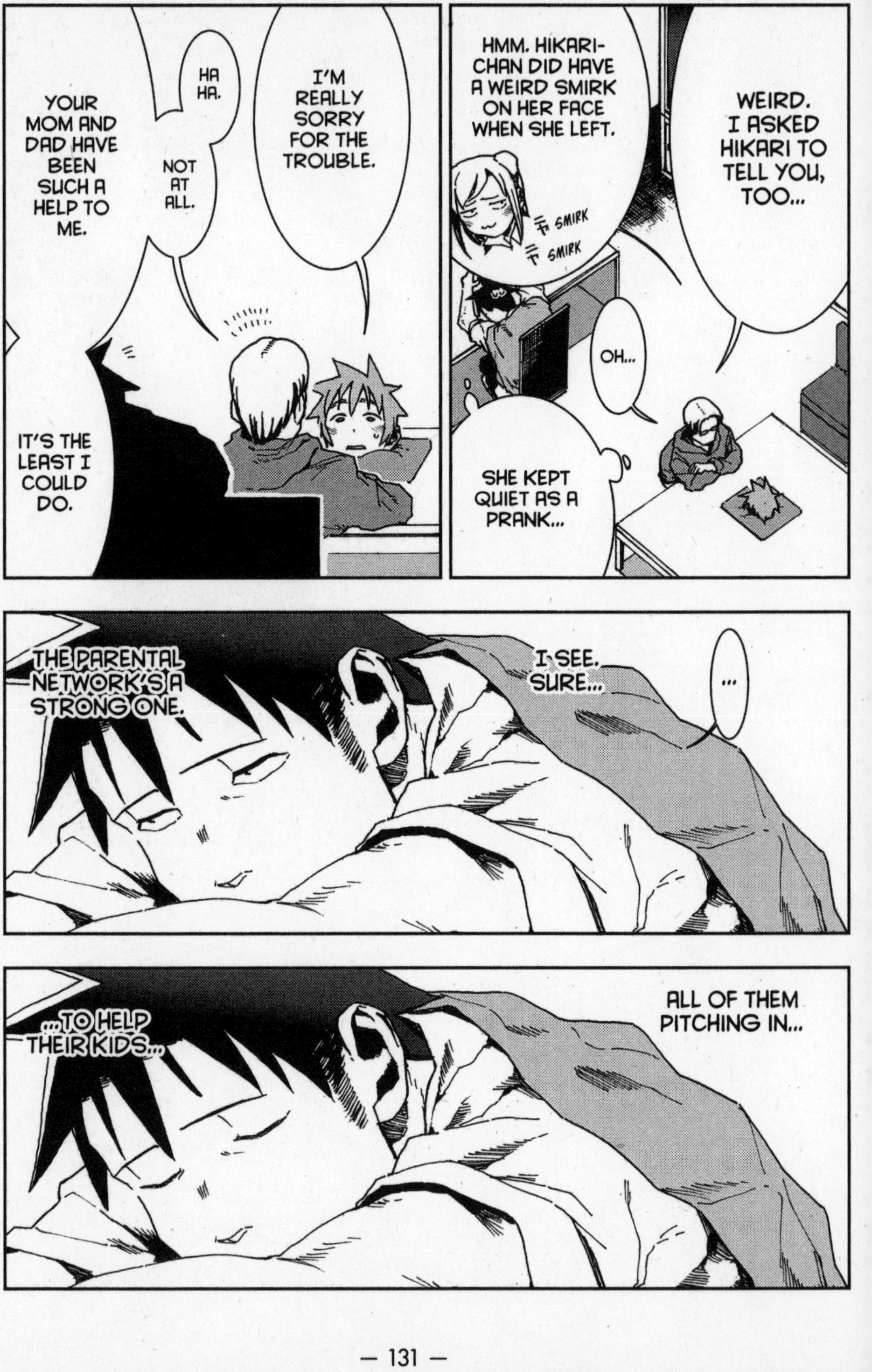
WEIRD. I ASKED HIKARI TO TELL YOU, TOO...
HMM. HIKARI-CHAN DID HAVE A WEIRD SMIRK ON HER FACE WHEN SHE LEFT.
SMIRK
SMIRK
OH...
SHE KEPT QUIET AS A PRANK...
I'M REALLY SORRY FOR THE TROUBLE.
HA HA.
NOT AT ALL.
YOUR MOM AND DAD HAVE BEEN SUCH A HELP TO ME.
IT'S THE LEAST I COULD DO.
...
I SEE. SURE...
THE PARENTAL NETWORK'S A STRONG ONE.
ALL OF THEM PITCHING IN...
...TO HELP THEIR KIDS...

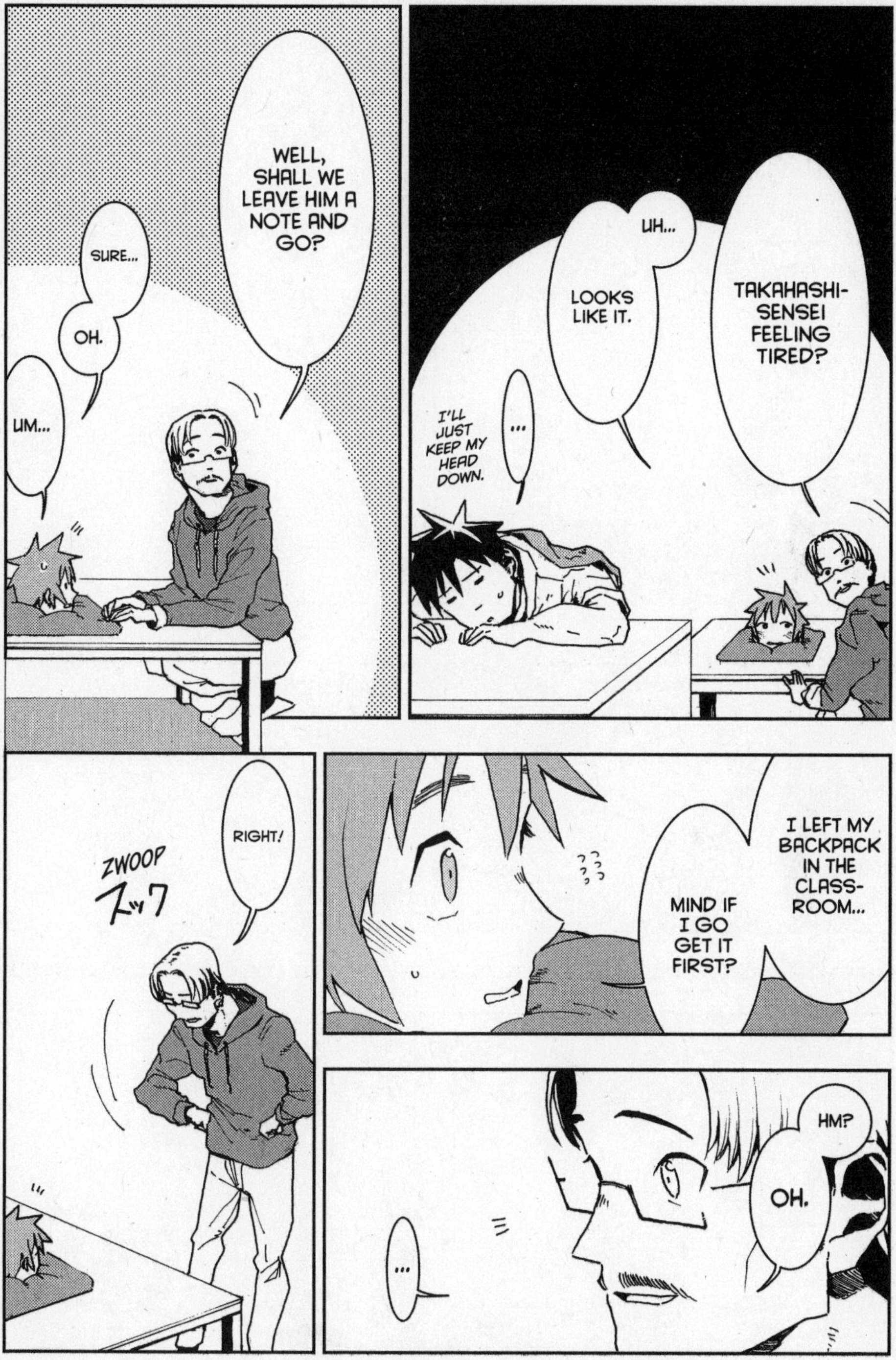
TAKAHASHI-SENSEI FEELING TIRED?
UH...
LOOKS LIKE IT.
...
I'LL JUST KEEP MY HEAD DOWN.
WELL, SHALL WE LEAVE HIM A NOTE AND GO?
SURE...
OH.
UM...
I LEFT MY BACKPACK IN THE CLASSROOM...
MIND IF I GO GET IT FIRST?
HM?
OH.
...
RIGHT!
ZWOOP

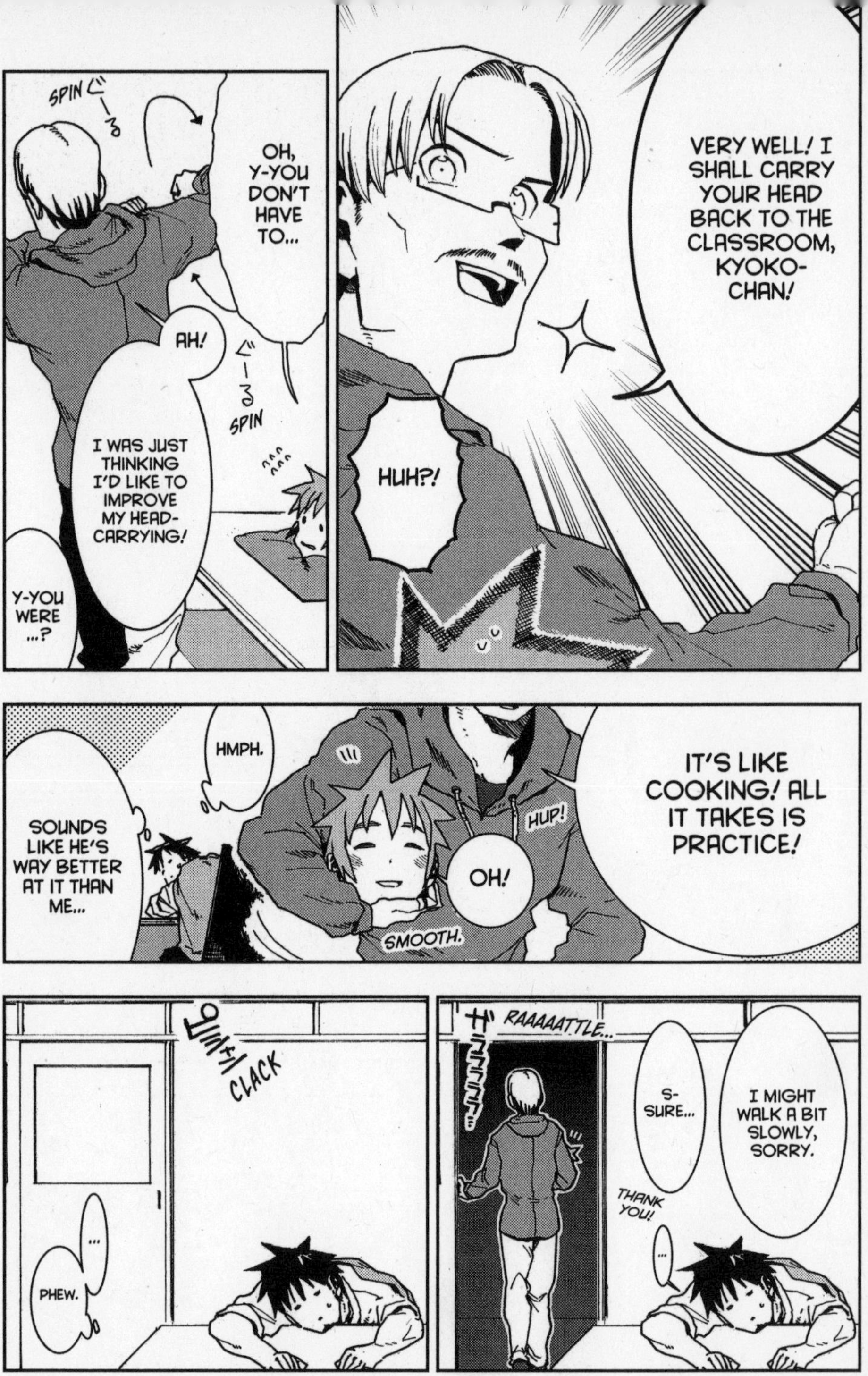
VERY WELL! I SHALL CARRY YOUR HEAD BACK TO THE CLASSROOM, KYOKO-CHAN!
HUH?!
SPIN
OH, Y-YOU DON'T HAVE TO...
AH!
SPIN
I WAS JUST THINKING I'D LIKE TO IMPROVE MY HEAD-CARRYING!
Y-YOU WERE ...?
IT'S LIKE COOKING! ALL IT TAKES IS PRACTICE!
HUP!
OH!
SMOOTH.
HMPH.
SOUNDS LIKE HE'S WAY BETTER AT IT THAN ME...
RAAAAATTLE...
I MIGHT WALK A BIT SLOWLY, SORRY.
S-SURE...
THANK YOU!
...
CLACK
...
PHEW.

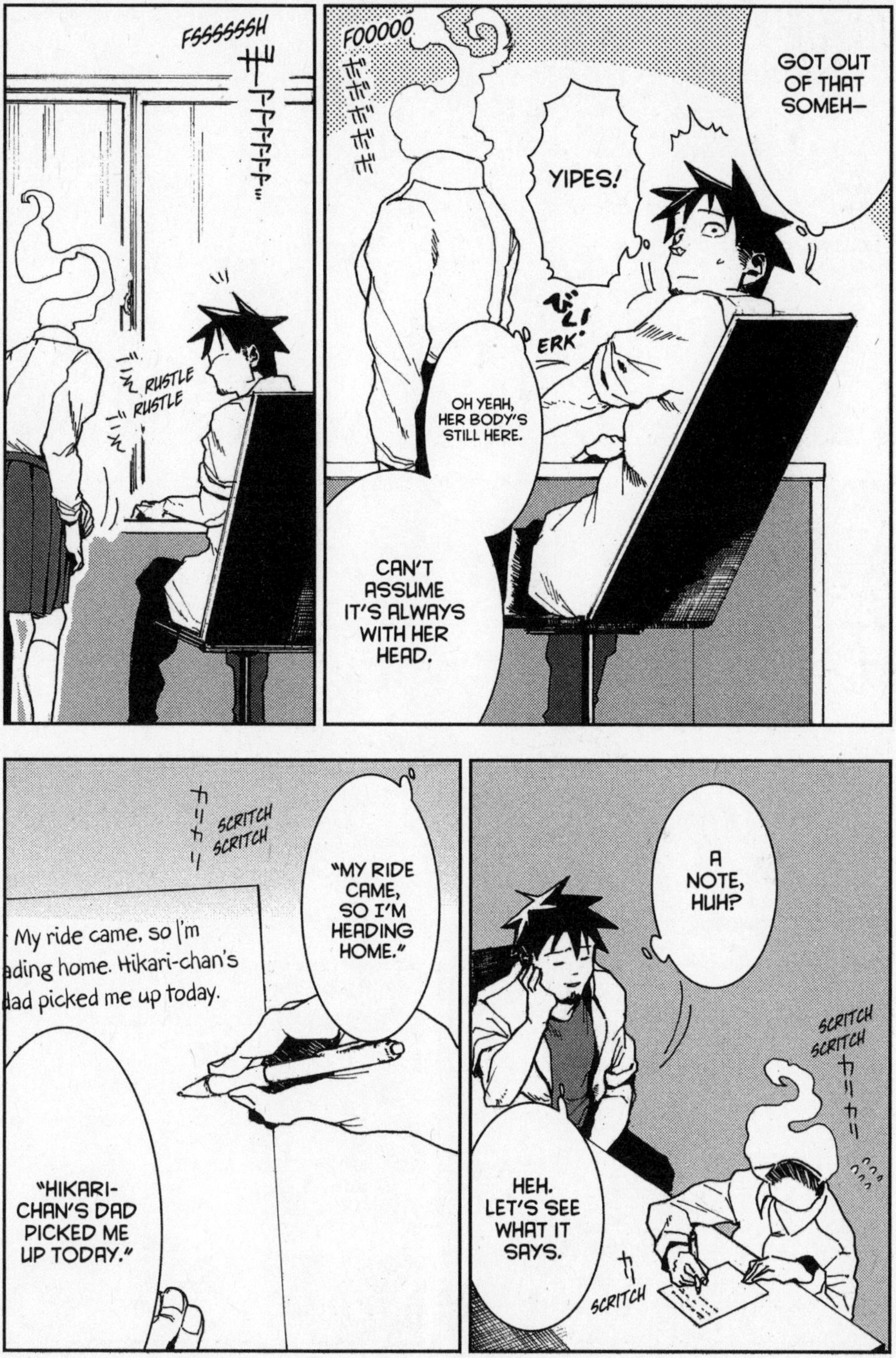
GOT OUT OF THAT SOMEH–
FOOOOO
ボボボボボ
YIPES!
ERK
OH YEAH, HER BODY'S STILL HERE.
CAN'T ASSUME IT'S ALWAYS WITH HER HEAD.
FSSSSSSH
ザァァァァァァ"
RUSTLE RUSTLE
ごそごそ
A NOTE, HUH?
SCRITCH SCRITCH
カリカリ
HEH. LET'S SEE WHAT IT SAYS.
カリ
SCRITCH
カリカリ
SCRITCH SCRITCH
My ride came, so I'm
ading home. Hikari-chan's
dad picked me up today.
"MY RIDE CAME, SO I'M HEADING HOME."
"HIKARI-CHAN'S DAD PICKED ME UP TODAY."

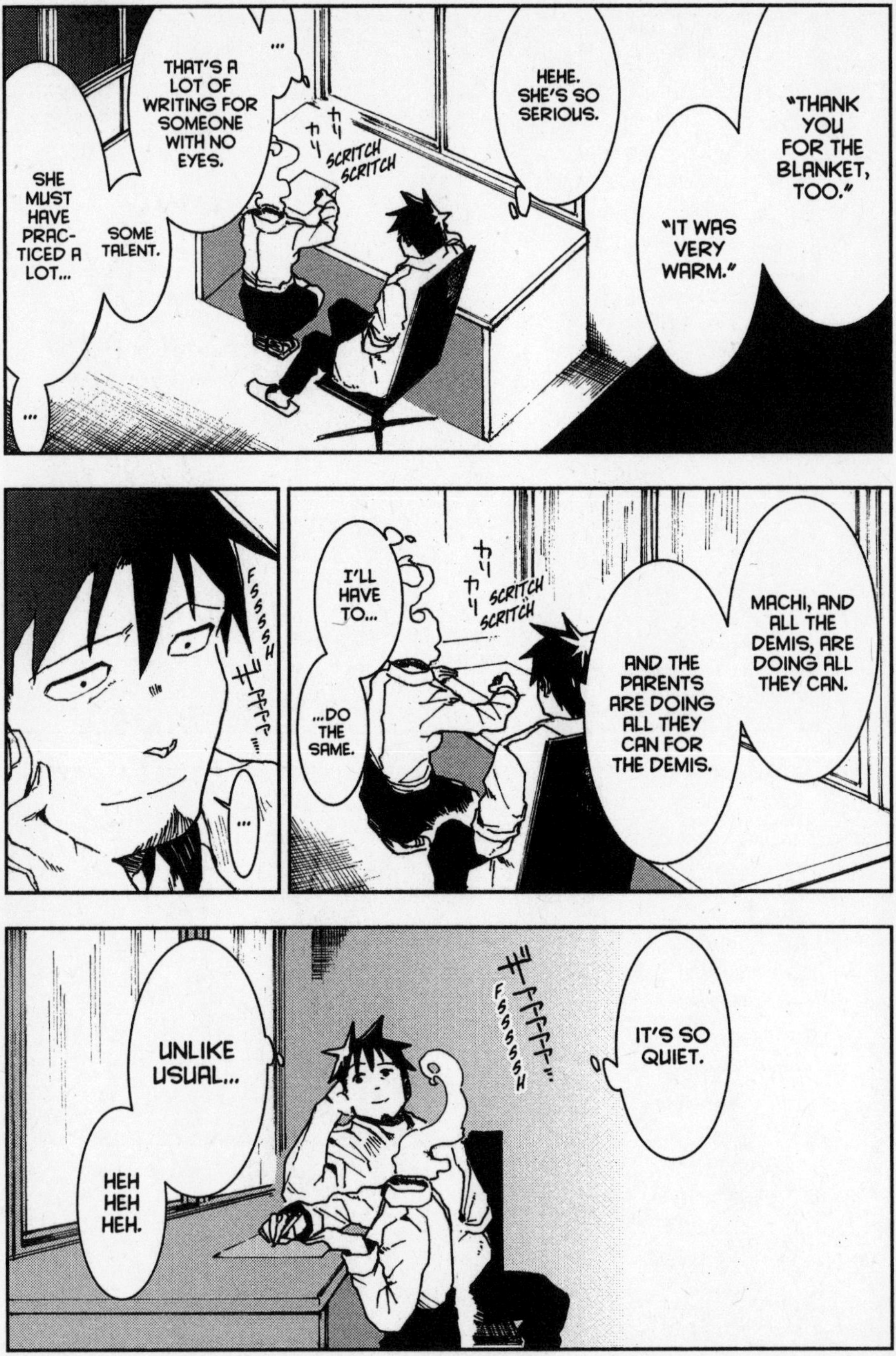
"THANK YOU FOR THE BLANKET, TOO."
"IT WAS VERY WARM."
HEHE. SHE'S SO SERIOUS.
...
THAT'S A LOT OF WRITING FOR SOMEONE WITH NO EYES.
カリ カリ
SCRITCH SCRITCH
SOME TALENT.
SHE MUST HAVE PRAC-TICED A LOT...
...
MACHI, AND ALL THE DEMIS, ARE DOING ALL THEY CAN.
AND THE PARENTS ARE DOING ALL THEY CAN FOR THE DEMIS.
カリ カリ
SCRITCH SCRITCH
I'LL HAVE TO...
...DO THE SAME.
FSSSSH
...
IT'S SO QUIET.
FSSSSSH
UNLIKE USUAL...
HEH HEH HEH.

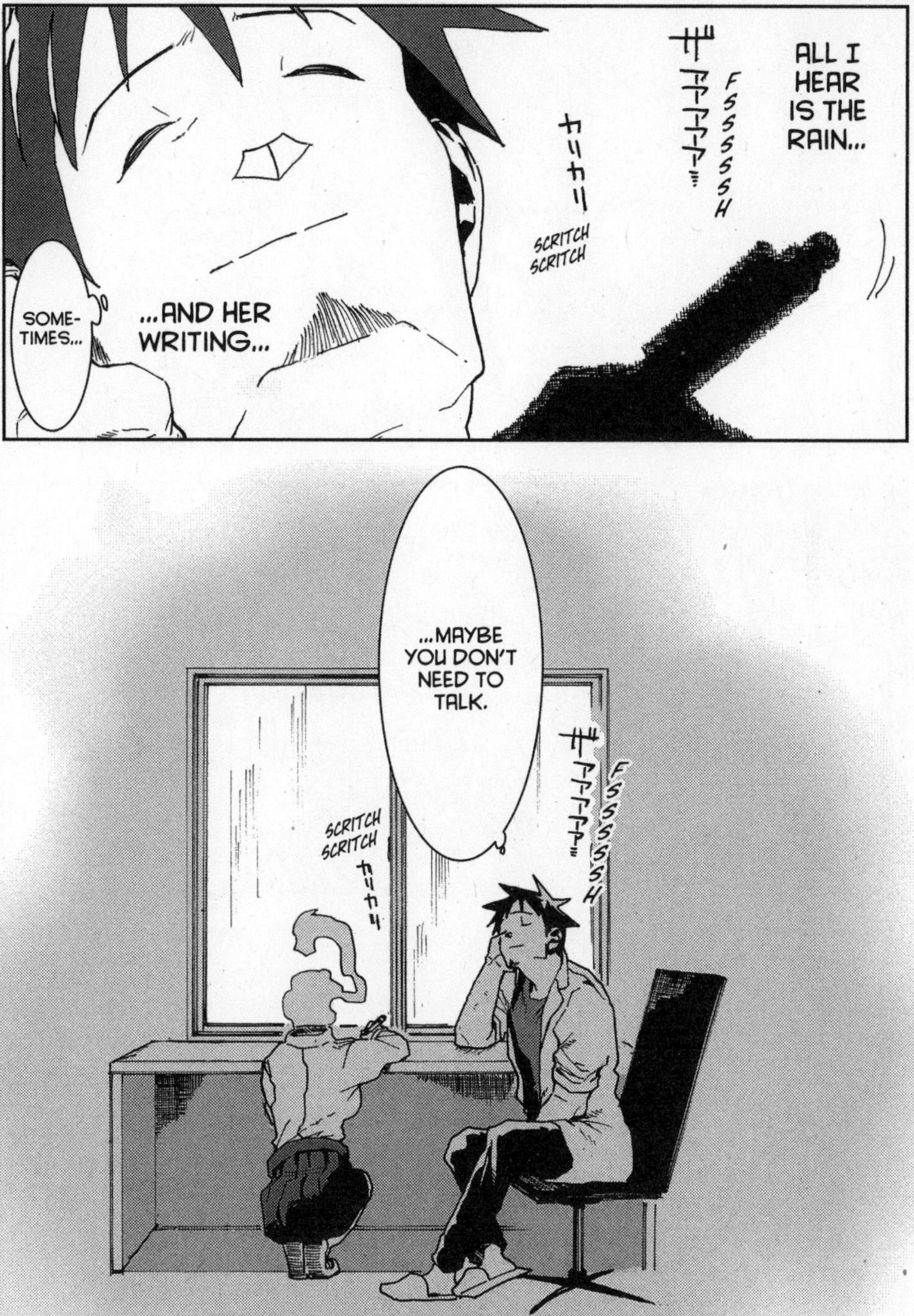
ALL I HEAR IS THE RAIN...
ザアアアア
FSSSSSH
カリカリ
SCRITCH SCRITCH
...AND HER WRITING...
SOME-TIMES...
...MAYBE YOU DON'T NEED TO TALK.
ザアアアア
FSSSSSSH
SCRITCH SCRITCH
カリカリ

VOLUME 3/END

ALL RIGHT, SEE YOU.
SURE!
THANK YOU!
OH, SAY...
ABOUT HIKARI'S LAST TEST... SHE FAILED... AGAIN.
TWITCH
...
...
AHEM...
LIKE FATHER, LIKE DAUGH-TER...

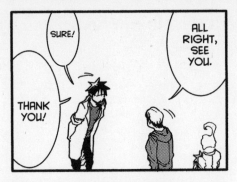

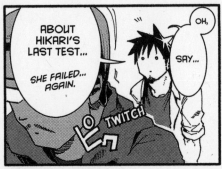

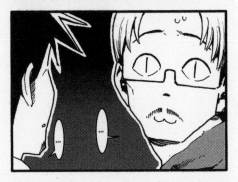

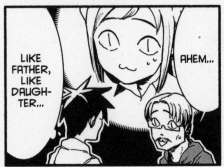

✿ Next time in *Interview with Monster Girls...*

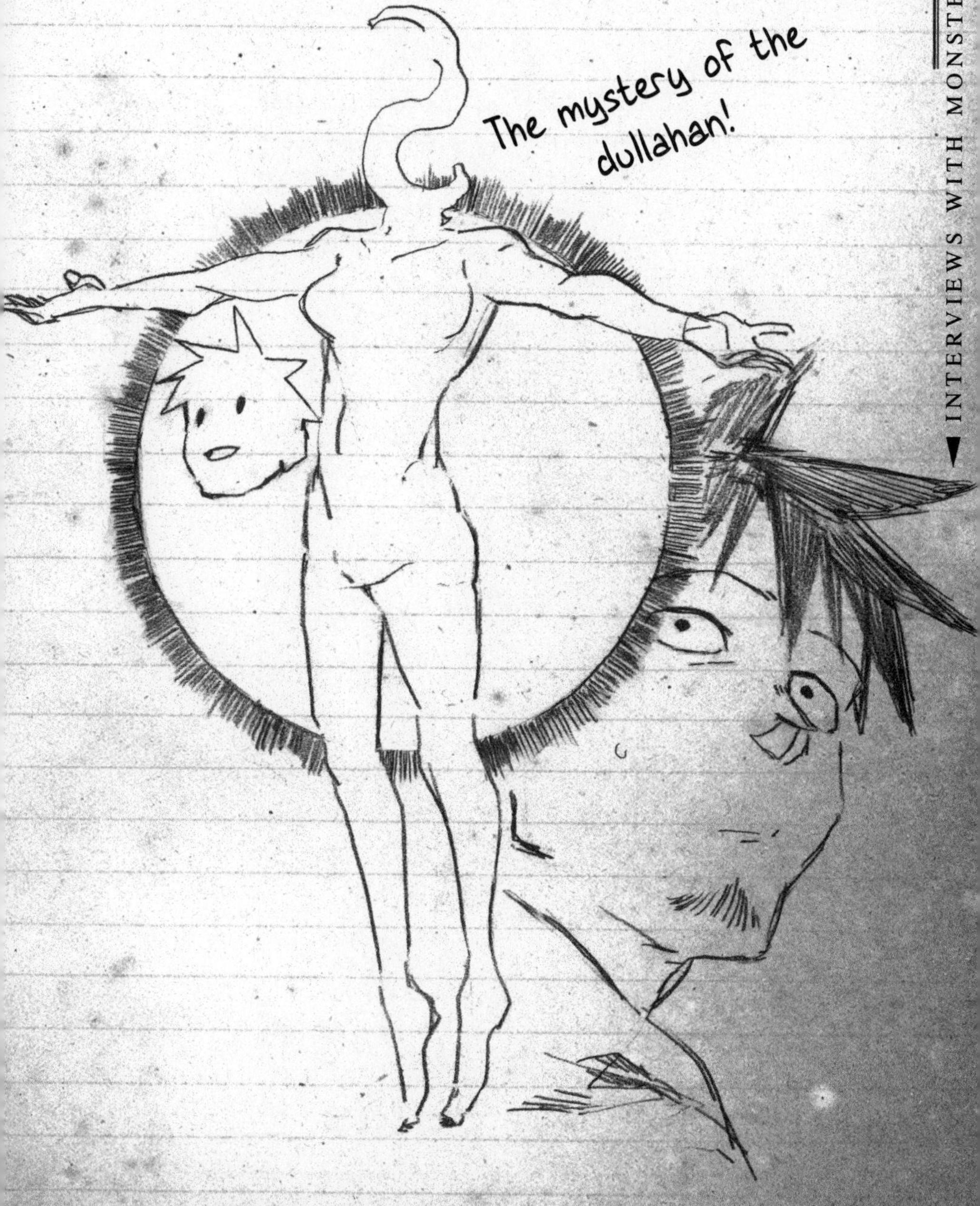
The mystery of the dullahan!

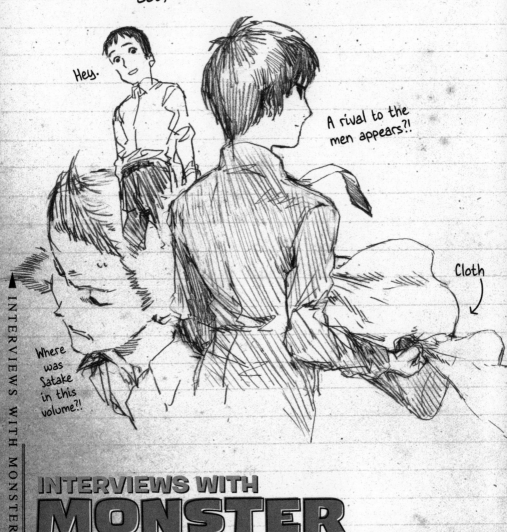

TRANSLATION NOTES

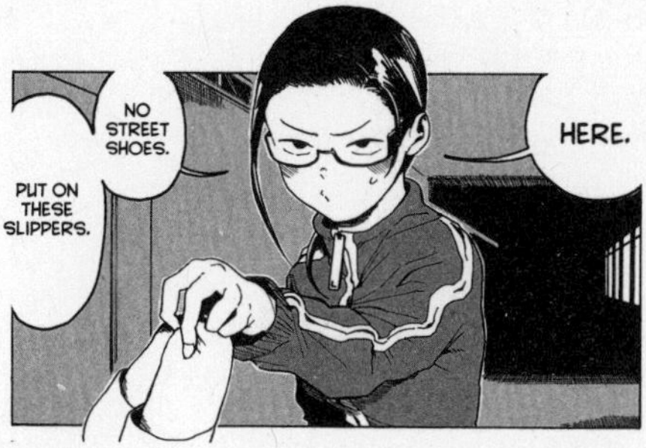
HERE.
NO STREET SHOES.
PUT ON THESE SLIPPERS.

No street shoes, page 7

Street shoes are almost never allowed in Japanese schools. Everyone who comes to a school—students, staff, and visitors alike—is expected to remove their shoes, trading them for a pair of slippers much like the one Sato-sensei is holding in this panel. (Students have a separate pair of shoes exclusively for use during gym class.)

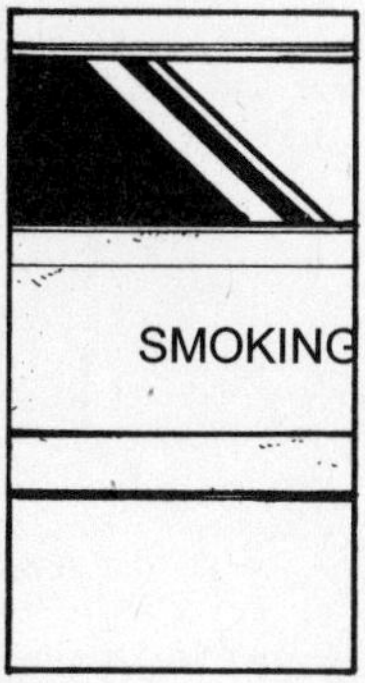
SMOKING

Smoking..., page 23

The sign says Smoking Room (only part of it is visible in the panel). Smoking is extremely common in Japan. However, in many places today, including most public buildings, it is restricted to designated areas, often a room where smoke will not interfere with other workers, staff, or students.

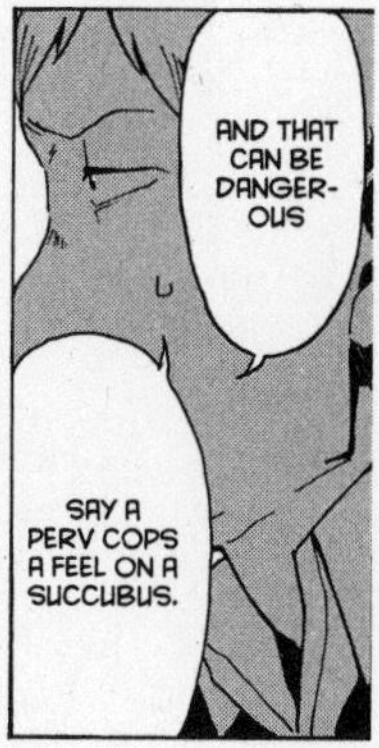
AND THAT CAN BE DANGER-OUS
SAY A PERV COPS A FEEL ON A SUCCUBUS.

Pervs, page 31

Sexual harassment of women remains a pervasive problem in Japan. (Perpetrators are called *chikan*, or perverts.) The press of bodies in a rush-hour train car, especially, can make it easy for a harasser to touch a victim without leaving the victim much recourse (or room to move away). This may be the kind of situation Ugaki has in mind, although, in Japan as anywhere, harassment is not limited to any single place or time.

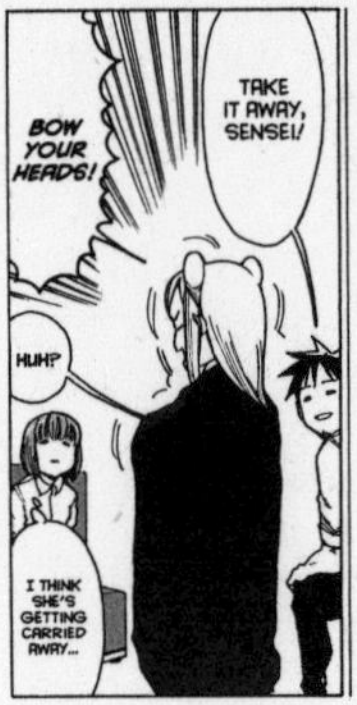
TAKE IT AWAY, SENSEI!
BOW YOUR HEADS!
HUH?
I THINK SHE'S GETTING CARRIED AWAY...

Sensei, page 61

Though Tetsuo is being somewhat facetious in using the word sensei to refer to Hikari here, the term does have a broader meaning than the common translation of "teacher." Anyone in a position of authority, or anyone to whose knowledge you defer, can be addressed as sensei. Among others, doctors, lawyers, instructors—and in this case, the adjudicator of a contest—can all be referred to as sensei.

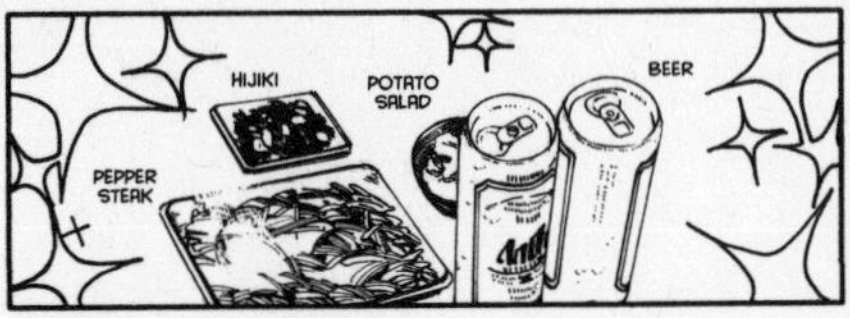
BEER
POTATO SALAD
HIJIKI
PEPPER STEAK

***Hijiki*, page 96**

Hijiki is one of several kinds of edible seaweed. (Sato-sensei's table here is full of classic Japanese beer snacks.)

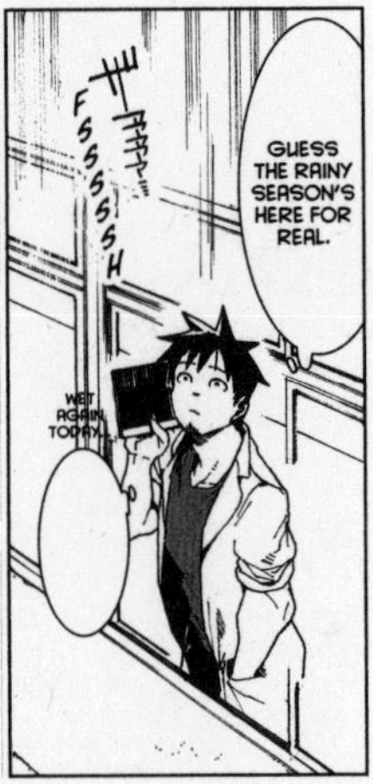
GUESS THE RAINY SEASON'S HERE FOR REAL.
FSSSSSH
WET AGAIN TODAY...

Rainy season, page 121

In Japan, rainy season, or *tsuyu*, lasts from around June to around July. True to its name, rain occurs frequently during this time—often not as a downpour, but as a persistent drizzle.

The required school bag, page 123

The bag used to carry school supplies is among the items that may be (and often is) dictated by the school dress code.

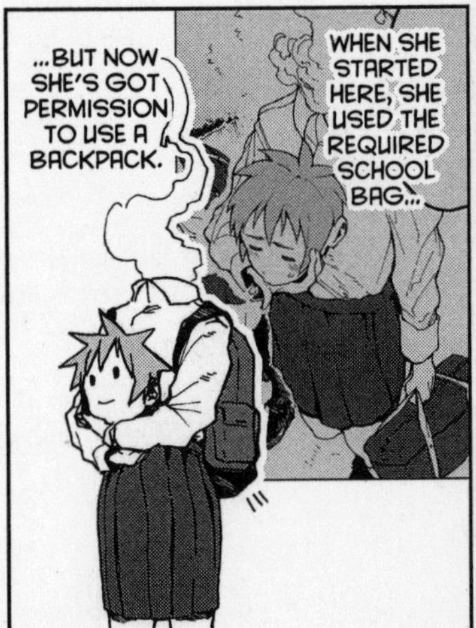
WHEN SHE STARTED HERE, SHE USED THE REQUIRED SCHOOL BAG...
...BUT NOW SHE'S GOT PERMISSION TO USE A BACKPACK.

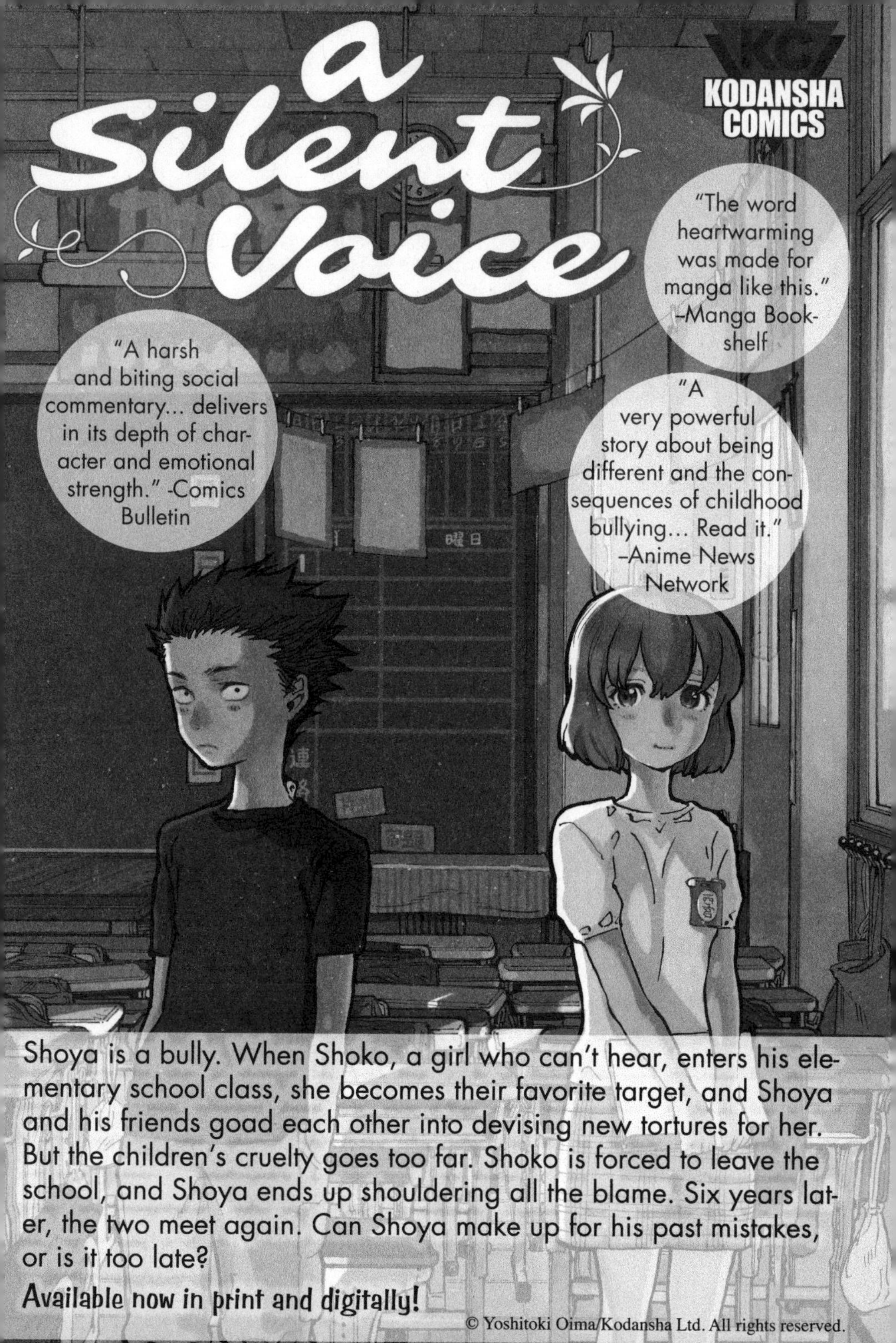

A Kodansha Comics Trade Paperback Original.

Interviews with Monster Girls volume 3 copyright © 2016 Petos
English translation copyright © 2017 Petos

Published in the United States by Kodansha Comics, an imprint of Kodansha USA Publishing, LLC, New York.

Publication rights for this English edition arranged through Kodansha Ltd., Tokyo.

First published in Japan in 2016 by Kodansha Ltd., Tokyo, as *Demi-chan wa Kataritai*, volume 3.

ISBN 978-1-63236-388-6

Printed in the United States of America.

www.kodanshacomics.com

9 8 7 6 5 4 3 2 1

Translation: Kevin Steinbach
Lettering: Paige Pumphrey
Editing: Lauren Scanlan
Kodansha Comics edition cover design: Phil Balsman

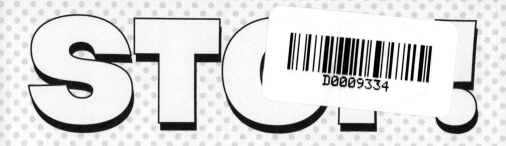
STOP!

You are going the wrong way!

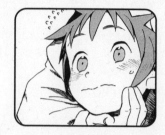

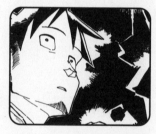

Manga is a completely different type of reading experience.

To start at the BEGINNING, go to the END!

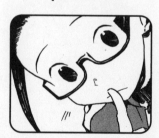

That's right! Authentic manga is read the traditional Japanese way—from right to left, exactly the opposite of how American books are read. It's easy to follow: just go to the other end of the book, and read each page—and each panel—from the right side to the left side, starting at the top right. Now you're experiencing manga as it was meant to be.